MUST WE
CONFESS
OUR SINS?

Guy Duininck

Must We Confess Our Sins?
ISBN: 978-0-929400-07-5

Copyright © 2020 by Guy Duininck

Published by Master's Touch Publishing Company
PO Box 35543
Tulsa, OK 74153 USA

Printed in the United States of America

Cover and book design by Barbara Rupps

Table of Contents

Preface 9

Introduction 13

1. Overview Of First John 25

2. John's First Epistle Was Written To Believers 35

3. The Early Gnostics 49

4. The Purpose Of John's First Epistle 71

5. Homologeō 107

6. John's Polemic 141

7. Sin And Sinning 179

8. Three Analogous Statements 211

9. The Catholic Church's Sacrament Of Confession 237

10. A Logical Look At I John 1:9 243

11. What Does I John 1:9 Really Mean? 263

12. What Should I Do If I Have Sinned? 291

Conclusion 343

Research Sources 347

Preface

In the first chapter of his first epistle, the apostle John wrote,

"If we confess our sins, he is faithful and just to forgive us our sins, and to cleanse us from all unrighteousness."

I John 1:9

For most Christians over many generations and throughout the world, John's words in I John 1:9 have been understood to mean that believers must sorrowfully admit to God the sins they commit in order to be forgiven and cleansed of those sins. It has been widely accepted that this admission of sins initiates God's forgiveness and cleansing of believers' sins and keeps them in right standing with Him. In today's church, the majority of Christians accept this interpretation, believing that they must admit to God the sins they commit so that He will forgive those sins, so that they can be cleansed from any stain of those sins, and so that their righteous standing with Him can be maintained.

For most Christians, across time and across church denominations, this interpretation of John's words in I John 1:9 has been happily accepted, is not a serious issue, and does not engender fear. Even if they sometimes fail to admit their sins to God, most Christians do not become anxious, thinking that they might be unforgiven and unclean, that their relationship with God might be in jeopardy, or that their eternal destiny is in question. Most Christians don't believe they have to live perfect lives or literally confess to God each and every sin they commit in order to be forgiven and cleansed of those sins. They trust that God's free gift of salvation through faith in Jesus Christ is greater than any of their failures; including a failure to confess to God the sins they have committed.

For some Christians, however, the commonly accepted interpretation of I John 1:9 has created a works mentality that has permeated their relationship with God. They believe that if they fail to confess to God the sins they have committed, they may not be forgiven of those sins, they may not be cleansed, their right standing with Him may be compromised, and their eternal destiny might be in jeopardy. Because they fully embrace the common interpretation of I John 1:9—that the forgiveness and cleansing of any sins they commit is contingent upon confessing those sins to God—they are hyper-diligent about confessing their sins to God, seeking to ensure that they are fully forgiven, that they stay cleansed, that their right standing with Him remains intact, and that their future in heaven is secure.

For a small percentage of Christians, the commonly accepted interpretation of I John 1:9 has caused serious doubts concerning their relationship with God. Some are anxious, wondering if the reason things are not going well for them, or the reason they were not healed, or the reason their prayers were not answered in the way they had hoped is because they have unconfessed sin in their lives. They fret religiously over this possibility, trying to determine if they might have forgotten to confess one of their sins to God. Some are fearful about what their eternal destiny will be if they die with unconfessed sin in their life. Unfortunately, some have even developed mental and emotional issues because of their persistent fear that if they fail to confess their sins to God, they will be unforgiven and unclean.

In more recent times, some ministers have expressed serious concerns about the common interpretation of I John 1:9 because that interpretation suggests the necessity of works on the part of believers—the work of confessing one's sins—in order to be forgiven and cleansed of sins and in order to maintain right standing with God. These ministers do not believe that the common interpretation of I John 1:9 harmonizes with the rest of the New Testament and its strong emphasis on the complete sufficiency of Jesus' finished work in dealing with the problem of sin. Being troubled by the long standing, familiar, and widely accepted interpretation of I John 1:9, they searched for a different interpretation; an interpretation that didn't suggest the necessity of believers doing the work of confessing their sins in order to be forgiven and cleansed of their sins and in order to maintain their righteous standing with God.

Some of these ministers discovered what they believe is a solution to the problem of the commonly accepted interpretation of I John 1:9. They concluded that the first chapter of John's first epistle, including I John 1:9, was not written to believers, but to the gnostic sinners of John's day. They believe that John's words in I John 1:9 constituted a presentation of the gospel of Jesus Christ to gnostic sinners—an invitation to believe on Jesus as Savior, to confess their sins to God, to come into the light, to be saved, and to be forgiven and cleansed of their sins. This view of I John 1:9 and this explanation of the first chapter of John's first epistle satisfied these ministers because it solved the problem of what they considered to be an unacceptable interpretation of I John 1:9. Unfortunately, however, the view of these ministers is, itself, quite problematic, having almost no support beyond their own persuasion that the common interpretation of I John 1:9 is not harmonious with the rest of the New Testament and must, therefore, be wrong.

Contemplating these two interpretations of I John 1:9—the long held, familiar, and common interpretation that believers must admit their sins to God in order to be forgiven and cleansed of those sins, and the less common interpretation that John's words were not written to believers, but to gnostic sinners as an invitation to be saved and forgiven of sins—you might suppose that you must choose one of them. I am persuaded, however, after my own prayerful study and careful consideration of I John 1:9, that there is another interpretation, a better interpretation, that is harmonious with all of the New Testament and with all of Scripture, that is consistent with the purpose of John's first epistle, that embraces the view that all of John's first epistle was written to and written for the benefit of believers, that makes perfect sense in its appropriate contexts, that properly interprets the English word "confess," and that is enlightening, encouraging, and freeing. It is this interpretation, a more accurate interpretation of I John 1:9, that I will present and argue for throughout this study.

Some who are aware that I worked on this study for more than four years have asked me why such an extensive and thorough study was necessary to explain just one verse in the Bible; especially since "everyone already knows what I John 1:9 means." My response has been that it is precisely because the church at large thinks it understands what I John 1:9 means that it was necessary to do such a thorough study and offer this amount of information. Because I was going to offer an interpretation of I John 1:9 that was different than the two currently accepted interpretations, it was necessary that I presented a thorough body of evidence in support of my interpretation.

It is my prayer that you will find this study of I John 1:9 to be enlightening, challenging, and helpful. Because it is an extensive study, you will get the most out of it if you read carefully from the beginning to the end. The facts you will learn about the apostle John and his first epistle, the information you will acquire about the activity of the errant early gnostics in the region of Asia minor at the time John wrote his first epistle, the discoveries you will make about the various important contexts in which I John 1:9 is situated, and the important meanings you will learn of various Greek words, especially the Greek word *homologeō*, will enrich your understanding of I John 1:9 and may result in you embracing the interpretation of I John 1:9 I present. Let's proceed now to our study and discover what I John 1:9 really means.

Introduction

It can happen sometimes that believers are so familiar with certain Scriptures and "already know what they mean" that they have not carefully studied those Scriptures to make sure that the meanings and common uses they have accepted are accurate. One of my favorite examples along these lines is the Old Testament story of Balaam and his donkey. Scripture tells us that while Balaam was en route to curse Israel, having been hired by king Balaak to do so, he was stopped abruptly by his donkey who saw an angel of the Lord holding a sword and blocking their path. Not wanting to be delayed, Balaam beat his donkey, trying to make her move forward. She refused to move, however, and by refusing to move saved his life. Balaam's donkey then spoke to Balaam, chiding him for mistreating her after all her years of faithful service. This familiar story found in Numbers 22:21–35 is the basis for the well known saying, "If God can speak through a donkey, He can speak through you!" Those who have never read this story, or haven't read it carefully, are unaware of the fact that although God indeed opened the donkey's mouth, God did not speak through the donkey. What Balaam's donkey said to Balaam were her own words; they were not God's words. As far as we know from Scripture, God has never spoken through a donkey or through any other animal. Unfortunately, this story has often been used to support a common, but inaccurate Christian belief that if God can speak through a donkey, He can certainly work through believers, even if they are unprepared.

Another example of believers being so familiar with a Scripture that they may not know what that Scripture means or even what it says are Paul's words from his second epistle to the Corinthians about the revelation of grace he received from the Lord. In that epistle, he wrote, "for when I am weak, then am I strong" (II Corinthians 12:9). Many believers, thinking they are quoting Paul's words, declare "When we are weak, He (God) is strong!" That is not, however, what Paul said and that was not what he was communicating. When Paul said, "when

I am weak, then am I strong" he was not communicating that when he was weak in his own strength, God would carry him. He was communicating that when he was weak in his own strength, he could receive the strengthening grace of the Lord Jesus and become strong in his inner man, enabled and empowered to face any test or trial, to overcome any temptation, and to continue running his race with steadfast patience. The wonderful New Covenant truth Paul revealed in II Corinthians 12:9 was that when believers are weak in their own human strength, they can receive the strengthening grace of the Lord Jesus in their inner man and, by means of that strengthening grace, be divinely enabled to do all things.

The situation of Christians being so familiar with a Scripture that they have never searched out what that Scripture really means is a problem with I John 1:9. John's words in I John 1:9 have been quoted so often, used so frequently in Christian materials, and spoken so many times from the pulpits of churches, that almost all Christians "know" what I John 1:9 means. As with the story of Balaam, however, and as with Paul's words to the Corinthians, most Christians, including ministers, have never carefully studied John's words to make sure that what they believe about I John 1:9 is actually correct. In this study, we will examine John's words in I John 1:9 closely and carefully and also study important relevant information in order to determine what John really intended to communicate by his words in this familiar verse of Scripture.

Dealing with Problem Scriptures

It can happen in our study of the Word of God that we come across a Scripture that might be considered a problem Scripture. A problem Scripture is a passage of Scripture that is either difficult to understand or that doesn't seem to harmonize with the rest of Scripture. Thankfully, we never have to panic over a problem Scripture because we know that God is not confused, even though we might be confused about something He said. Because we know that God is not confused, we can be confident that every Scripture can be accurately interpreted, correctly understood, and properly harmonized with all of Scripture. We simply need to take our time, be diligent in our study, lean upon the Holy Spirit to guide us, and do our heartfelt best to, "rightly (divide) the word of truth." There are, however, several things we must be careful about when dealing with problem Scriptures.

First, we must not lift any Scripture out of its proper place—out of its general and immediate contexts—and assign it a meaning that fits our time, our culture, our preferred narrative, or our fancy. We must leave Scriptures where they belong and examine them honestly and carefully in their general and immediate contexts and in the context of the time, the place, and the people to whom they were first addressed. If a Scripture is detached from its proper context, it can take on a meanings that was never intended and even be grossly misinterpreted. If a Scripture is removed from its proper context, it can be misused to communicate things it was never intended to communicate. Scriptures must be left where they belong.

Second, we must ask important questions about problem Scriptures like: "Who was the author of the words we are studying?" "Who were the people this particular author was writing to?" "What was transpiring at the time the author was inspired to write these words?" "What was the main purpose of the author's writing?" These questions and others like them are very important to our being honest and careful as we investigate a Scripture to discover what it truly means.

Third, we must study the important words used in a problem Scripture. We must learn what those words meant in their original language and discover how they were commonly used at the time that Scripture was written. We must seek to know what those words would have meant to their original audience. Taking the time and making the effort to learn the various possible meanings of important words in a problem Scripture greatly increases the probability that we will discover what that Scripture really means.

Fourth, we must consult the teachings of others who are of a right spirit, who love God and His Word, who are intelligent and scholarly, and who can contribute historical context, correct meanings of words, and other important insights to the Scriptures we are studying. No matter how independent we wish to be or how much we want to be only Spirit taught, we do ourselves and others a great disservice if we ignore what other godly, wise, mature, and right-spirited ministers, scholars, and believers have said about a particular Scripture.

Fifth, we must humbly ask the Father and the Lord Jesus to help us as we study problem Scriptures. After all, it is their Word we are studying and seeking to understand. We must also lean upon the all knowing Holy Spirit of Truth, the author of Scripture, as He does His important work of teaching us all things, guiding us into all truth, and assisting us as we seek to, "rightly (divide) the word of truth." There are no more important words we can utter as we study problem Scriptures than the words, "Please help me, Holy Spirit."

If we will take our time, studying diligently, humbly, and prayerfully, and deal honestly with problem Scriptures, we can come to a good understanding of their best meanings and learn how they fit with the rest of Scripture. In this process, we may discover that some Scriptures which seemed to be problem Scriptures are actually beautiful and deeply meaningful Scriptures that are harmonious with all of Scripture and can enlighten, enrich, challenge, and encourage us.

Dealing With the Problem of I John 1:9

Because some confusion and even consternation has recently arisen over I John 1:9, causing it to become a problem Scripture for some, I decided to do a thorough study and write a book detailing my study, providing information for others to use for their own study of this important Scripture. My hope is that the information I provide will help believers everywhere to reach a good understanding of I John 1:9 and will aid ministers in resolving the problems with both of the interpretations of I John 1:9 I mentioned in the Preface—the interpretation that Christians must confess their sins to God in order to be forgiven and cleansed of those sins and to maintain their righteous standing with Him and the interpretation that I John 1:9 and the first chapter of John's first epistle was written to gnostic sinners as an evangelistic message.

I feel certain that when I John 1:9 is studied carefully, utilizing the aid of the Holy Spirit, the aid of all Scripture, the aid of prayer, the aid of careful thought, and the aid of all good information available, we will reach an interpretation of I John 1:9 that is accurate, that fits its immediate and general contexts, that harmonizes with John's first epistle, that is harmonious with the teaching of the New Testament, and that fits well with all of Scripture. When I John 1:9 is properly interpreted and rightly understood, it will no longer bring fear to some believers and confusion to others, but will bring light, clarity, and confidence to all, as Scripture is intended to do. It is my prayer that the information I provide in this study will help many to reach an accurate and enlightened understanding of what I John 1:9 really means.

Outline

The style I employed in writing "Must We Confess Our Sins?" is similar to the style John employed in his first epistle. His writing was not linear, as was typical to Paul and other New Testament authors, but was circular. He would introduce a theme, say some things concerning that theme, and then leave that theme and introduce a new theme. Later, he would circle back to his earlier theme and address it again, sometimes with different words and from a different point of view. Then he would move on to another new theme, only to return again to previous themes later in his epistle.

In each of the early chapters of this study, I introduce one significant element of information—a historical point of view, a contextual insight, the definition of a word, or some particular fact—that is important to a right interpretation of I John 1:9. As I move forward to new chapters and new elements of information, I sometimes circle back and revisit information I introduced in a earlier chapter, addressing that information from a different point of view. As I move from chapter to chapter, I don't move forward in a straight line, but circle around I John 1:9, looking at it from various points of view.

As we consider I John 1:9 from the various points of view of each chapter, we will get a very good look at John's words and gain insights that will help us understand what he intended to communicate. I believe that my "circling around I John 1:9" approach will be effective for this study, bringing clarity and insight to John's words, helping us to discover their truest meaning. Because I used this circular approach, you will notice some repetition of information as you move from chapter to chapter. I originally tried to avoid this repetition of information, but upon further reflection concluded that circling around the main subject and sometimes repeating the same information would be an effective approach for this study and a good way to reach a well informed, complete, and accurate understanding of I John 1:9.

In chapter one, I present a brief, general overview of First John. We will learn who wrote this epistle, when it was written, to whom it was written, and why it was written. We will discover the style and nature of this epistle and the heart passion of the person who wrote it. We will also learn a little bit about what was going on spiritually in the region of Ephesus at the time this epistle was written. This brief, general overview will orient us properly to First John, preparing us for the rest of our study.

In chapter two, I begin circling around I John 1:9, looking at it from the point of view that John's first epistle, including the first chapter of his epistle and I John 1:9, was written to and intended for believers; specifically for John's spiritual children. This simple fact is extremely important to a correct interpretation of I John 1:9. If it were true, as some say, that the first chapter of John's first epistle was written to gnostic sinners, that would profoundly alter the immediate context of I John 1:9 and, therefore, significantly influence the meaning of I John 1:9, leading us to an errant interpretation. If we approach I John 1:9 as if it was written to gnostic sinners, we will be looking at it from a wrong point of view and will misunderstand the meaning of John's important words.

In chapter three, I introduce information about a group of individuals that caused great concern to the apostle John; a group I refer to as the errant early gnostics. Some of these errant early gnostics may have actually once fellowshipped with the community of faith, but had been deceived, had embraced error, and had left the sound body. It is essential that we understand the beliefs and teachings of the errant early gnostics because it was their teachings, their lifestyle, and their efforts to influence the community of faith that caused John such deep concern and gave rise to his first epistle. If we don't know anything about the beliefs and the lifestyle of the errant early gnostics, we will lack information that is critical to a correct understanding of what John was communicating to believers in I John 1:9.

In chapter four, I reveal John's purpose for writing his first epistle. Knowing "why" John wrote his epistle is essential to an accurate understanding of "what" he wrote in his epistle; including his words in I John 1:9. In this chapter, we will discover the source of John's deep concern for believers he loved and learn why he penned such serious words of warning and instruction. We will become aware of what was going on spiritually in the region where he was living that motivated him to write. Discovering "why" John wrote his first epistle and looking at I John 1:9 from this point of view is essential to a right interpretation and correct understanding of "what" he meant by his words.

In chapter five, I present important information about the Greek word *homologeō* John used in I John 1:9 that the English word "confess" is translated from. It is essential that we understand the meaning of this word because the meaning of the English word "confess," which has significantly influenced the interpretation of I John 1:9, means something different than the Greek word *homologeō*. Because the English word "confess" carries a strong sense of, "admitting an offense to an authority," or, "acknowledging one's sins to a priest," John's words in I John 1:9 have been infused with the strong sense of, "the verbal admission of sins and of personal guilt to God." Understanding the meaning of the Greek word *homologeō* and discovering how it was used in the New Testament, especially by the apostle John in his first two epistles, will help us understand what *homologeō* would have meant to John's original audience and what it meant in I John 1:9. Knowing what the Greek word *homologeō* would have meant to John's original readers is critical to a correct interpretation and an accurate understanding of his words in I John 1:9.

In chapter six, I reveal an important fact about John's first epistle that few are aware of, but that is crucial to a right understanding of I John 1:9. We will learn that the section of his epistle from I John 1:5 through I John 2:11 is a polemic. A polemic is a strong written or spoken attack against the opinions or beliefs of others. It is a pithy argument against and a robust refutation of the philosophies or beliefs of another person or group. John's words in I John 1:5 through I John 2:11 constitute a strong, logical, carefully crafted argument against early gnostic error on the subject of sin and sinning. Understanding that this portion of John's first epistle is a polemic against early gnostic error on the subject of sin and sinning is critical to a correct interpretation of his words in I John 1:9 because it is in the immediate context of his polemic that I John 1:9 sits.

In chapter seven, I reveal that throughout his first epistle, John dealt strongly, clearly, and often with the subject of sin and sinning. I point out the various passages where he addressed the subject of sin and sinning and give a brief commentary on his words in those passages. Understanding that one of the primary reasons John wrote his first epistle was to confront early gnostic error on the subject of sin and sinning and to provide believers with sound New Covenant teaching on that subject is essential to determining the best interpretation of his words in I John 1:9.

In chapter eight, I focus on three passages in John's first epistle that I call "three analogous statements." These three statements are found in I John 1:7, I John 1:9, and I John 2:1-2. I use the term "three analogous statements" to describe these passages because they each express the same New Covenant truth concerning the forgiveness of believers' sins. Using different words, these statements express the wonderful reality that our wise God designed and put in place in the New Covenant a divine remedy to deal with the sins believers commit after they are saved. The blood of Jesus Christ is continually cleansing believers of all sin. Believers have an advocate with the Father, Jesus Christ; and the same Jesus Christ is the propitiation for their sins. And believers are continually being forgiven and cleansed of sins they commit by their Father God because He is faithful and just. Examining these three analogous statements, knowing that they each express the same basic New Covenant truth about the forgiveness of believers' sins, will further enhance our understanding of what John's words in I John 1:9 mean.

In chapter nine, I present information that identifies the role of the Catholic church in shaping the belief of the larger body of Christ concerning I John 1:9. The Catholic church has seven sacraments it holds dear and practices; one of those sacraments is the Sacrament of Confession. The Sacrament of Confession is the practice members of the Catholic church follow when they go to ordained Catholic priests and verbally acknowledge their sins to them so that they can be forgiven and absolved of those sins. Although protestant Christians do not follow this sacrament of the Catholic church, the Sacrament of Confession and the mental image of believers going to a priest to confess their sins has significantly influenced how churches and believers throughout the world "see" and understand John's words, "If we confess our sins."

In chapter ten, I examine the common interpretation of I John 1:9—that believers must admit each and every sin they commit to God in order to be forgiven and cleansed of those sins—from a logical point of view, considering the significant implications of that interpretation. Considering the significant implications of the common interpretation of 1 John 1:9 will help us determine if that interpretation agrees with and is harmonious with other important New Covenant truths or if it is contrary to and not harmonious with other important New Covenant truths. Thinking logically and carefully about I John 1:9, as well as prayerfully and humbly, will aid us considerably as we seek the right interpretation and the best understanding of John's important words in that verse.

In chapter eleven, I focus directly on I John 1:9, offering insights into John's words based on everything we learned in previous chapters. After having looked at I John 1:9 from many different points of view in previous chapters, and after having examined I John 1:9 more particularly in this chapter, I offer an interpretation of John's words that expresses what I believe to be the most accurate interpretation of I John 1:9 and the truest meaning of his words in that verse. I also offer several paraphrases of John's words in I John 1:9 to express more clearly what he intended to communicate.

In chapter twelve, I present important thoughts for your consideration based on everything we will learn in this study. I especially focus on how believers should relate to God and communicate with Him if they have sinned or if they are engaged in a lifestyle of sinning. The things I cover in this chapter are significant take aways from this study. They are truths from God's Word and nuggets of wisdom that we, as true believers, can implement into our daily lives as we walk with our Father in the light. All our learning from this study will only be information if we don't implement what we have learned as we seek to please our Father God and bear fruit in His kingdom.

Finally, I wrap up this study in two short, final chapters. In the chapter called "Conclusion," I briefly summarize the study and reiterate my interpretation of I John 1:9, tying everything back to the Preface and the Introduction, neatly wrapping things up. And in the final brief chapter called "Research Sources," I present some of the sources I consulted in my research for this study. As a reader, you may find it both interesting and comforting to know that some of the important information I presented in this study was either gleaned from or supported by other reputable authors and scholars.

Get Ready to Study

When you first picked up this book, you may have wondered, "Why would anyone write such an extensive book on just one verse of Scripture?" My purpose for writing this book was to set out a significant amount of information—from Scripture, from history, from Bible commentaries and dictionaries, and from my own contemplations— that would weigh upon, bear upon, and shine light upon John's words in I John 1:9. Because of the profound shaping influence the interpretation of I John 1:9 can exert on believers' lives and their relationship with

God, I wanted to offer much important information to help ministers and believers correctly interpret John's words. The right interpretation of I John 1:9 will help believers to rightly orient themselves toward God and to relate to Him properly where the matter of sin and sinning is concerned.

If the most familiar and common interpretation of I John 1:9 is the correct interpretation of I John 1:9, then believers are not forgiven of sins they commit unless and until after they have admitted each one of those sins to God in a time of confession. If the most familiar and common interpretation of I John 1:9 is correct, then the overwhelming majority of believers must make significant adjustments in their personal spiritual lives, cultivating a regular practice of confessing their sins to God lest they find themselves continually in an unforgiven and unclean state, without right standing with God. If the most familiar and common interpretation of I John 1:9 is the correct interpretation of I John 1:9 and believers do not engage regularly in the practice of confessing their sins to God, they will often be in an unforgiven, unclean state and will not be in right standing with God.

If the less common interpretation of I John 1:9 is correct—the interpretation that I John 1:9 was not written to believers, but to early gnostic sinners as an evangelistic message—then believers don't need to concern themselves with John's words in I John 1:9. After all, if his words were an invitation to lost sinners to be saved and to be forgiven and cleansed of their sins through the action of "the confession of sins," then his words have no specific relevance to those who are already saved.

If the interpretation of I John 1:9 that I will be offering and arguing for throughout this study is correct, then believers will be able to greatly rejoice and joyfully praise the Father God and the Lord Jesus Christ because they understand that the remedy for the sins they commit has already been put in place in the New Covenant and is functioning. Realizing that in I John 1:9, John was not describing a required performance of the admission of sins to God that believers must engage before they can be forgiven and cleansed of sins they have committed, believers will be deeply thankful to the Father God for His great foresight and wise plan and will praise Jesus Christ for His profound work, not only in procuring their salvation by the shedding of His blood, but also in maintaining their forgiven status, their cleanness, and their righteous standing with God by the ongoing cleansing of His ever effectual blood and by His work as the propitiation for their sins and their advocate with the Father. If the interpretation of I John 1:9 that I offer in this study is correct, believers will be comforted understanding that they are not part of a works oriented forgiveness of sins covenant, but are continually being forgiven of sins they commit by the blood of Jesus and by their Father God who is faithful to His own promises and just to keep the terms of the New Covenant that He designed and set in place.

As you begin this study, I encourage you to set aside whatever understanding of I John 1:9 you currently have and carefully and prayerfully consider the things I have written. Open your heart and mind to God's Word, to the Holy Spirit, and to the words of this study and come to your own best heart-motivated, Spirit guided, carefully studied, and well reasoned interpretation of I John 1:9.

I

Overview Of First John

The authorship of the first epistle of John has traditionally been attributed to the apostle John, one of the original twelve apostles that Jesus called to follow Him, to minister with Him, and to lead the early church. Nearly all historians agree with this opinion and there is no reasonable argument against this view. The apostle John was not only one of Jesus' original twelve apostles; he was also one of the inner core of Jesus' three close companions along with Peter and James. These three apostles who were the closest to Jesus, who went places with Him that the other apostles did not go, and who were described by Paul as pillars in the church at Jerusalem went on to become the primary spiritual leaders in the early church. According to historians, John was a young man when Jesus first called him; most likely in his mid to late teens. At the time he wrote his first epistle, however, the apostle John was an elderly man and the only remaining apostle of the Lamb. The other original apostles were dead, martyred for their faith.

Most historians agree that in the later years of his life, John was living and ministering in the region of Ephesus. This suggests that he may have succeeded both Paul and Timothy as the primary spiritual leader in that region. Some scholars say that John may not only have taken over the church at Ephesus, but may have taken leadership of all the churches in the region. The words of Irenaeus, bishop of Lyons, lend support to this view saying of the church in Ephesus that Paul had started it, but that John remained permanently among the believers there. According to others, it might have been the case that Timothy was the pastoral leader in the church at Ephesus while John ministered on a more expanded scale throughout the region. In any case, most scholars agree that John was living in Ephesus and most likely wrote his first epistle there sometime between 85 and 95 A.D.

It is apparent from John's first epistle that he was a respected Christian leader of wide influence and that he was well known to believers and local assemblies in the region of Ephesus. Interestingly, in his second and third epistles, he introduced himself simply as, "the elder." It is also apparent from John's first epistle that he had a deep affection and sincere concern for believers and for the church. The fact that he addressed believers as, "my little children," as, "children," and as, "beloved," reveals the depth of his affection for them and the closeness of his relationship with them. John's first epistle not only revealed his deep affection for believers, however. It also conveyed his serious concern for his spiritual children as he warned of dangerous error and dangerous individuals and boldly defended foundational truths of the Christian faith.

The Style of John's First Epistle

John's first epistle does not conform to the general characteristics of most other New Testament epistles. It was not addressed to a specific person or church and it had no greeting at the beginning or benediction at the conclusion. Interestingly as well, it contained no words of thanksgiving to God or to the Lord Jesus for all they had done. As with the gospel he wrote, John did not identify himself in his first epistle or make any specific reference to his calling, his authority, or his position in the church. The absence of his name and of any explanation of his place in the church suggests that he was well known to his readers and felt no need to identify himself or invoke his position in order to strengthen his authority in writing.

In contrast to the linear style of writing that the apostles Paul and Peter and James employed in their epistles, John's first epistle moved in circles, forming an advancing sequence of thoughts. He would introduce a thought, move on from that thought, and then return to that thought later in his writing. When he returned to a previous thought, it was often to restate that thought and add strength to it. This style he employed was not unlike the parallel structure of Hebrew poetry where the second verse of a couplet often carried the same meaning as the first and strengthened it by restating it.

John's first epistle may have been a written homiletic; a sermon or message that could be read by many believers and by many different congregations. In fact, his epistle may have been an encyclical; a written message intended to reach all the churches of Asia. Some historians suggest that messengers may have carried John's epistle from city to city and from church to church where it could be read for the benefit of the general assemblies in those places. It is possible that what Paul exhorted the Colossian believers to do with the epistle he wrote to them was also done with John's first epistle. Paul had exhorted the Colossians with these words,

> "When this epistle is read amongst you, cause that it be read also in the church of the Laodicians; and that ye likewise read the epistle from Laodicea."
>
> *Colossians 4:16*

An early section of John's first epistle was written in the style of a polemic—a strong written or spoken argument against another person's or another group's opinions, beliefs, or practices. One cannot read his first epistle and fail to notice that much of it was, indeed, a skillful, carefully crafted, sometimes harsh argument against the errant teachings and ungodly lifestyle of some and a strong and thorough argument for fundamental Christian truth and for a godly lifestyle in the light.

The Nature of John's Epistle

The apostle John's first epistle was pastoral in nature, written from the heart of a true spiritual leader who had a great concern for the people of God he knew and loved. John was bound in heart to his spiritual children. His intense personal feelings for them are everywhere evident in his epistle, revealed by the tender language he used. In I John 2:1, for example, he wrote,

"My little children, these things write I unto you..."

I John 2:1

Not only in this passage, but also in I John 2:18, I John 2:28, and I John 3:18, John referred to his readers as his "little children." Clearly, he had a father's heart for these believers and felt a true shepherd's concern for them. His desire to protect his little children from dangerous error and from the consequences of that error is clearly expressed throughout his epistle. The deep affection John felt for the believers under his care created the pastoral tone of his epistle.

Although John wrote his first epistle with tenderness and compassion, he also demonstrated apostolic authority and even harshness in his writing; especially when referring to doctrinal error and to those who were peddling it. Although gentle when addressing his spiritual children, he was strident when referencing those who were errant and who wanted to seduce his spiritual children. He characterized those who were promoting error and an ungodly lifestyle as liars, antichrists, children of the devil, seducers, deceivers, and false prophets. He was not afraid to warn his spiritual children of teachings that were dangerous or to label individuals who would seduce them with very negative descriptors.

John's first epistle was a mix of pastoral care, fatherly encouragement, and sound teaching on the one hand, and serious warnings and harsh rhetoric directed against error and those who were promoting it on the other hand. Throughout his epistle, both his deep affection for his spiritual children and his intolerance for those who would pervert the truth and damage his spiritual children was on display. John's writing voice, then, was not only the voice of a father and a shepherd, but was also the voice of an apostle, a prophet, a herald, and a theologian. Writing with passion and authority, John expected his words to be considered and heeded.

John's Audience

John did not state in his first epistle who he was writing to or reveal where they lived. It is most likely, however, that the immediate recipients of his letter were Christians living in Ephesus and the surrounding area of the Roman province of Asia. Because he did not specifically address a person or a local church, many scholars believe that his letter may have been a circular sermon, intended to be read by believers in various places; primarily among the Asiatic churches of which Ephesus was the center. This geographic area would have included the seven churches mentioned in the first three chapters of the book of Revelation. It is possible, since John's first epistle was written twenty-five or thirty years after Peter's first epistle, that it reached a larger territory and greater scope of believers than Peter's epistle. It may have been read by some of the same believers who read Paul's epistles to the Ephesians, to the Colossians, and to the churches of Galatia.

Although John's first epistle contains no detailed information about who he was addressing and gives no clue as to the specific locale of the recipients, what can be said about his intended audience, based on the content of his epistle, is that they were Christians, that they were well-known to him, and that they were facing a serious threat from false teaching and false teachers. This threat seemed to be coming not only from without, but also from within their own Christian community (I John 2:19). Some of the believers John addressed were new converts to Christianity and young in the faith. Others were more mature in the faith. In fact, John referred to some as "fathers" and revealed that some had heard the message of Christ, "from the beginning" (I John 2:24; 3:11).

The Situation

More important than the geographic location John wrote from or the geographic location of the believers he wrote to was the spiritual situation that gave rise to his first epistle. The deeply concerned tone and authoritative nature of his first epistle reveals that he was addressing a situation that was already negatively affecting the church and could become a much greater problem. In one place, he wrote,

"These things have I written unto you concerning them that seduce you."

I John 2:26

John's words throughout his first epistle reveal that certain individuals were causing trouble for the community of faith he loved. The strength of the negative labels he used to identify these opponents of the faith—antichrists, false prophets, liars, deceivers, and seducers—revealed the depth of his negative feelings about them and indicated how dangerous he believed their influence was. His words in 1 John 2:19—"they went out from us"—suggest that some of the seducers had once been part of, or at least had engaged with, the Christian community. The strong words John employed throughout his first epistle leave no doubt that believers he loved were being negatively influenced and that their steadfast faith in Christ was being threatened.

Although we will delve deeper into these things later in our study, I will briefly identify the trouble makers and the errors that John referred to, both directly and indirectly, throughout his first epistle. What was happening in the region of Ephesus where John lived and was ministering is that early forms of gnostic teaching and lifestyle were being promoted. Exactly what early gnosticism looked like at the time John wrote his first epistle is difficult to pin down, not only because gnosticism was in its infant stages, but also because it was an amalgamation of many different teachings—Jewish, Christian, pagan, and other. Most scholars agree, however, that although John was not addressing and warning about fully developed gnosticism, he was, indeed, addressing and warning about dangerous early elements of gnostic belief and lifestyle. His message was intended to protect his spiritual children from heretical teachings and to ensure that their fellowship with God in the light continued.

Throughout his first epistle, John addressed two of the most dangerous doctrines that grew out of the early gnostics' core belief in dualism. One of those errant doctrines was their teaching about Jesus of Nazareth. The early gnostics did not believe that Jesus of Nazareth was the eternal God who had come to earth in a human body to save men from their sins. They did not believe that He was the Son of God. They did not believe that He was the Christ; the anointed one. They did not believe that He was the Messiah or Savior. They believed, rather, that Jesus of Nazareth was one of several "enlightened teachers" or "redeemers" who had been sent to earth by God as a messenger to bring *gnosis* (special knowledge) to those who were seeking.

A second errant doctrine of the early gnostics was their teaching that men had no sin nature, that men did not need to be saved from their sins, and that sinning didn't matter because the pure spirit of man had no meaningful connection to the evil body. Because of this disconnect between spirit and body, they believed that nothing a person did in their body could affect their spirit, their spiritual life, or their relationship with God.

John warned about early gnostic error concerning the divinity of Jesus Christ and His incarnation with words like these,

> *"Beloved, believe not every spirit, but try the spirits whether they are of God: because many false prophets are gone out into the world. Hereby know ye the Spirit of God: Every spirit that confesseth that Jesus Christ is come in the flesh is of God: And every spirit that confesseth not that Jesus Christ is come in the flesh is not of God: and this is that spirit of antichrist, whereof ye have heard that it should come; and even now already is it in the world."*
>
> I John 4:1-3

John had addressed this same error earlier in his epistle when he wrote,

> *"Who is a liar but he that denieth that Jesus is the Christ? He is antichrist, that denieth the Father and the Son."*
>
> I John 2:22

Later in his epistle, John confronted this same errant doctrine when he wrote,

> *"And ye know that he (Jesus) was manifested to take away our sins..."*
>
> I John 3:5

John also addressed the early gnostic error concerning sin and sinning throughout in his first epistle. For example, in I John 1:8, he wrote,

> *"If we say that we have no sin* (which the early gnostics said), *we deceive ourselves, and the truth is not in us."*
>
> I John 1:8

John followed up and expanded on this statement two verses later when he wrote,

> *"If we say that we have not sinned* (which the early gnostics said), *we make him a liar, and his word is not in us."*
>
> I John 1:10

Not only did the early gnostics believe that their spirit was pure and sinless and that they didn't need a Savior to save them from their sins; they also believed that nothing they did in their bodies could affect their spirit or their spiritual life. That is why they said, "we have not sinned."

In I John 2:1, John clearly expressed that one of the main reasons he wrote his first epistle was so that believers would not embrace this errant teaching concerning sin and the lifestyle of sinning that was being promoted in the region. He wrote,

> *"My little children, these things write I unto you, that ye sin not...."*
>
> I John 2:1

The apostle John's many words of warning in his first epistle about the errant teachings of the early gnostics, both concerning who Jesus of Nazareth was and concerning the subject of sin and sinning, may confirm the accuracy of the warning Paul had delivered to the Ephesian elders three decades earlier when he left the region of Ephesus. He had warned those Holy Ghost chosen spiritual leaders that not only would savage wolves seek to invade the church from outside, but that false teachers would arise from within their own group and, "speak perverse things...to draw away disciples after them" (Acts 20:29-30). It seems that Paul's words of warning had come true. False teachers were seeking to infiltrate the church with their error. And even once sound believers had been deceived and were speaking perverse things. Some had gone out from the body and were trying to seduce others to depart from the truth and from the sound body. The Ephesian church and other churches in the region were facing significant spiritual trouble; trouble that was coming not only from outside the church, but also from those who had once been part of the church; perhaps, as Paul had warned, even from those who had once been Holy Ghost appointed spiritual leaders.

More than any other New Testament epistle, John's first epistle features the errant teachings of early gnosticism. It contains strong arguments against those teachings and stern warnings about the ungodly lifestyle those teachings both gendered and supported. John's specific warnings about and teachings against the two major errors of the early gnostics—their errant teaching about who Jesus of Nazareth was and their errant teaching about sin and sinning—can be found throughout his first epistle.

Conclusion

This brief overview helps orient us to John's first epistle and gives us a base of knowledge to start from as we delve into our study. We now know who wrote the first epistle of John, know why it was written, and know to whom it was written. We know something of the style of John's first epistle and are familiar with its general purpose. We also know something about the two early gnostic errors John addressed and contended against throughout his first epistle. One of those errors, very pertinent to our study of I John 1:9, was their error concerning sin and sinning.

We can now proceed to examine various important facts that pertain specifically to I John 1:9. The things we learn in upcoming chapters as we circle around I John 1:9 and look at it from various points of view will provide us with the information and the context we need to reach an accurate interpretation and a good understanding of what John really meant by his words in I John 1:9.

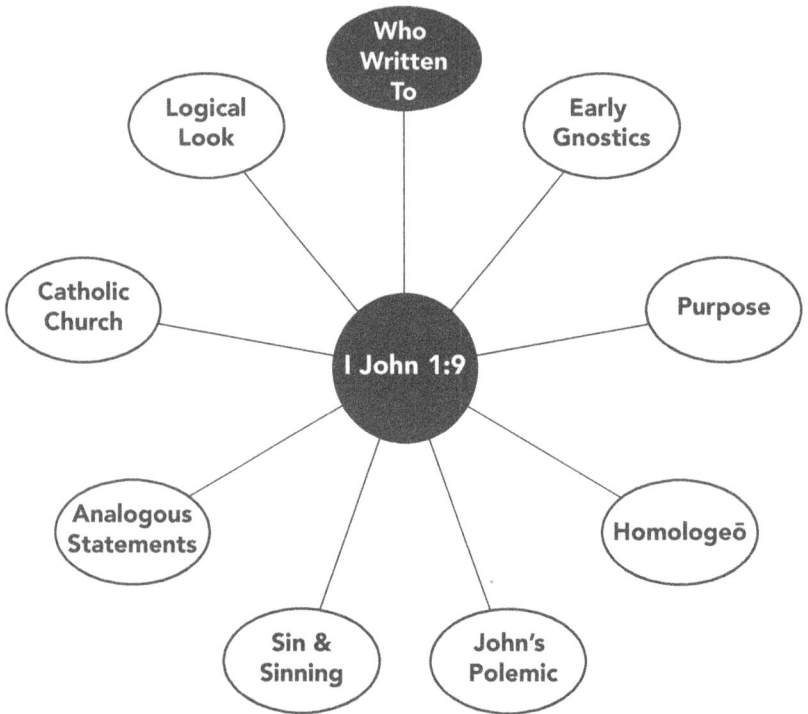

II

John's First Epistle Was Written To Believers

In order to arrive at a correct interpretation of any Scripture, we must determine who was being addressed in that Scripture. To make that determination, we must ask and answer the questions, "Who was the author of these words writing to?" or, "Who was the speaker of this message speaking to?" The correct answer to these questions is essential to reaching a correct interpretation of any Scripture.

For example, if we were reading the words Jesus spoke to the rich young ruler as recorded in Luke's gospel, we must ask the question, "Who was Jesus speaking to?" If we determined that He was speaking not only to the rich young ruler, but to all His disciples in every place and in every generation, then His instruction to, "sell all that you have and give it to the poor," would pertain to every person who ever chose to follow Him. In that case, every disciple of Jesus should heed His words, sell everything they have, and give the proceeds to the poor. In this passage of Scripture, however, Jesus' words were not an instruction directed to all His disciples in every place and in every generation, but were an instruction directed to the rich young ruler whose heart was divided between loving and following after wealth and loving and following after Jesus. Jesus' instruction to the rich young ruler to sell everything he had and give the proceeds to the poor does not apply to every disciple of Jesus. Understanding who Jesus was speaking to in this situation is very important to a correct interpretation and application of His words.

If we were reading the Old Testament Scriptures where God gave specific instructions to His covenant people Israel about sacrifices, feast days, and specific aspects of temple service, we must ask ourselves, "Do these instructions that God gave to His people Israel pertain to us as New Testament believers and must we follow them?" If we determined that every instruction God gave to Old Covenant Israel also applied to us as New Covenant believers, then we should follow those instructions. We should offer certain sacrifices at certain times for certain sins. We should forego eating certain foods. We should observe special feast days. We should honor the Sabbath day by not working. And we might have to stone to death anyone who violated the Sabbath. If, on the other hand, we determined that some of the instructions God gave to Old Covenant Israel pertained only to them and were only applicable to those living under the Old Covenant dispensation, then we would not have to follow those instructions.

Sometimes it is easy to determine who an author of Scripture was addressing. For example, several authors of New Testament epistles stated specifically who they were writing to. We know that the first and second epistles to the Corinthians, both written by the apostle Paul, were written to believers in the city of Corinth (I Corinthians 1:2; II Corinthians 1:1). A number of things in those two epistles pertained specifically to the Corinthian believers and to unique situations in the church there. We know that Paul's epistle to the Romans was directed to believers in Rome that he had never met; some who were Jewish and some who were Gentile (Romans 1:7; 15:22-24). We know that Paul's epistle to the Galatians was written to believers in the region of Galatia who were being targeted by Judaizers attempting to persuade Gentile converts that they must be circumcised in order to be saved.

Peter was not as specific in his two epistles about who he was addressing. We know, however, that his first epistle was written to believers who had been scattered throughout Pontus, Galatia, Cappadocia, Asia, and Bithynia; many of them Jewish converts to Christianity (I Peter 1:1). In his first epistle, Peter identified a subset of believers he called "elders" and offered them specific instructions pertaining to their unique role in the church (I Peter 5:1-4). His instructions to those elders were not directed to all believers and must be interpreted and applied with that important fact in mind.

Concerning the epistle to the Hebrews, it is not so clear who the intended recipients were. We can deduce, however, both from its many exhortations and from its general content that it was written to Jewish converts to Christianity who were suffering significant affliction and considering abandoning their faith in Jesus Christ and returning to Judaism. We know that the Hebrew epistle was intended to be an exhortation because the author concluded it by encouraging his readers to receive his, "brief word of exhortation" (Hebrews 13:22).

As in Peter's first epistle, sometimes within an epistle certain individuals were addressed. For example, in his epistle to the Ephesians, Paul addressed wives and gave them specific instructions (Ephesians 5:22). Then he addressed husbands and gave them specific instructions (Ephesians 5:25). When husbands read what Paul wrote to the wives, they must remember that those words were not written to them. Otherwise, they might misuse those words to leverage themselves over their wives by demanding that they submit. And when wives read Paul's exhortation to husbands, they must remember that those words were not written to them. Otherwise, they might misuse those words and criticize their husbands for not being more loving.

As we can see from these examples, it is critical to the interpretation and application of any Scripture to determine who the intended recipient was. This crucial aspect of Scripture interpretation also applies to John's first epistle and to I John 1:9. In order to rightly understand John's first epistle and accurately interpret his words in I John 1:9, it is essential to know who he was writing to. If we don't know "who" he was writing to, we will not correctly understand "what" he was communicating. In this chapter, therefore, we will look at John's words in I John 1:9 from this very important view, asking and answering this question, "Who were John's words in I John 1:9 written to and intended for?"

Who Was John's First Epistle Written To?

There is a significant amount of support for the point of view that John's first epistle was written to believers. There is very little support, on the other hand, for the point of view some have articulated that the first chapter of John's first epistle, including I John 1:9, was written to gnostic sinners. Let's consider several things that support the point of view that John's whole first epistle was written to believers.

First, almost all Bible scholars agree that John's first epistle was written to believers John knew and loved. Although some Christians don't have much faith in scholars or scholarship, it is important to realize that being a scholar, a theologian, or a Christian historian does not indicate that one is not a serious Christian or a passionate, devoted follower of Jesus Christ. In fact, many who have written serious theological works and authored books about church history did so because they felt called by God to do so. They did their work seriously and prayerfully and their views should be given careful consideration. Whether some Christians realize it or not, many of the things they know and believe were things studied out, interpreted, established, and communicated by serious and devoted Christian scholars.

The fact that almost all Bible scholars agree that John's first epistle was written to and written for the benefit of Christians is significant. If the opinions of experts were divided on this matter, or if only a few Bible scholars believed that John's first epistle was written to Christians, then we would be less confident about this point of view. But the overwhelming weight of evidence from serious and studious scholars informs us that John's first epistle—his whole epistle, including the first chapter and I John 1:9—was written to and written for the benefit of Christians.

Second, although John did not name a specific recipient for his epistle, he revealed a number of times throughout his epistle who he was writing to. The fact that he did not open his epistle with a specific greeting to Christians as he did in his other two epistles and as most New Testament authors did is not a legitimate basis for an argument that the first chapter of his epistle was not written to believers. There are numerous passages throughout his first epistle where John addressed his readers with terms that make it abundantly clear he was writing to believers. For example, in I John 2:1 he wrote,

"My little children, these things write I unto you, that ye sin not."

I John 2:1

By characterizing his readers as "My little children," John not only revealed that he was writing to believers; he revealed that he was writing to believers he knew and loved.

In I John 2:7, John addressed his readers as "Brethren" when he wrote,

"Brethren, I write no new commandment unto you…"

I John 2:7

The fact that John addressed the recipients of his words as "Brethren" reveals that he was addressing fellow believers; those who were in the same family of God that he was in.

In I John 4:1, John wrote,

"Beloved, believe not every spirit, but try the spirits to see if they be of God."

I John 4:1

By referring to his readers as "Beloved," John revealed that he was writing to believers that he loved, that he knew, who were part of the family of faith, and who he felt a spiritual responsibility for.

In I John 4:6, John again addressed those he was writing to as "little children" and revealed that they were born of the same God he was born of; in other words, they were believers. He wrote,

"Ye are of God, little children…"

I John 4:6

In I John 4:13, John wrote,

"Hereby know we that we dwell in him, and he in us, because he hath given us of his Spirit."

I John 4:13

With these words, John identified his readers as those who, like him, dwelt in God, revealing that they were believers. He also wrote that God had, "given us of his Spirit." The Holy Spirit is God's wonderful gift to those who believe His gospel and have confessed their faith in Jesus Christ. The recipients of these words from John were clearly believers.

In I John 5:19, John wrote,

"And we know that we are of God…"

I John 5:19

By using the word "we" in this passage and saying, "we are of God," John again revealed that both he and his readers were believers.

In I John 5:13, John wrote,

"These things have I written unto you that believe on the name of the Son of God; that ye may know that ye have eternal life, and that ye may believe on the name of the Son of God."

I John 5:13

In this verse, John identified those he was writing to as, "you that believe on the name of the Son of God," and as those who, "have eternal life." Again, there is no doubt that John was addressing believers.

Throughout his epistle, John made it abundantly clear that he was writing to believers. Is it possible that the individuals he addressed in all of the verses we just considered were a completely different group of individuals than those he addressed in chapter one? When he said in I John 5:13, "These things have I written unto you that believe," was he referring to a group of individuals that he only began to address in I John 2:1, or was he referring to the same individuals he had been addressing from the beginning of his epistle? It is far more likely that John's whole first epistle was written to and written for the one group of individuals he clearly identified throughout his epistle as believers.

The apostle John gave no indication in his first epistle that he was addressing two different groups of individuals and gave no indication that he changed audiences in I John 2:1. It is not logical, then, to assume that he was addressing two different groups of individuals;

gnostic sinners in chapter one and believers in the remainder of his epistle. There is no good reason to doubt that all the words of John's first epistle, including his words in chapter one and in I John 1:9, were addressed to and intended for believers.

Third, John was often specific in his first epistle about who he was addressing. In one place, he even delineated between the different spiritual ages of believers, addressing some as "little children," some as "young men," and some as "fathers" (I John 2:12-14). The fact that John went to this length to identify the various spiritual ages of believers makes it illogical to suppose that if he was writing to gnostic sinners in chapter one, he would not have made an effort to identify them as such.

If, as some suggest, John's intention was to reach gnostic sinners with the gospel of Jesus Christ in the first chapter of his first epistle, he would not have failed to identify and specifically address them. Nowhere in his first epistle, however, did he address anyone as unbelievers or sinners. Because John was so specific throughout his first epistle about who he was writing to and why he was writing, it is not logical to conclude that he was addressing gnostic sinners in the first chapter, but somehow failed to make that clear.

Fourth, many times in his first epistle, John stated explicitly why he had written. He said he had written that, "your joy may be full" (I John 1:4). He said he had written, "that ye sin not" (I John 2:1). He said he had written because, "ye know (the truth)" (I John 2:21). He said he had written to warn believers of seducers (I John 2:27). He said he had written so that believers would know they had eternal life and so that they would have a certainty about what they believed (I John 5:13). Among all the specific statements John made about why he had written his first epistle, there was not a single statement or even an indication expressing that one of the reasons he had written was for the purpose of converting sinners to faith in Jesus Christ. In an epistle where he made obvious efforts to be clear about why he had written, John made no mention that one reason he had written was for the purpose of presenting the gospel to sinners. Rather, in every mention of why he had written, he made it apparent that he had written to believers and had written for their benefit.

Fifth, in both his statement expressing why he had written in I John 2:1 and in his final summary statement expressing why he had written in I John 5:13, John was clear that his whole epistle, including the first chapter, was written to and intended for believers. Notice his important statement in I John 2:1,

> *"My little children, these things write I unto you, that ye sin not."*
>
> I John 2:1

What things was John referring to when he told his little children, "these things write I unto you?" Was he referring to things he had not yet written, but intended to write? Or was he referring to things he had already written? It seems that by his words, "these things," John was referring to things he had already written in chapter one. He had already written that the message he heard from the beginning was that God was light and in Him was no darkness at all (I John 1:5). He had already written about those who claimed to be in fellowship with God, but were walking in darkness (I John 1:6). He had already written about the serious error of saying, "we have no sin," and, "we have not sinned" (I John 1:8, 10). And had already written about the forgiveness and the cleansing of sins of those who walked in the light and who confessed their sins (I John 1:7, 9). It seems abundantly clear that when John wrote, "My little children, these things write I unto you," he was referring to things he had already written to his "little children"—to believers—in chapter one.

When John made his final summary statement in I John 5:13 expressing why he had written his first epistle, he made it perfectly obvious that his whole epistle, including the first chapter and I John 1:9, was written to and intended for believers. He wrote,

> *"These things have I written unto you that believe on the name of the Son of God; that ye may know that ye have eternal life, and that ye may believe on the name of the Son of God."*
>
> I John 5:13

Is it possible that by his words, "These things have I written unto you," John was referring only to things he began to write about in I John 2:1? If that was what he intended for his spiritual children to understand, no doubt he would have said, "The things I have written in this epistle that are intended for you who believe are only the things that come after the words, 'If we say that we have not sinned, we make him a liar, and his word is not in us' (I John 1:10)."

It is highly unlikely that John would have expected his spiritual children to somehow know that he wasn't addressing them in the first chapter of his epistle. It seems clear, then, that his words in I John 5:13 were meant to confirm once again to believers he loved that every thing he had written in his epistle was written to, "you that believe on the name of the Son of God." As in the other places in his first epistle where he stated explicitly why he had written, John's summary statement in I John 5:13 made it clear that all the words of his epistle, including his words in chapter one and his words in I John 1:9, were written to and intended for believers; for those who were born of God, who were in Christ Jesus, and who had received eternal life.

Nowhere in his first epistle did John give any indication that he was addressing two different groups of people. If, as some assert, he was addressing unsaved gnostic sinners in chapter one and believers he loved in the rest of his epistle, he certainly failed to make that crucial fact clear. Because John's first epistle was so carefully and thoughtfully laid out, contains such exquisite arguments, and is filled with many specific statements about why he had written, it is highly improbable that he would have switched from addressing unsaved gnostic sinners in chapter one to addressing believers he loved in I John 2:1 without even mentioning it.

Who Was I John 1:9 Written To ?

Those who believe that the first chapter of John's first epistle was an evangelistic message written to gnostic sinners also believe, of course, that John's words in I John 1:9 were written to and intended for gnostic sinners. Because the common interpretation of I John 1:9

indicates the necessity of works on the part of believers to initiate God's forgiveness of their sins, they believe that I John 1:9 could not have been written to believers. The New Covenant, they would say, is a covenant of faith, not of works. The fact that the common interpretation of I John 1:9 does not seem to harmonize with the rest of the New Testament and its emphasis on the finished work of Christ is not, however, a valid reason for concluding that the first chapter of John's first epistle could not have been written to believers. To claim that the first chapter of John's first epistle must have been written to gnostic sinners simply because the common interpretation of I John 1:9 is troubling is not the way to solve what is actually not a problem when I John 1:9 is properly interpreted and correctly understood.

Although it is true that John's first epistle contains a significant amount of information about and argument against the beliefs of the early gnostics, his epistle was not directed to gnostic sinners, but to members of the Christian community who were being exposed to their dangerous error. John's spiritual children needed to be put on alert concerning that error and reminded of fundamental truths of the Christian faith so that they did not abandon the faith they had embraced. I John 1:9 was not an evangelistic message and was not written to gnostic sinners. It was, rather, one of many important statements John penned in his first epistle for the benefit of believers he loved. His words in I John 1:9 were not written for the purpose of saving sinners, but were written for the purpose of warning, teaching, and reinforcing the faith of believers, lest they be deceived and go astray.

Those who believe that the first chapter of John's first epistle was written to gnostic sinners will interpret I John 1:9 as part of an evangelistic message when, in fact, it is a significant part of John's strong warning and critical teaching to believers who were in danger of being misled by seductive and dangerous error. This serious mistake concerning who John's audience was in the first chapter of his first epistle will cause those who make it to forfeit critical truth essential to a right interpretation of I John 1:9. To reiterate, it is absolutely essential to a right interpretation of I John 1:9 to embrace the fact that John's whole first epistle was written to believers; including the first chapter and his words in I John 1:9.

Why Is This View of I John 1:9 Important?

In this chapter, we looked at John's words in I John 1:9 from our first point of view, asking and answering this important question: "Who were John's words in I John 1:9 addressed to and intended for?" We learned that John's words in I John 1:9 were written to and intended for the benefit of believers who were being exposed to errant doctrine and, therefore, at risk of being deceived. If we are mistaken on this important matter, suppose that I John 1:9 was written to and intended for gnostic sinners, and interpret John's words from that point of view, we will completely misunderstand what he was communicating and forfeit the important revelation contained in I John 1:9.

Knowing who I John 1:9 was written to is absolutely essential to a correct interpretation of I John 1:9. If it were true, as some believe, that I John 1:9 and the first chapter of John's first epistle were written to and intended for gnostic sinners, then John's words in I John 1:9 would have no special relevance to believers beyond indicating that John loved sinners and wanted them to be saved. If it were true, as some believe, that I John 1:9 and the first chapter of John's first epistle were written to and intended for gnostic sinners, then believers could skip past his words in the first chapter and move to I John 2:1 where, as some say, he began to address believers. If, on the other hand, John's words in the first chapter of his epistle and in I John 1:9 were addressed to believers and were written for their spiritual benefit, then believers must read his words, study his words, and interpret his words from that point of view.

In order for us to accurately interpret and correctly understand John's words in I John 1:9, his first epistle must be embraced as a single, cohesive message written to believers he loved who were encountering dangerous error. When John's first epistle is embraced this way and I John 1:9 is interpreted in this light, it will become clear that John's words in I John 1:9 fit beautifully with all his teaching in his first epistle and harmonize wonderfully with his other epistles, with the rest of the New Testament, and with all of Scripture. Embracing the fact that all of John's first epistle was written to and intended for believers is absolutely essential to a correct interpretation, a good understanding, and a right application of I John 1:9.

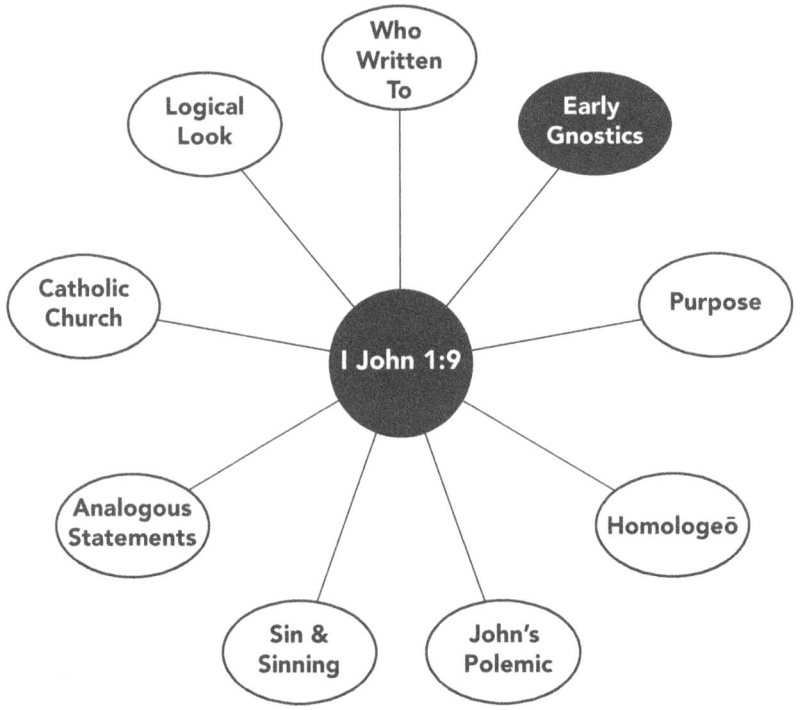

III

The Early Gnostics

You may wonder why it is necessary to include a chapter in this study that focuses on the beliefs and teachings of the early gnostics. This chapter is necessary because much of what the apostle John wrote about in his first epistle was a warning about and an argument against the errant teachings and ungodly lifestyle of some who would later be known as gnostics. If we don't know something about what these early gnostics believed and taught and are unaware that one of the primary reasons John wrote his first epistle was to warn believers about their errant teachings and their ungodly lifestyle, we will lack the context necessary to a good understanding of what he was communicating in his first epistle. That also means, of course, that we will not be able to ascertain with the clarity that accompanies right context and accurate perspective what John really meant when he wrote, "If we confess our sins, he is faithful and just to forgive us our sins and to cleanse us from all unrighteousness." Being familiar with the beliefs and the lifestyle of the early gnostics, especially the particular errors John was addressing in his first epistle, is essential to a good understanding of his first epistle and to a right interpretation of I John 1:9.

The Early Gnostics

It can be difficult to precisely understand the early gnosticism that was present in the region of Ephesus at the time John wrote his first epistle. One reason for this is because the early church made a concerted effort to eradicate all traces of early gnosticism and early gnostic teaching. Another reason is because much of what was written about the early gnostics was written by their opponents; the spiritual leaders of the early church who were gravely concerned about their error. Bishop Irenaeus, for example, who supervised the church in Lyons around 180 A.D., wrote five volumes against gnosticism entitled, "The Destruction and Overthrow of Falsely So-called Knowledge." He began his five volumes by promising to set forth the views of those who were teaching heresy and to reveal that their views were inconsistent with God's truth. What we know about gnosticism through early church leaders is colored by their opposition to that error.

Another reason it can be difficult to know the beliefs of the early gnostics is that they rarely put their teachings into writing. One reason they didn't often document their teachings was because they believed that putting spiritual revelations into a physical form corrupted them. A fairly recent discovery of gnostic writings has been helpful, however, in revealing some of their early beliefs. In the 1940s, at Nag Hammadi in Egypt, a buried jar was discovered with a number of rolled up manuscripts that are considered to be partially gnostic in nature. Some scholars say these manuscripts might be from as early as 150 A.D. and that the jar may have been left behind by a small, secluded gnostic community trying to avoid persecution. They may have buried their manuscripts to keep them from prying eyes, but then were never able to recover them.

Although the most significant historical period of gnostic influence was from about 135-160 A.D., the general philosophy of the gnostics and their beliefs, teachings, and lifestyle can be traced as far back as the beginning of the church. Some historians suggest that gnostic philosophy and beliefs actually predate Christianity. In any case, it is evident from historical writings and from the New Testament epistles that the teachings of early gnosticism were present at the time of the early church and were exerting a negative influence on the church, even though those teachings were not yet codified or labeled as gnostic.

Some historians refer to the individuals of John's day who held the errant beliefs and lived the ungodly lifestyle that would later be identified as gnosticism as "protognostics." They use this term because these individuals were an early version, a prototype, of the later gnostics. Throughout our study, I will refer to the individuals of John's day who embraced, lived, and taught what would later be referred to as gnosticism as "errant early gnostics." I think "errant early gnostics" is the best way to identify these individuals because although gnosticism was not yet galvanized into an identifiable belief system at the time John authored his first epistle, the errant teachings and ungodly lifestyle of those who would later be identified as gnostics were clearly in play and dangerous to believers and the church.

What Did the Gnostics Believe?

Gnosticism, which borrowed elements of belief from many sources, professed to be based on *gnosis*, the Greek word for "knowledge" or "insight." *Gnosis*, according to the gnostics, was a transcendental knowledge of God and His redemptive purpose. It was the special, superior knowledge gnostics believed they had received which guided them toward a state of enlightenment and, finally, salvation. For the gnostics, *gnosis* was essential and its acquisition was of chief importance.

Many early gnostics combined Christian teachings with their own allegorical teachings and with mystical interpretations of the Old Testament. Some beliefs included elements of Greek philosophy; especially Platonic dualism, Stoicism, and the teachings of Heraclitus (who was from Ephesus). Often thrown into this "gnostic mix" was basic paganism.

Some early gnostics believed that they alone truly understood Christ's message and that other streams of thought within Christianity had misunderstood who Jesus was, had misunderstood His mission, and had misinterpreted His sayings. Because the element of spiritual pride was widespread among the gnostics and because their pursuit was "deep revelation," they were proud of themselves when they believed they had achieved it. Some second century gnostics proclaimed themselves to be so enlightened and perfect that no one could compare to them with respect to the immensity of their knowledge, including Paul and Peter and other early apostles.

Gnosticism was broadly based on the philosophy of dualism. Gnostics believed that everything in the universe was either good or evil, spirit or matter, light or dark. In general, they believed that spirit was good and pure, that matter was evil and dark, and that spirit and matter could have no enduring relationship with each other. Their belief in the dual nature of the world and the dual nature of man earned them the epithet "dualists."

Gnostics believed that a good God (spirit) could not have created the evil physical world (matter) because a good God would be too pure and too perfect to have anything to do with an evil, material universe, much less create it. They believed, rather, that the good God had created lesser divinities and that one of those lesser divinities, Wisdom, who had an evil desire to know the unknowable God, had formed an evil god that created the universe of matter. This evil god kept people in bondage in material matter and tried to prevent their pure spirits from ascending back to God after the death of their physical bodies.

For gnostics, human nature expressed this duality found in the universe. The spiritual part of man—the inner spirit, which they believed was good and pure—consisted of light and a spark of the true God. This spiritual component, considered to be a fragment of the divine essence, was often referred to as "the divine spark." The physical part of man—the body, which they believed was evil—was made by the false creator god. Human beings, then, consisted of an eternal spiritual component that was good and pure—the spirit—and a perishable physical component that was evil—the body.

Gnostics believed that the spark of the purely spiritual in people longed to be reunited with God, but was unable to do so because it was trapped in the physical (evil) world of matter; especially the evil body. Most people, according to their belief, were ignorant of the divine spark of the purely spiritual that was resident in them. This ignorance was due to the influence of the false creator and his archons who were intent upon keeping men and women unaware of their true nature and eternal destiny.

Gnostics did not believe that every person was able to gain the secret knowledge necessary to enlightenment and salvation. *Gnosis* was only available, rather, to a special few called the pneumatics. Only these spiritually elite could gain the special knowledge necessary to be enlightened and saved and only these spiritually elite had within themselves the capacity for liberation from the evil matter of the world and the shackles of the body. The gnostics considered themselves to be these spiritually elite individuals. In fact, some gnostics who claimed to be Christians considered themselves to be spiritually superior to the average Christian.

The gnostic concept of salvation, like other gnostic concepts, was somewhat subtle. Although some believed that there might be potential present in every man and woman for *gnosis*, and thus salvation, they also acknowledged that *gnosis* must be stimulated and facilitated from an outside source in order to arise within the human consciousness. This outside help was necessary, they believed, because knowledge of the true human condition was withheld by the very nature of human existence. A revelation, or *gnosis*, from an outside source was needed to alert people to their condition, to awaken the indwelling divine spark from its slumber, and to bring about enlightenment and salvation.

Gnostics believed that the outside stimulation which awakened people to their condition was supplied by messengers of light who came forth from the true God to aid humans in their quest for *gnosis*. These messengers came from the world of light, penetrated the barrier of the spheres, outwitted the archons, awakened the human spirit from its earthly slumber, and imparted saving knowledge. These messengers, or redeemers, who came from the spirit realm often came in a disguise. Many gnostics believed that Jesus of Nazareth was one of these special messengers of light who came to earth to impart *gnosis*. Only a few special messengers are mentioned by name in gnostic writings, the most important being Seth (the third son of Adam), Jesus, and the prophet Mani.

According to gnostic teaching, the spirit of man, imprisoned in the body and ignorant of whence it came, found salvation from its condition in two stages. In this present life, salvation was an awakening or an enlightenment which was affected through *gnosis*. Then, equipped with saving *gnosis*, the spirit of man was prepared for the second stage of salvation; liberation at death from the bonds of the world and from the evil body of flesh and a return to its own native realm of light.

For gnostics, the only hope of salvation—of reaching the spiritual realm and being reunited with God in the light—was by receiving enlightenment. And it was only by the special revelation of secret, esoteric knowledge—only by *gnosis*—that a person could be enlightened. By the aid of *gnosis*, a person who was enlightened could, at death, overcome the "gate-keepers" who would attempt to hinder the spirit on its journey to the realm of light. They believed that as the spirit of the enlightened person traveled upward, it would leave behind at each sphere the psychical vestment put upon it by the spirit's downward flight at birth. The spirit would finally be stripped of all foreign accretions, such as individual personal identities and a body, and be reunited with God in the realm of light.

For gnostics salvation was not about being forgiven of sins, not about escaping eternal punishment in hell, and not about the physical resurrection of the body at some point in the future. Salvation was about being freed from ignorance and then, at the end of one's physical life, escaping from the realm of evil matter into the realm of good spirit and light. The gnostics believed that physical death always released the divine spark of man from its lowly prison in the body. If, however, there had been no substantial work of *gnosis* undertaken prior to death, the divine spark would be hurled back to the evil material world and re-embodied within the slavery of that world.

Gnostics did not believe that they needed to be saved from their sins because they didn't believe that anyone had a sin nature or was a sinner. They believed, rather, that man's spirit was good and pure because it came from God and, therefore, did not need to be saved. This belief fit with their view that Jesus of Nazareth was a wonderful teacher and a messenger of light, but was not the Savior sent to the world by God to save men from their sins. After all, if no one was a sinner and no one sinned, then no one needed a Savior to save them from their sins. The early gnostics believed that what was truly necessary was for people to be enlightened to the "truth" that they were already pure, not for them to come to the realization that they were sinners who needed a Savior.

For nearly all gnostics, Jesus held a central place; although they denied that He was the Son of God, denied that He was the Christ in human form, denied His physical death and resurrection, and denied that He was the Savior of the world. Some gnostics believed that Jesus was pure spirit and only had a phantom body; that He only appeared to be human to His followers. Some believed that at His birth, Jesus was a "psychic Christ" that passed through Mary like water passes through a tube, but that He never assumed human flesh.

For most gnostics it was inconceivable that the Christ, who was a divine and exalted spirit being, would choose to inhabit an evil, human body. Therefore, the Christ could not have become flesh, could not have become the historical Jesus of Nazareth, and could not have been the Son of God in human form. Most gnostics denied the incarnation; they denied that Jesus of Nazareth was the Son of God who had come to earth in a genuine human body. They also did not believe that the Christ, who they saw as a true emissary sent from the Supreme God, could have been overcome by the evil of the world and died. Because gnostics denied the incarnation of God as Jesus Christ the man, they also denied the doctrine of Jesus' atoning work to provide salvation from sin for all mankind.

Gnosticism and Morality

Gnostics believed that because the human spirit came from God, it was pure and light. Concerning the human body, however, they believed that along with all other matter, it was essentially evil and dark. As pertaining to humanity, then, they believed that the eternal spirit was pure while the physical body was evil. They also believed that the spirit and the body had no effective connection with each other. This core belief led to two main lifestyle expressions among gnostics; some were ascetic and some were libertarian.

The ascetic gnostics tried to separate themselves from all earthly evil in order to avoid contamination. They believed that because the physical body was evil, it must be denied in order for the spirit to gain salvation. Some gnostics beat, starved, and denied their physical selves, practicing a rigid asceticism in which their bodies were kept under strict control. Some shunned marriage and certain foods and delighted in self-abasement; even inflicting pain on their bodies. Paul's epistle to the Colossian church may suggest that ascetic gnostics were influencing believers in Colosse (Colossians 2:20-23). It is also possible that in his first letter to Timothy, Paul was referring to early acetic gnostics when he wrote about those who had departed from the faith because they had listened to seducing spirits and were now, "forbidding to marry and commanding to abstain from meats" (I Timothy 4:1-4).

The libertarian gnostics, although they shared the same fundamental beliefs as the ascetics, had an opposite lifestyle expression. They believed that those who were truly enlightened—those who had received *gnosis* and "knew"—understood that although man had a body, he was essentially a spirit and, therefore, was good and pure because spirit was good and pure. The libertarian gnostics believed that no immoral deed done in the flesh could ever penetrate the enlightened spirit. Many of them lived according to their carnal desires, believing that nothing they did in their body could affect their pure spirit or their spiritual life. They believed that they could satisfy every appetite and use their body in any way they pleased since only what they did in their spirit truly mattered. To the libertarian gnostics, all things were permitted. Some actually denied that sin existed at all, completely disregarding God's moral code found in Scripture. They lived as they pleased while saying, "I am enlightened and in fellowship with God; I have no sin; I have not sinned" (I John 1:6, 8, 10).

One of the libertarian gnostics' favorite metaphors for their "truth" was that of a ring of pure gold set in a pile of pig dung. They said that in the same way that a golden ring could sit in dung and be surrounded by dung, but not be penetrated and tainted by the dung, so they could live in sin and commit sin, but not be tainted by sin—sin could not penetrate and defile their pure spirit. They believed that at some point in the future it was only the spirit that would be saved, so it didn't really matter what they did in the present with their physical bodies. Of the Carpocratian gnostics, Irenaeus (bishop of Lyon and a leading Christian theologian of the 2nd century) reported they were so abandoned in their recklessness that they claimed they could practice anything whatsoever, no matter how ungodly, since conduct was only good or evil in the eyes of man. Iranaeus also said in his writings that some gnostics claimed that they had attained to such spiritual heights that they were free to act however they pleased and did not need to fear anything from any authority.

Concerning life on earth the general principle of gnostic conduct was a hostility toward the world of matter because the world and the body were evil; they were the source of ignorance and the cause of the slumber of the soul. The ascetic gnostics deduced from the possession of *gnosis* their obligation to avoid further contamination and, therefore, tried to keep their contact with the world to a minimum. The libertine gnostics derived from the possession of *gnosis* their privilege of absolute freedom and lived as carnally as they pleased while claiming to be enlightened; often professing a relationship with God and sometimes even claiming to be Christians. It seems that it was the libertine gnostics and their error concerning sin and sinning that the apostle John was warning about and dealing with in his first epistle.

Early Spiritual Leaders and Early Gnosticism

Some Christian historians believe that the teachings and the lifestyle of those who would later be called gnostics were some of the most dangerous heresies and lifestyle challenges the first century church faced. Because of the danger of these heresies and the dark lifestyle of many early gnostics, first generation spiritual leaders dealt with them often in their writings. Paul's epistle to the Colossians, his epistle to the

Ephesians, and his letters to Timothy and Titus all contained warnings and corrective teaching that appear to be a response to early gnostic heresy. As well, Peter's epistles, Jude's epistle, and John's first two epistles contain significant warnings and corrective teachings addressing error that would later be identified as gnostic.

In his various epistles, Paul referred to the wisdom and knowledge that came from God and did not concern itself with idle speculations, angelic visitations, fables, and immoral lifestyle; all things that were characteristic of the early gnostics (Colossians 2:1-23; I Timothy 1:1-10, 15; II Timothy 2:16-19; Titus 1:10-16). Paul may have been refuting early gnostic claims of special revelation and profound knowledge in his epistle to the Colossians when he wrote,

> *"For I would that ye knew what great conflict I have for you, and for them at Laodicea, and for as many as have not seen my face in the flesh; That their hearts might be comforted, being knit together in love, and unto all riches of the full assurance of understanding, to the acknowledgment of the mystery of God, and of the Father, and of Christ; In whom are hid all the treasures of wisdom and knowledge. And this I say, lest any man should beguile you with enticing words."*
>
> *Colossians 2:1-4*

The serious inward struggle and deep concern Paul experienced for believers in Colosse may have been due to the unhealthy spiritual influence of errant early gnostics in the region. His assertion that, "all the treasures of wisdom and knowledge," were hidden in the Father and in Christ would have both refuted early gnostic teaching about who Jesus of Nazareth was and strengthened believers' grounding in New Covenant truth so that no one could, "beguile (them) with enticing words." The early gnostics sometimes tried to lure true believers away from sound faith by boasting that they had deep revelation and special knowledge and that they were the ones who truly "understood mysteries." Paul declared, however, that all the treasures of wisdom and knowledge were hidden in the very Father and the very Son of

God and Lord Jesus Christ the early gnostics denied. The fact that Paul even referred to God as Father and referred to Christ in his words to the Colossians was a strong refutation of the early gnostic teaching that Jesus of Nazareth was not God's Son or the Christ.

Paul may also have been addressing early gnostic error when he warned believers in Colosse with these words,

> *"Beware lest any man spoil you through philosophy and vain deceit... and not after Christ. For in him* (Christ) *dwells all the fullness of the godhead bodily. And you are complete in him who is the head of all principality and power..."*
>
> *Colossians 2:9*

The early gnostic teaching that Jesus of Nazareth was not the Son of God incarnate in human flesh and was not the Christ, but was only an exalted messenger of *gnosis* posed a threat to the very foundation of Christianity—the foundational truth that Jesus of Nazareth was God incarnate in flesh, that He was the Son of God, that He was the Christ, that He was the Savior of sinners, and that He was sufficient in all things. Paul wanted to be sure that true believers were grounded in the truth that the fullness of the Godhead dwelt bodily in Jesus of Nazareth; that He was the eternal Word made flesh. Then their faith would not be spoiled by philosophy that was not grounded in Christ.

Paul may have been addressing the early gnostics' preoccupation with angelic revelations, their boasts of superior spirituality, and the ascetic view of life that some of them held when he exhorted the Colossian believers with these words,

> *"Let no man beguile you of your reward in a voluntary humility and worshipping of angels, intruding into those things which he hath not seen, vainly puffed up by his fleshly mind, And not holding the Head* (Christ)*...Which things have indeed a shew of wisdom in will worship, and humility, and neglecting of the body: not in any honour to the satisfying of the flesh."*
>
> *Colossians 2:18-19, 23*

It seems that early in the life of the church, foundational Christian truths were being challenged by early gnostic teaching. Paul was laboring in teaching and in prayer to combat this influence and to make sure believers remained grounded in God's truth and secure in their faith. He did not want them to be led away from the soundness of their faith by errant teachings coming from false teachers, but to be, "Rooted and built up in him (Christ Jesus) and stablished in the faith" (Colossians 2:7). He wanted them to understand that Jesus of Nazareth was not just some exalted teacher, but that, "in him (Jesus Christ) dwelleth all the fullness of the Godhead bodily," and to know that they were, "complete in him" (Colossians 2:9-10). He wanted them to know that they were circumcised in Christ from the sins of their old carnal life, that they were buried and risen with Him to new life, and that they were forgiven of all their sins because of His suffering and death (Colossians 2:11-13). These incredible things could never have been accomplished by the teachings of an exalted messenger of *gnosis*, but they had been accomplished by Jesus Christ of Nazareth who was the Son of God and the Savior of the world. Many of the warnings Paul presented throughout his epistle to the Colossians would have alerted them to the serious errors of the early gnostics.

In his first letter to Timothy, Paul spoke of some who had "swerved" from the faith and, "turned aside unto vain jangling" (I Timothy 1:6). He may have been referring to early gnostics who had once fellow-shipped with the sound body of Christ, but had departed in pursuit of deeper revelation and "went out from among us" as John mentioned in his first epistle (I John 2:19). Paul reminded Timothy that he had left him in Ephesus to deal with these "swervers" and their errant teachings when he wrote,

> "As I besought thee to abide still at Ephesus, when I went into Macedonia, that thou mightest charge some that they teach no other doctrine, Neither give heed to fables and endless genealogies, which minister questions, rather than godly edifying which is in faith..."
>
> I Timothy 1:3-4

The "fables and endless genealogies" that Timothy was to charge others not to teach or to pay attention to were things characteristic of the early gnostics. They were fascinated with various creation accounts, with genealogies, with mystical stories, and with other speculations.

Just a few verses later in his letter to Timothy, Paul wrote,

> *"This is a faithful saying, and worthy of all acceptation, that Christ Jesus came into the world to save sinners; of whom I am chief."*
>
> I Timothy 1:15

Paul characterized his saying that, "Christ Jesus came into the world to save sinners," as a, "faithful saying, and worthy of all acceptation." He meant by these words that his saying was absolutely trustworthy and should be embraced as truth. Paul may have written these strong and clear words to Timothy because of the errant teachings of the early gnostics that were spreading in the region of Ephesus where Timothy was living and serving. Paul's faithful saying that, "Christ Jesus came into the world to save sinners," was not only an absolutely foundational statement of Christian truth; it was also a direct refutation of early gnostic error concerning Jesus of Nazareth. He may have emphasized this most basic truth to Timothy to help keep him steady in the faith and to help him hold the church steady against the infiltration of early gnostic error.

One other thing the apostle Paul wrote to his young son in the faith, Timothy, may have been intended as a direct attack on early gnostic error concerning who Jesus of Nazareth was. He wrote,

> *"And without controversy great is the mystery of godliness; God was manifest in the flesh…"*
>
> I Timothy 3:16

Paul did not want Timothy to entertain error or pass along error concerning Jesus of Nazareth or what He had done. According to Paul's words, Jesus was, "God…manifest in the flesh." This strong and concise statement of truth was completely antithetical to the errant teaching of the early gnostics who claimed that Jesus of Nazareth was just an exalted messenger of truth.

The apostle Peter may have been referring to errant early gnostics and their activity when he wrote these words of warning in his second epistle,

> "But there were false prophets also among the people, even as there shall be false teachers among you, who privily shall bring in damnable heresies, even denying the Lord that bought them, and bring upon themselves swift destruction...For when they speak great swelling words of vanity, they allure through the lusts of the flesh, through much wantonness, those that were clean escaped from them who live in error. While they promise them liberty, they themselves are the servants of corruption: for of whom a man is overcome, of the same is he brought in bondage. For if after they have escaped the pollutions of the world through the knowledge of the Lord and Saviour Jesus Christ, they are again entangled therein, and overcome, the latter end is worse with them than the beginning."
>
> II Peter 2:1-2, 18-20

Although we cannot be certain that the false teachers Peter was referring to in this passage were early gnostics, his words were perfectly descriptive of the licentious early gnostics who were active during his ministry. He referred to "false teachers among you" in the same way the apostle John wrote about "many false prophets" and "seducers" who had once been part of the sound body, but had gone out. Peter characterized these false teachers as those who used ultra alluring language to draw people back into lustful and unclean living. His words, "they promise them liberty," were certainly descriptive of the early gnostics who claimed to be pure in spirit and free to indulge in sin. Peter said that these false teachers brought in damnable heresies, "even denying the Lord that bought them." In other words, they went so far as to deny that Jesus of Nazareth was the Savior of sinners. This was, in fact, the gravest error of the early gnostics. Peter's words in his second epistle were certainly descriptive of the errant early gnostics.

Jude may also have been warning about errant early gnostics in his epistle when he wrote,

"Beloved, when I gave all diligence to write unto you of the common salvation, it was needful for me to write unto you, and exhort you that ye should earnestly contend for the faith which was once delivered unto the saints. For there are certain men crept in unawares, who were before of old ordained to this condemnation, ungodly men, turning the grace of our God into lasciviousness, and denying the only Lord God, and our Lord Jesus Christ."

Jude 3-4

Jude exhorted believers to earnestly contend for the faith they had embraced and were established in. Why would these believers have to, "earnestly contend for the faith?" Because there was an attack against the faith. Danger was present, Jude wrote, because of "certain men" who were perverting the true message of grace, who were promoting lustful and lascivious lifestyle, who were, "denying the only Lord God, and our Lord Jesus Christ," and who were working their way into the church unawares. Jude's words were descriptive of early gnostic lifestyle and accurately characterized the error they were seeking to promote into the church; the error that Jesus of Nazareth was not the Lord God or the Lord Jesus Christ. Later in his epistle, Jude described these "certain men" as those who, "(walked) after their own lusts," and, "(spoke) great swelling words" (Jude 16). His words accurately depict what we know about the arrogant speaking and ungodly lifestyle of many errant early gnostics.

Jesus and Early Gnosticism

Jesus may have been referring to early gnostics and their dangerous error when He spoke to several of the spiritual leaders of the seven churches in Asia minor as recorded in Revelation two and three. Some of the things He said inferred the errant beliefs and ungodly practices that would later be connected to gnosticism. For example, He referred to some in the church at Thyatira who had been influenced and seduced by a false prophetess named Jezebel as those who had embraced errant doctrine and who, "(knew) the depths of Satan." Apparently, some in the church in Thyatira had not only embraced error, but were exploring how far they could descend into sin, carnality, and perversion. False doctrines and lustful lifestyle were characteristic of the early gnostics. Also, the presence of the false prophetess Jezebel in the church could imply gnostic influence since many gnostics believed in an exalted spiritual role for women, often giving them places of leadership.

Twice in His words to the spiritual leaders of the seven churches, Jesus mentioned a group called the Nicolaitans (Revelation 2:6, 15). Many historians believe that the Nicolaitans were a sub-group of the early gnostics. Jesus' words about the Nicolaitans make it abundantly clear that He did not care for them or for their doctrine. His animosity toward them was apparent when He said this to the spiritual leader of the church at Pergamos,

> "*So hast thou also* (you have in your church) *them that hold the doctrine of the Nicolaitans, which thing I hate.*"
>
> *Revelation 2:15*

Jesus chided the spiritual leader and the church in Pergamos for having some in their midst who, "(held) the doctrine of the Nicolaitans." About their doctrine, He strongly stated, "which thing I hate." Clearly, the doctrine of the Nicolaitans was not only errant, but was a threat to Jesus' church.

On the other hand, Jesus commended the spiritual leader and the church in Ephesus for hating the deeds of the Nicolaitans. He said to them,

> "*But this thou hast* (this you have done well), *that thou hatest the deeds of the Nicolaitans, which I also hate.*"
>
> *Revelation 2:6*

Jesus characterized the Ephesian believers' hatred for the deeds of the Nicolaitans as a good thing and remarked that He also hated their deeds. For Jesus to state that He hated both the doctrine and the deeds of the Nicolaitans, their doctrine and their deeds must have been significantly ungodly and spiritually dangerous to His church.

History reveals that Nicolaitans of the second century believed and taught that the deeds of the flesh had no effect upon the spirit of man and no relation to salvation. Some of them embraced antinomianism, believing that they could freely partake in sin and carnal deeds, the law of God no longer binding upon them since they had participated in the saving work of Jesus. While the teachings of the first century Nicolaitans are not completely clear, Scripture suggests and historians believe that their primary sins were idolatry and sexual immorality. This seems to be supported by Jesus' words to the spiritual leaders and churches in Pergamos and Thyatira concerning fornication and eating things sacrificed to idols.

Some historians believe that the false prophetess Jezebel who was permitted a place of leadership in the church in Thyatira was part of the Nicolaitans and an early gnostic teacher. Jezebel caused significant trouble in the church in Thyatira, bringing her ungodly influence to bear both through teaching and seduction. Concerning her influence, Jesus said,

> "Notwithstanding I have a few things against thee, because thou sufferest that woman Jezebel, which calleth herself a prophetess, to teach and to seduce my servants to commit fornication, and to eat things sacrificed unto idols."
>
> Revelation 2:20

Jesus spoke harsh words to the spiritual leader and the church in Thyatira because of who and because of what they permitted to gain a place of influence there. He also denounced Jezebel because she had corrupted the church with her false teaching, had seduced some of God's servants to commit fornication, and had refused to repent.

According to historians, among some early gnostic groups like the Nicolaitans, women were given leadership roles and were respected as spiritual leaders. One reason they were granted these roles was because some gnostics believed that Eve was formed before Adam and was, therefore, superior to him. This belief that Eve was superior to Adam is evident in the role assigned to her as Adam's awakener in the gnostic "Apocryphon of John." In that text, Adam was in a deep sleep, and it was only Eve's liberating call that aroused him. In another piece of gnostic literature entitled "On the Origin of the World," Eve, whose mystical name was Zoe, was represented to be the daughter and messenger of the Divine Sophia, the feminine aspect of the supreme Godhead. In that passage, Eve was sent to raise up Adam who had no spiritual soul. She called Adam to rise up, and he awoke. When he awoke, he told Eve that she would be called mother of the living because she was the one who gave him life.

Being considered to have spiritual sensitivities that superseded the spiritual sensitivities of men, it was not unusual among the early gnostics that women held places of leadership. Some early gnostics even taught that men could gain revelation and spiritual depths through sexual relations with women. This belief that women were spiritually superior to men was likely acceptable because the whole region of Ephesus was already strongly influenced by goddess worship. Early gnostic belief in the spiritual superiority of women may have given rise to this instruction Paul offered to Timothy, who served as a spiritual leader in Ephesus,

> *"But I suffer not a woman to teach, nor to usurp authority over the man, but to be in silence. For Adam was first formed, then Eve. And Adam was not deceived, but the woman being deceived was in the transgression."*
>
> I Timothy 2:12-14

The belief in the primacy of Eve in creation was common among early gnostic groups and produced many writings portraying the creation event with Eve preceding Adam. It is not surprising, then, that Jezebel and other false women prophetesses and teachers had made their way into the leadership ranks in churches that embraced elements of early gnostic belief. Their wrong beliefs and teachings opened the door to ungodly lifestyle. It seems from the words recorded in Revelation that Jesus Himself opposed the doctrine and the lifestyle of the errant early gnostics, being deeply disturbed about their influence in the churches.

Early Church Leaders and Early Gnosticism

Although gnosticism was not categorized as a specific belief system until the beginning of the second century, the beliefs, teachings, and lifestyle that later galvanized and became known as gnosticism were present and influencing the church at the time John wrote his first epistle. First century spiritual leaders like the apostle John, the apostle Paul, the apostle Peter, Jude, and even Jesus offered words of warning and corrective teaching that strongly indicate they were dealing with the false teachings and the ungodly lifestyle of early gnostics.

Many errors that would later be identified with gnosticism continued after the time of the first century church and the early apostles. Because these errors persisted, there were many refutations offered by early church fathers who were theologians and apologists. Some of the more important works written against early gnostic error were Irenaeus' "Against Heresies," Hippolytus' "Refutations of All Heresies" Epiphanius' "Panarion," and Tertullian's "Against Marcion." Irenaeus, who lived from 130 to 200 A.D., had firsthand experience with gnostic teaching. He referred to those who blasphemed the Creator as agents of Satan. Hippolytus wrote a graphic description of certain gnostics who called themselves the Naasenes (from the Hebrew *nahas*, "snake") or Ophites (from the Greek *ophis*, "snake"). These worshipers of the serpent believed they had received secret knowledge from the serpent; the same special knowledge he had offered to Eve in the garden.

Irenaeus characterized the Nicolaitans—who he believed to be followers of Nicolas, one of the seven men who had been chosen to serve as deacons in the early church at Jerusalem (Acts 6:2-6)—as those who led lives of unrestrained indulgence. He connected the Nicolaitans to early gnosticism when, referring to the apostle John in some of his writings, characterized him as one who had been seeking by teaching to remove the error being propagated by the Nicolaitans and by a man named Cerinthus.

Cerinthus was, in fact, a well known proponent of early gnostic error in the region of Ephesus. The earliest surviving accounts about him can be found in Irenæus' refutation of gnosticism "Against Heresies" written about 170 C.E. According to Irenaeus, Cerinthus was educated in the wisdom of the Egyptians and claimed angelic inspiration. His doctrine was a mix of Egyptian thought, current mysticism, and Christian doctrine. Cerinthus taught that God did not create the world. He also denied the divinity of Jesus, saying that Jesus was a mere man who, at His baptism, was empowered by "the Christ" which guided and empowered Him during His earthly ministry. According to Cerinthus, just moments before Jesus died on the cross, "the Christ" left Him and He died as a mere mortal.

Cerinthus, who lived until about 150 A.D., was a contemporary of Polycarp, a well known disciple of the apostle John. It is possible that Cerinthus was active in Ephesus during the later years of John's life. Tradition tells a story of the fervent opposition of the apostle John to this man and his teaching. This tradition says that on one occasion, John discovered that he and Cerinthus were visiting the same public bath house. This discovery caused him to run out of the bath house yelling, "Let us fly, that the steam fall not on our heads, since Cerinthus, the enemy of the truth, is therein."

Why Is This View of I John 1:9 Important?

In this chapter, we learned about the errant early gnostics—what they believed and what they were teaching in the region of Ephesus during the earliest days of the church. This information provides us with critical context and an important lens through which to view John's words in his first epistle and in I John 1:9. If we didn't know anything about what was going on spiritually in the region of Ephesus at the time John wrote his first epistle and didn't know anything about the errors and the nature of the seducers and liars and antichrists he was warning about, we would lack the context necessary to a right interpretation of his words in I John 1:9.

In order to truly understand John's first epistle and to reach a correct interpretation of I John 1:9, we must realize that when he penned his epistle it was because he, like Paul and Peter and Jude, felt compelled to deal with serious doctrinal errors and the accompanying ungodly lifestyle that was encroaching upon the church and affecting believers—doctrinal errors and ungodly lifestyle that would later be classified as gnosticism. John wrote his first epistle to warn believers of the dangerous errors these seducers and liars and antichrists were promoting and to argue against those errors, setting forth essential Christian truth to refute them.

If we were unaware that in his first epistle, John was dealing with early gnostic errors concerning who Jesus of Nazareth was and concerning the subject of sin and sinning, we would be left with the options of interpreting his words in a complete vacuum, interpreting his words in the context of the time and the culture in which we live, or interpreting his words based on our own beliefs, assumptions, or preferences. If we attempted to interpret John's words without a good understanding of what he was dealing with in his first epistle, we would misinterpret much of what he wrote and not discern the truest and most accurate meaning of his words in I John 1:9.

Understanding that the apostle John wrote his first epistle to warn believers about dangerous early gnostic error concerning who Jesus of Nazareth was and concerning sin and sinning and to ensure that his spiritual children did not embrace their errors or their ungodly life-style shines a bright light on all of John's first epistle, including his important words in I John 1:9. A good understanding of early gnostic error and the ungodly lifestyle the apostle John was warning about and arguing against in his first epistle greatly increases the possibility that we will arrive at a correct interpretation and a good understanding of his important words in I John 1:9.

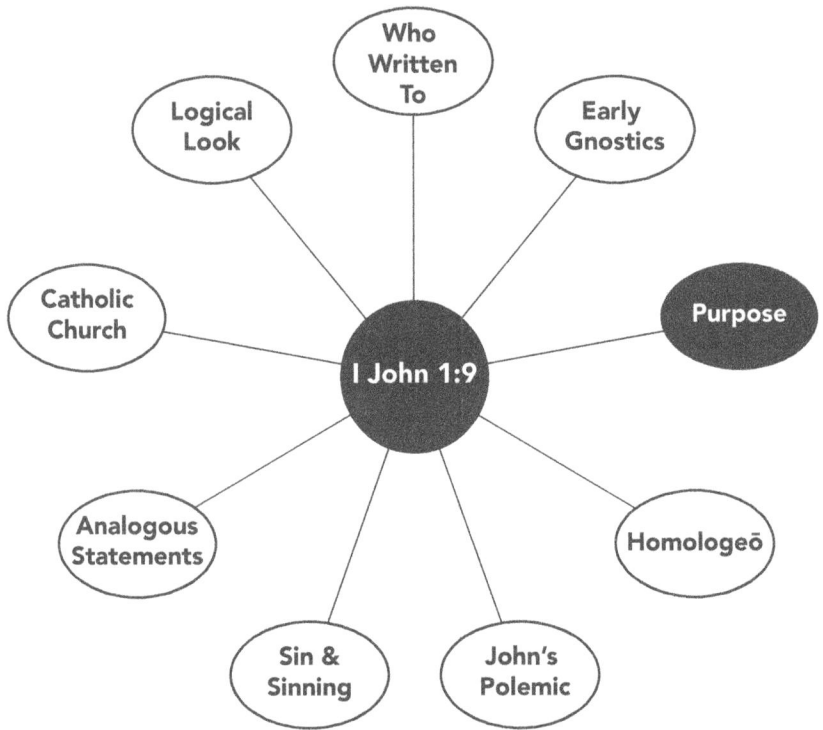

IV

The Purpose Of John's First Epistle

No matter which part of the Bible we are reading or what specific Scripture verses we are studying, in order to truly understand what we are reading or studying, we must ask and correctly answer this question: "What was the author's purpose for writing?" If we don't correctly answer this important question, we will likely end up with a wrong interpretation, a wrong understanding, and a wrong application of what we are reading or studying.

Understanding an author's purpose for writing is essential to discovering the truest meaning of the words they have written. For example, if a man wrote a note to a friend, saying, "Be sure to set your alarm clock," we would not know the truest meaning of his words if we didn't know why he wrote them. Perhaps he wrote those words as general advice for his friend because he believed there was value in starting each day with a schedule. Perhaps he wrote those words so that his friend didn't miss an early morning flight. Perhaps he wrote those words as a mild rebuke because his friend often showed up late to meetings. We could easily misunderstand the truest meaning and real intent of the man's words, "Be sure to set your alarm clock," if we didn't know his purpose for writing them.

This same principle applies to the apostle John's words in I John 1:9. In order to accurately interpret his words and gain the truest sense of what he was communicating, we must understand his purpose for writing those words. But to truly understand his purpose for writing those words, we must understand his purpose for writing his first epistle. We must, therefore, ask and answer this very important question: "Why did the apostle John write his first epistle?" Discovering why John wrote his first epistle will prevent us from attaching interpretations and meanings to his words in I John 1:9 that are foreign to his purpose for writing and which, therefore, are most likely not accurate. Our goal in this study is to discover the truest meaning of John's words in I John 1:9, not to impose a meaning on his words. We must discover, then, what he intended his words to mean to those who first read them. Discovering his purpose for writing his first epistle will aid us greatly in that endeavor.

In this chapter, we will look at I John 1:9 from the point of view of John's purpose for writing his first epistle. When we know why he wrote his first epistle and what he hoped to accomplish by writing it, we will have a clearer view of his words in I John 1:9, a better understanding of how those words fit in the overall message of his epistle, and, therefore, a more accurate understanding of what his words in I John 1:9 really mean. Understanding the apostle John's purpose for writing his first epistle is essential to an accurate interpretation and a correct understanding of his words in I John 1:9.

Why Did John Write His First Epistle ?

Sometimes we have to make an educated guess as to why an author of Scripture wrote what they wrote because they did not state their purpose for writing. There is no need for us to speculate about why the apostle John wrote his first epistle, however, because he stated five specific reasons for writing. In addition to his stated reasons for writing, we can infer his general purpose for writing by examining his epistle and linking what we learn with a good understanding of what was going on spiritually in the region where he was living and serving. When we put all that information together, we will have a good understanding of John's general purpose for writing his first epistle. That information will, in turn, aid us in discovering the best meaning of his words in I John 1:9.

In the first part of this chapter, we will examine the five specific statements John penned revealing why he wrote his first epistle. In the second part of this chapter, we will consider what was going on spiritually in the region where John was living and ministering at the time he wrote his first epistle and link that information with what he wrote to gain further insight into why he wrote his epistle.

One: That Your Joy May Be Full

The first statement John penned revealing why he wrote his first epistle is found in I John 1:4. There he wrote,

"And these things write we unto you, that your joy may be full."
I John 1:4

John had opened his epistle with the strong declaration that he and others had heard, had seen, and had touched the eternal God in the person of Jesus of Nazareth. He wrote,

"That which was from the beginning, which we have heard, which we have seen with our eyes, which we have looked upon, and our hands have handled, of the Word of life...For the life was manifested, and we have seen it, and bear witness, and shew unto you that eternal life, which was with the Father, and was manifested unto us..."
I John 1:1-2

John's words, "that which was from the beginning...the Word of life...the life was manifested...that eternal life," referred to Jesus of Nazareth, the eternal Son of God, who had been sent to earth by His Father and had lived and ministered on earth in a human body. John opened his epistle with these powerful and revelatory words about Jesus of Nazareth to remind believers of the most fundamental reality of their faith; the reality that Jesus of Nazareth was the eternal God who had manifested on earth in the flesh. Firmly grounded in this essential truth, John's spiritual children could share in the same rich fellowship with the Father and with Jesus Christ that he and others were experiencing. John expressed his desire that believers enjoy this rich fellowship with the Father and with His Son, Jesus Christ when he wrote,

"That which we have seen and heard declare we unto you, that ye also may have fellowship with us: and truly our fellowship is with the Father, and with his Son Jesus Christ."

I John 1:3

Although John's words in this verse express his desire that his spiritual children enjoy rich and authentic fellowship with the Father and with His Son, Jesus Christ, his words were far more than words of encouragement about fellowshipping with God. They were also a powerful declaration of truth about who Jesus of Nazareth was and a stout rebuke of early gnostic error which claimed that Jesus of Nazareth was not God incarnate, was not the Son of God who had come in the flesh, was not the Christ, and was not the Savior of the world, but was one of several important messengers of *gnosis.*

John intended the bold opening declaration of his epistle concerning Jesus of Nazareth's eternal pedigree to be a deep cut of the two-edged sword of truth. One edge of that sword was meant to deal a destructive blow to early gnostic error that was spreading in the region and had the potential to undermine the very foundation of Christianity—their errant teaching that Jesus of Nazareth was not God in the flesh, was not the Son of God, and was not the Christ, but was one of several high ranking messengers of *gnosis.* The other edge of the sword of truth was meant to pierce believers' hearts, alerting them to the error being spread in the region and confirming them in fundamental truth about who Jesus of Nazareth was. John's seemingly simple exhortation about fellowshipping with the Father and "with his Son Jesus Christ" was much more than a sincere wish for believers; it was a strong declaration that Jesus of Nazareth was, in fact, the Son of God and the Christ.

Disagreeing adamantly with the error of the early gnostics and determined to expose their error and to set forth foundational truth that would strengthen believers in their faith, John opened his epistle with a strong statement declaring that Jesus of Nazareth was the eternal Son of God manifested in the flesh and with an exhortation to believers to fellowship with the Father and with His Son, Jesus Christ.

He wanted his spiritual children to experience the joy and the richness of their relationship with the Father and the Son, just as he and others were experiencing. John clearly expressed this desire and revealed one of his purposes for writing his first epistle with these simple words,

"And these things write we unto you, that your joy may be full."
                                                        I John 1:4

Two: That You Sin Not

In I John 2:1, John penned this statement revealing another reason he wrote his first epistle,

"My little children, these things write I unto you, that ye sin not."
                                                        I John 2:1

Due to the subversive influence of the early gnostics in the region where the apostle John was living and ministering, it is not surprising that he wrote to warn believers not to embrace their errant teachings or join them in their sinful lifestyle. John had introduced the issue of early gnostic error concerning sin and sinning in the first chapter of his epistle when he wrote about those who claimed that they had fellowship with God, but were walking in darkness (I John 1:6). He had already expressed what many early gnostics believed and said when he wrote, "If we say that we have no sin, we deceive ourselves," and, "If we say that we have not sinned, we make him (God) a liar, and his word is not in us" (I John 1:8, 10). Now John informed his spiritual children that he had written to them so that they would not be deceived by this errant teaching and engage in a sinful lifestyle.

The apostle John was deeply concerned about the negative influence of the early gnostics on his spiritual children because their seductive teaching and dark lifestyle was completely contrary to God's truth. They taught that those who were "spiritually enlightened"—those who had received *gnosis*—knew that man was essentially a spirit and was, therefore, good and pure because the spirit came from God and was good and pure. They taught that because the pure spirit of man was not connected to the evil body, no carnal deed done in the body could taint a person's pure spirit or have any affect on their relationship with God. Based on this belief, many early gnostics taught that indulgence in immorality, drunkedness, lying, stealing, coveting, and other carnal deeds had no real effect on a person's spirit, on their spiritual life, or on their relationship with God According to many of them, the "truly enlightened" could live as they pleased and it would have no effect on their spiritual life.

John wrote his first epistle to expose this errant early gnostic teaching about sin and sinning as false and to exhort true believers to abide in the truth, to remain in the light, and to continue to live in ways that were consistent with the faith they claimed. If they testified that they were in the light, then they should walk in the light. If they said that they were walking in fellowship with God, then they should not be fellowshipping with sin. If they said that they were righteous, then they should be living righteously. John was forcefully clear throughout his first epistle that the true Christian life, unlike the life of many early gnostics, was not one of empty verbal declarations about being enlightened, but was a life fully integrated with the teachings of God's Word. True believers not only said that they were righteous, that they were in the light, and that they were in fellowship with God; they actually lived righteously, walked in the light, and lived in authentic fellowship with God. Their daily living was harmonious with their spoken claims.

When John penned the words, "these things write I unto you, that ye sin not," in I John 2:1, he was saying something far more comprehensive than, "The reason I am writing to you is because I don't want you to sin." He was saying something more like this:

"My little children, I am writing to you because of the false and dangerous teaching concerning sin and sinning that is spreading in the region where you live. I don't want you to fall prey to this error which claims that sin doesn't really exist and that sinning doesn't really matter and that an enlightened person can do whatever they please in their body and it will not affect their spiritual life. I don't want you to embrace this dark error and follow the seducers who promote it, thinking that it doesn't matter to God if you sin and supposing that sinning won't affect your life. A lifestyle of sinning is not only a violation of God's will and unpleasing to Him; a lifestyle of sinning will ruin you. So please do not embrace grievous error concerning sin and sinning and indulge in a sinful lifestyle. I wrote to warn you about this."

Three: Because You Know The Truth

A few verses later, John expressed a third reason he had written his first epistle. He wrote,

"I have not written unto you because ye know not the truth, but because ye know it, and that no lie is of the truth."

1 John 2:21

John's words in this verse are fascinating. He informed believers that he had not written to them because they didn't know the truth, but because they did know the truth. These words reveal that he didn't write his epistle to present the gospel to sinners or to introduce new truths to believers, but wrote it because believers who had already heard, who had already embraced, and who were already walking in the truth—some, in fact, from the beginning (I John 2:24)—were now being challenged concerning the validity of the truths they had embraced. John didn't want his spiritual children to abandon the truth they already knew and embrace a lie.

John was deeply concerned because believers he cared for were being exposed to dangerous lies. The lies they were hearing were not, "of the truth." In other words, what they were hearing was not part of God's truth or part of the body of sound doctrines that belonged to Christianity. John wrote to remind his spiritual children of essential truths they had already embraced, to confirm them in those truths, and to make sure they understood that some things they were hearing were lies, were not of God's truth, and should not be embraced.

Immediately following his statement revealing why he had written his first epistle, John wrote,

> "Who is a liar but he that denieth that Jesus is the Christ? He is antichrist, that denieth the Father and the Son. Whosoever denieth the Son, the same hath not the Father: he that acknowledgeth the Son hath the Father also."
>
> I John 2:22-23

With these words, John connected the lies he mentioned in I John 2:21 with the liars of I John 2:22. The lies he was warning his spiritual children about did not come from God, from His Word, or from true spiritual leaders, but from liars. One of the lies that liars were promoting in the region of Ephesus was that Jesus of Nazareth was not the Christ, that He was not God's Son, and that God was not His Father. John said that by denying the Son, these liars denied the Fatherhood of God. According to John, those who denied the Sonship of Jesus and denied that God was His Father were not in relationship with God; they, "hath not the Father." Those, on the other hand, who acknowledged the Son, "hath the Father also."

Foundational truths about Jesus of Nazareth and other foundational truths of the Christian faith were being challenged by liars-deniers-antichrists who were active in the region where the apostle John lived and was serving. He wrote his first epistle to remind believers of those foundational truths and to warn them of dangerous lies and liars. He wanted to fortify believers' faith foundations, making it less likely that they would be dislodged from the truth. Like the apostle Paul who traveled from place to place strengthening and confirming churches in the truth, John was strengthening and confirming believers in the truth through his writing.

Four: Concerning Them That Seduce You

At the time John wrote his first epistle, believers in the region of Ephesus were being exposed to dangerous error. Some who were promoting that error had once been part of, or had at least acted as if they were part of, the sound body of Christ. John was referring to those individuals when he wrote,

> *"Little children, it is the last time: and as ye have heard that anti-christ shall come, even now are there many antichrists; whereby we know that it is the last time. They went out from us, but they were not of us; for if they had been of us, they would no doubt have continued with us: but they went out, that they might be made manifest that they were not all of us."*
>
> *1 John 2:18-19*

Who was John referring to when he said, "They went out from us?" He was referring to individuals who had once seemed to be part of the body of Christ, but had departed. John labeled them as anti-christs and characterized them with these words,

> *"Who is a liar but he that denieth that Jesus is the Christ? He is antichrist, that denieth the Father and the Son. Whosoever denieth the Son, the same hath not the Father: he that acknowledgeth the Son hath the Father also."*
>
> *I John 2:22-23*

Some who had once seemed to be part of the sound body of Christ were characterized by John as antichrists and liars who denied that Jesus of Nazareth was the Christ and the Son of God. Not only had these individuals embraced serious error themselves; they were endeavoring to spread that error back into the body of Christ. John was explicit in his warning about these antichrist-liars because if believers embraced the error they were promoting, it would destroy the foundation upon which their faith rested. In fact, any believer who embraced this error would be abandoning the faith by which they had been saved.

For most modern day believers, the possibility that any true believer would embrace the gross error that Jesus of Nazareth was not the Christ and was not the Son of God seems almost non-existant. But because the antichrists John was warning about had once fellowshipped as if they were part of the sound body of Christ and may have even cultivated close relationships with some believers, there was an increased possibility that believers would be susceptible to their influence. John was clear, however, that these antichrists who went out from the community of faith had never truly been part of the body of Christ. If they had been, he said, they would not have departed. The fact that they departed made it "manifest"—made it clear and obvious—that, "they were not all of us."

The apostle John's deep concern about the nefarious activity of antichrists and liars in the region and about the negative influence they might exert on believers motivated him to write his first epistle. He made that abundantly clear when he said,

> *"These things have I written unto you concerning them that seduce you."*
>
> *I John 2:26*

With these words, John revealed that one of his primary purposes for writing his first epistle was to warn his spiritual children about dangerous individuals who were trying to seduce them. The English word "seduce" in I John 2:26 comes from the Greek verb *planaō* which means, "to cause one to stray, to lead astray, to lead someone aside from the right way, to lead into error and sin." That was exactly what the seducers John was warning about were endeavoring to do. They were attempting to peddle their error into the church in the hope of seducing believers away from the truth, causing them to stray from the sound body and into error and sin.

John wrote his first epistle not only to set forth a clear distinction between God's truth and dangerous error, but also to warn about and expose those who were promoting that dangerous error. He wrote to warn believers to beware of dangerous individuals who were endeavoring to draw them away from the sound body, away from sound doctrine, and into errant doctrines and an ungodly lifestyle. John did not want his spiritual children to suppose that just because a person had once seemed to have been part of the community of faith that they were sound in faith, were trustworthy, and should be listened to. He did not want believers to naively suppose that any person who said, "We are in fellowship with God," was truly in fellowship with God. He did not want his beloved brothers and sisters in Christ to think that every person who claimed to be a prophet was truly a prophet. That is why he told them that, "many false prophets have gone out into the world," and exhorted them to, "test the spirits to see if they be of God" (I John 4:1). He did not want believers he loved to simply accept that anyone who said, "I am enlightened and speak for God," was actually enlightened and spoke for God.

John wanted his spiritual children to be fully aware that there were liars-seducers-antichrists-false prophets who were active in the region where they lived. They might even be personally acquainted with some of these individuals because some had gone out from among them. If his spiritual children failed to realize that some who claimed to be speaking for God, claimed to be prophets, and claimed to be specially enlightened were actually liars, seducers, false prophets, and antichrists, they would be susceptible to their seduction. One of the main reasons John wrote his first epistle, then, was to warn believers, "concerning them that seduce you," who may have, "(gone) out from us, but they were not of us."

Five: That You May Know You Have Eternal Life

Near the end of his first epistle, John wrote these beautiful words,

"These things have I written unto you that believe on the name of the Son of God; that ye may know that ye have eternal life, and that ye may believe on the name of the Son of God."

I John 5:13

John's final statement about why he wrote his first epistle was a summary statement. His words reveal that he wrote it to reassure those who had already believed on the name of the Son of God and to confirm to them what they already knew—that they were forgiven and saved from sin, that they were in the truth, and that they were in relationship with God through faith in Jesus Christ. He wrote so that they could, "know (with confidence) that ye have eternal life," and so that they would continue to, "believe on the name of the Son of God."

John didn't want his spiritual children to worry that if they refused to embrace the errant teachings they were hearing from the "spiritually superior" early gnostics and had not received special *gnosis* like those with "deeper revelation," they would be missing something in their relationship with God. He wanted them to understand that they didn't have to join the early gnostics and become "super spiritual" and "specially enlightened" because they were already living in the truth, were already walking in the light, and were already fellowshipping in an authentic relationship with God through faith in Jesus Christ. He wanted his spiritual children to be confident in the truth they had already embraced—that Jesus was the Son of God, that He was the Christ, that He was their Savior, that He had destroyed the works of the devil, that He had cleansed them of their sins, and that He had given them the gift of eternal life. He wanted them to be confident that they were in right standing with God through faith in Jesus Christ and to rest assured that they had eternal life in Him. He wanted them to know that they were standing firm on the foundation of Jesus Christ, the Son of God and their Savior, and that was where they should remain.

John's General Purpose for Writing

Each of the five specific reasons John offered about why he wrote his first epistle were part of his larger and more general purpose for writing. That larger and more general purpose was to expose, to warn about, and to deal with the false teachers and false teachings that were proliferating in the region where he lived; false teachers and false teachings that were negatively influencing believers and could get a toe-hold in the church. Most Bible scholars agree that the teachings John identified and argued against throughout his first epistle were the teachings of gnosticism in their primitive form. Although those errant teachings were not yet solidified in writing and were not yet specifically characterized as gnostic teachings, it is apparent from history that the teachings he identified and argued against in his first epistle were, indeed, early gnostic errors. John wrote his first epistle to warn his spiritual children about those errors to prevent them from being seduced back into the darkness they had been delivered from through faith in Jesus Christ.

The two main early gnostic errors John identified and argued against throughout his first epistle were both outgrowths of the early gnostic philosophy of dualism. Dualism asserted that everything in the universe was either good or evil, spirit or matter, light or dark. In general, dualism presented that spirit was good, pure, and light, that matter was evil, corrupt, and dark, and that spirit and matter, not being connected, could have no enduring relationship with each other. Out of this dualistic philosophy grew the two dangerous early gnostic errors John dealt with throughout his first epistle; errors that had the potential to infect and even undermine the church and to damage the spiritual lives of true believers.

The most grievous early gnostic error John dealt with was their teaching that Jesus of Nazareth was not God manifested in the flesh, was not the Son of God, and was not the Christ, but was one of several special messengers of *gnosis* sent to the dark world to bring enlightenment. The other very dangerous early gnostic error John dealt with—an error that bears significantly on his words in I John 1:9—was their teaching that men did not have a sin nature, but a pure spirit from God, and, therefore, did not need a Savior to save them from sin. This error included the belief of some early gnostics that they could live carnal and fleshly lives without consequence because nothing they did in their corrupt body could affect their pure spirit or their relationship with God. Let's examine the places in his first epistle where the apostle John addressed these two dangerous errors and see how he dealt with them.

Early Gnostic Error Concerning Jesus of Nazareth

The most grossly errant early gnostic teaching John exposed, warned of, and argued against in his first epistle was their teaching about Jesus of Nazareth. Most early gnostics considered Jesus to be one of several leading enlightened teachers or "messengers" who had been sent to earth to bring *gnosis* and to enlighten the people. They did not believe that He was God in the flesh, that He was the Son of God, that He was the Christ, or that He was the Savior the Father had sent into the world to save men from their sins and to defeat death and Satan. The reason early gnostics did not accept that Jesus of Nazareth was God's Son incarnate in a human body was because they were convinced that God, a pure and perfect spirit, would never choose to inhabit an evil, human body. Throughout his first epistle, John warned about and argued against this significant error that could do serious damage to the very foundation of the Christian faith.

Knowing what the early gnostics believed about Jesus of Nazareth and being aware that they were promoting their dangerous error in the region where he lived, it is no surprise that John opened his first epistle with bold and vigorous declarations about who Jesus of Nazareth was. He wrote,

> *"That which was from the beginning, which we have heard, which we have seen with our eyes, which we have looked upon, and our hands have handled, of the Word of life...For the life was manifested, and we have seen it, and bear witness, and shew unto you that eternal life, which was with the Father, and was manifested unto us..."*
>
> I John 1:1-2

The apostle John declared that Jesus of Nazareth was, "that which was from the beginning," and said that He was, "the Word of life...the life...that eternal life." He expressed with bold simplicity and without reservation that Jesus of Nazareth was God.

Throughout his first epistle, John exposed and argued against early gnostic error concerning Jesus of Nazareth. In the second chapter of his epistle, he wrote,

> *"Who is a liar but he that denieth that Jesus is the Christ? He is antichrist, that denieth the Father and the Son. Whosoever denieth*

the Son, the same hath not the Father: he that acknowledgeth the
Son hath the Father also."

I John 2:22-23

The early gnostics denied that Jesus of Nazareth was the Christ and the Son of God and denied that God was His Father; in other words, they did not acknowledge the Son. John did not soft-speak or write in ecumenical tones when referencing the early gnostics, but fearlessly characterized them as liars, as antichrists, and as those who, "hath not the Father." He was stout and harsh with his words, leaving no room for doubt in the minds of his readers about the error of these liars-deniers or about his own feelings toward them.

John followed his bold words exposing deniers and antichrists in I John 2:22-23 with a strong exhortation to his spiritual children. He wrote,

"Let that therefore abide in you, which ye have heard from the begin-
ning. If that which ye have heard from the beginning shall remain in
you, ye also shall continue in the Son, and in the Father."

I John 2:24

John's words in this passage were in stark contrast to his words in I John 2:22-23, both in content and in tone, and drew a clear line of demarcation between those who denied that Jesus of Nazareth was the Christ and the Son of God (early gnostics) and those who believed and acknowledged that Jesus of Nazareth was the Christ and the Son of God (true believers). According to John, those who did not believe that Jesus of Nazareth was the Son of God were not, "in the Son, and in the Father." Only true believers could, "continue in the Son, and in the Father," and they would only do so if what they had heard from the beginning remained in them. What had these believers heard from the beginning that should "remain in (them)?" They had heard the truth of the gospel that God so loved the world that He sent His only begotten Son, Jesus Christ, to earth in order to save men from their sins, to reconcile them to Himself, and to give them eternal life.

Making a clear distinction between true believers and early gnostic deniers later in his epistle, John wrote,

> *"Hereby know ye the Spirit of God: Every spirit that confesseth that Jesus Christ is come in the flesh is of God: And every spirit that confesseth not that Jesus Christ is come in the flesh is not of God: and this is that spirit of antichrist, whereof ye have heard that it should come; and even now already is it in the world."*
>
> I John 4:2-3

According to John, those who did not acknowledge—who did not speak in agreement with God—that Jesus Christ had come in the flesh were not of God, but were speaking by "that spirit of antichrist." These individuals were the errant early gnostics who were active in the region of Ephesus. John wanted believers to be aware that what the early gnostics believed and taught about Jesus of Nazareth was not just a different point of view, but was serious error inspired by the spirit of antichrist. He was explicit and unambiguous with his words when he stated that any person who did not confess—who did not speak in agreement with God—that, "Jesus Christ is come the flesh," was not of God and was not speaking by the Spirit of God, but was speaking by "that spirit of antichrist."

John followed his harsh words describing those who peddled error about Jesus of Nazareth with these encouraging words directed to true believers,

> *"Ye are of God, little children, and have overcome them: because greater is he that is in you, than he that is in the world...We are of God: he that knoweth God heareth us. Hereby know we the spirit of truth, and the spirit of error."*
>
> I John 4:4, 6

In this passage, John reminded believers that because they were born of God, the greater One, the Holy Spirit of truth, lived in them. The Holy Spirit of truth who indwelt them, he said, was greater than the spirit of error at work in the world, speaking through antichrists and deceivers. The greater Holy Spirit who lived in them, said John, would help them overcome the error they were hearing, would help them recognize those who were promoting it, and would keep them safe in God's truth.

According to John, both the Spirit of truth and the spirit of error were at work in the world where his spiritual children lived. The spirit of error, working through liars and antichrists, was seeking to make inroads into the church and into the hearts and minds of true believers. But the greater Spirit of truth was also at work. He was at work within believers to help them overcome the spirit of error. Moved himself by the Holy Spirit of truth, John penned his first epistle to warn believers of error, of seducers, and of false teaching and to exhort them to continue in the truth they had already embraced, being confident in the Holy Spirit who indwelt them.

Just a few verses later, John again set forth fundamental Christian truth about who Jesus of Nazareth was and what He had done. He wrote,

> "In this was manifested the love of God toward us, because that God sent his only begotten Son into the world, that we might live through him. Herein is love, not that we loved God, but that he loved us, and sent his Son to be the propitiation for our sins."
>
> I John 4:9-10

According to the apostle John, Jesus of Nazareth was God's, "only begotten Son," who had been sent into the world that men, "might live through him." Jesus was sent, he wrote, "to be the propitiation for our sins." The multiplied number of times John repeated fundamental and absolutely essential truths about who Jesus of Nazareth was and what He had done suggests that the early gnostic error being fostered in the region required a robust rebuttal and a repeated response. Just a few verses earlier he had written,

> "And ye know that he (Jesus) was manifested to take away our sins; and in him (Jesus) is no sin...For this purpose the Son of God was

manifested, that he might destroy the works of the devil."

I John 3:5, 8

The Amplified Bible renders John's words this way,

"You know that He appeared (in visible form as a man) in order to take away sins...The Son of God appeared for this purpose, to destroy the works of the devil."

I John 3:5, 8 Amplified Bible

According to John, Jesus of Nazareth was, "the Son of God... manifested." And He had come to earth, John revealed, for a much greater purpose than simply to bring *gnosis* and enlighten people, as the early gnostics believed and taught. He was, "manifested to take away our sins." He was, "manifested, that he might destroy the works of the devil." The English word "manifested" comes from the Greek word *phaneroō* which means, "to make visible, to expose to view, to appear, to be plainly recognized." According to John's words in I John 3:5 and 8, Jesus of Nazareth, the Son of God, was made visible, came in the flesh, and appeared on earth for profound and eternal reasons; to, "take away our sins," and, "that he might destroy the works of the devil."

In chapter three of his epistle, John penned a succinct statement revealing that Jesus of Nazareth was the eternal God. Note his simple, but cogent words,

"Hereby perceive we the love of God, because he laid down his life for us..."

I John 3:16

Notice that John did not write, "Jesus of Nazareth laid down His life for us." He wrote, rather, that, "God...he laid down his life for us." These simple, but profound words confirmed once again to John's spiritual children that Jesus of Nazareth was God.

In chapter four, John penned his most succinct statement about who Jesus of Nazareth was, about what He had done, and about how profoundly important it was what one believed about Him. He wrote,

> *"And we have seen and do testify that the Father sent the Son to be the Saviour of the world. Whosoever shall confess that Jesus is the Son of God, God dwelleth in him, and he in God."*
>
> *I John 4:14-15*

With these rich and powerful words, John set forth with absolute clarity the foundational truth that Jesus of Nazareth was the Son of God who had been sent to earth, "to be the Saviour of the world." Those who confessed—who believed and spoke in agreement with God's testimony—that Jesus was the Son of God were in relationship with God; God dwelt in them and they dwelt in Him. Those who did not confess—who did not believe and speak in agreement with God's testimony—that Jesus was the Son of God were not in relationship with God; they did not dwell in God and God did not dwell in them. In this passage, John not only expressed with clarity who Jesus of Nazareth was; he also made it clear that those who did not confess that Jesus was the Son of God were not in relationship with God.

John reiterated this same foundational truth of the Christian faith in chapter five when he wrote,

> *"If we receive the witness of men, the witness of God is greater: for this is the witness of God which he hath testified of his Son. He that believeth on the Son of God hath the witness in himself: he that believeth not God hath made him a liar; because he believeth not the record that God gave of his Son. And this is the record, that God hath given to us eternal life, and this life is in his Son. He that hath the Son hath life; and he that hath not the Son of God hath not life."*
>
> *I John 5:9-12*

The truth John set forth so clearly and beautifully in these verses was absolutely antithetical to early gnostic teaching. Because the early gnostics didn't believe that men were sinners or that men sinned, they didn't believe there was any need for a Savior. For them, Jesus of Nazareth was not a Savior, but was a messenger of *gnosis*. But God testified something very different about Jesus of Nazareth. He testified that Jesus was His Son and declared that, "eternal life...is in His Son." According to John, anyone who did not believe this record God gave of his Son, "made (God) a liar," and they, "hath not life."

Just a few verses earlier in chapter five, John had written,

"Who is he that overcometh the world, but he that believeth that Jesus is the Son of God."

I John 5:5

According to John, no person could overcome the world and be freed from sin, from darkness, from corruption, from Satan, and from death by being enlightened, as the early gnostics taught. Sin had to be dealt a death blow. Satan's works had to be destroyed. Men had to be delivered from sin, darkness, death, and corruption, and be made alive unto God. How could this happen? It could only happen by believing that Jesus of Nazareth was the Son of God. Early gnostic teaching about Jesus of Nazareth was wrong, and John wanted to make sure his spiritual children realized that.

Near the end of his first epistle, John wrote these simple and plain words,

"And we know that the Son of God is come..."

I John 5:20

Again and again in his first epistle, John penned words that expressed with absolute clarity that Jesus of Nazareth was the Son of God. In I John 5:20, he stated succinctly, "we know that the Son of God is come."

Why did John deal so strongly with the issue of who Jesus of Nazareth was? He did so because believers in the region were being negatively influenced, perhaps even unsettled in their faith, by teachings they were hearing from errant early gnostics. Perhaps they were wondering if Jesus of Nazareth really was the Son of God. Perhaps they were questioning if He was the promised Messiah of Scripture who had come to die for their sins. Perhaps they were doubting that their sins were really forgiven and that their salvation was secure. Perhaps they were uncertain that they had received eternal life and wondered if they had just bought into some fantastical story. To ensure that his spiritual children remained steadfast in the faith and were not seduced into the error of the early gnostics, the apostle John penned many clear and powerful statements in his first epistle about who Jesus of Nazareth was and exhorted believers to remain steadfast in the truth they had embraced.

The many passages from John's first epistle we have just examined make it clear that one of his primary purposes for writing was to confront and to correct the error being promoted by early gnostics about who Jesus of Nazareth was and to confirm believers in their faith. That is why he argued with authority and with simplicity that Jesus of Nazareth was God incarnate; that He was God in a human body, the Word made flesh (I John 1:1). That is why he stated that Jesus Christ was the Son of God (I John 5:5, 9-12) and declared that anyone who denied that Jesus was the Christ was a liar (I John 2:22-23). That is why he asserted that Jesus of Nazareth was God manifested in the flesh, "to take away our sins," and to, "destroy the works of the devil" (I John 3:5, 8). More than twenty times in his brief epistle, the apostle John made statements asserting that Jesus of Nazareth was the Son of God, that He had come in the flesh, and that He was the Christ. Jesus of Nazareth was far more than a high ranking enlightened messenger sent to earth to bring *gnosis,* as the early gnostics claimed. Jesus of Nazareth was the Word of God in the flesh, the Son of God, the Christ, and "the Saviour of the world" (I John 4:14).

Early Gnostic Error Concerning Sin and Sinning

There was another very significant early gnostic error the apostle John addressed throughout his first epistle. That error, which pertains specifically to our study of I John 1:9, was their belief and teaching concerning sin and sinning. Based on their philosophy of dualism, early gnostics taught that the spirit of man was good and pure because it came from God while the body of man was evil and corrupt. They believed that because good spirit and evil body could never truly integrate, it didn't matter what carnal things a person did in their body; it would not affect their spirit, their spiritual life, or their relationship with God. For many early gnostics, there was no such thing as sin. That is why they could say, "we have fellowship with God," while they walked in darkness (I John 1:6). That is why they could say, "we have no sin," and, "we have not sinned," while they lived according to their sinful and carnal pleasures (I John 1:8, 10). That is why they could say, "I know him," but not keep God's commandments (I John 2:4).

To counter the dangerous early gnostic error about sin and sinning that was being promoted throughout the region, the apostle John wrote his first epistle, warning his spiritual children about that error and reminding them of fundamental truths of God on that subject. For example, he wrote words like these,

> "For all that is in the world, the lust of the flesh, and the lust of the eyes, and the pride of life, is not of the Father, but is of the world."
>
> I John 2:16

John wanted his spiritual children to understand that things like the lust of the flesh and the lust of the eyes and the pride of life—things that many early gnostics said were of no concern whatsoever for the "truly enlightened"—were not of the Father and were not part of a life lived in fellowship with God in the light. He wanted believers to have clarity about what was "of the Father" and what was "of the world." He wanted his spiritual children to understand that indulging in carnal lusts and fleshly appetites and hatred toward others was contrary to God's Word, against His commandments, a violation of His will, and was, indeed, sin and unrighteousness.

It is clear from John's writings that believers he loved were being influenced, perhaps even seduced, by early gnostic teaching concerning sin and sinning. He wrote his first epistle to alert them concerning what they were hearing from those he characterized as liars, seducers, antichrists, and false prophets. He wanted to be sure they knew that what they were hearing was not just errant teaching; it was dangerous teaching.

John's deep concern about the errant teaching of the early gnostics concerning sin and sinning motivated him to implore his spiritual children with words like these,

"My little children, these things write I unto you, that ye sin not."
                                                              I John 2:1

Prior to these words in I John 2:1, John had made three very powerful statements that exposed early gnostic error concerning sin and sinning. In chapter one, he had written,

"If we say that we have fellowship with him, and walk in darkness, we lie, and do not the truth."
                                                              I John 1:6

This first statement John made about sin in his first epistle accurately depicted what early gnostics believed, what they said, and how they lived. They claimed, "we have fellowship with him (God)," but they, "walk(ed) in darkness." According to John, anyone who made claims that they were walking in fellowship with God while they walked in darkness was lying and not doing the truth. He had stated in I John 1:5 that, "God is light, and in him is no darkness at all." Anyone, then, who claimed, "we have fellowship with (God)," but habitually walked in darkness was lying and not living in the truth.

Two verses later, John penned words which again expressed the serious error of the early gnostics concerning sin and sinning. He wrote,

"If we say that we have no sin, we deceive ourselves, and the truth is not in us."
                                                              I John 1:8

In this statement, John succinctly expressed one of the core beliefs and teachings of the early gnostics—their belief and teaching that, "we have no sin." Debunking that error, he stated that any person who said, "we have no sin," was deceiving themselves and the truth was not in them. John's declaration was not only a statement of truth; it was also an indictment of early gnostic belief and teaching. Their errant thinking, which he characterized as being self-deceived (*planaō*), was not a minor mistake in thinking that could easily be rectified. Their error, rather, was a serious self-delusion, a falling away from the truth, and a journey into sin and darkness. According to him, those who said, "we have no sin," were void of the truth. John used strong and harsh words to characterize the errant early gnostics, endeavoring to ensure that his spiritual children recognized the falseness of their beliefs and refused their teaching.

Two verses later, John penned words which again characterized and debunked early gnostic error concerning sin and sinning. He wrote,

> *"If we say that we have not sinned, we make him* (God) *a liar, and his* (God's) *word is not in us."*
>
> I John 1:10

John's words in this verse clearly expressed what the early gnostics believed and said about sin and sinning. Because they believed that no carnal act or fleshly deed done in the body was sin, they could walk in darkness, persist in sensual practices and a covetous lifestyle, and confidently say, "we have not sinned." According to John, however, believing and saying such things was tantamount to calling God a liar. By disagreeing with what God clearly said about sin and sinning, the early gnostics set themselves against Him, implied that what He had said about sin was a lie, and revealed that His Word was not in them. John characterized those who believed and taught this error with harsh and biting words. His stout language was intended to bring his spiritual children to attention, ensuring that they recognized and avoided this profoundly false teaching.

In an interesting and powerful section of teaching found in I John 3:4-10, John offered an extended address on the subject of sin and sinning. He began with these words,

> *"Whosoever committeth sin transgresseth also the law: for sin is the transgression of the law."*
>
> I John 3:4

John's first three words, "Whosoever committeth sin," were written as if it was obvious that people sinned. His simple statement was a sharp jab at the errant teaching of the early gnostics who said that there was no sin and that they had not sinned. John did not want his spiritual children to be misinformed on the important subject of sin and sinning. And he surely did not want them to be led away from the truth by early gnostic lies. He wanted his spiritual children to be clear about the fact that sin existed and to understand that anyone who was living contrary to what God had instructed in His Word was transgressing the law and sinning.

Continuing along these lines, John wrote,

"And ye know that he (Jesus) *was manifested to take away our sins; and in him* (Jesus) *is no sin."*

I John 3:5

Again, John set forth fundamental New Testament truth, stating that Jesus of Nazareth was manifested on earth to, "take away our sins," revealing that there were, indeed, sins to be taken away. John reminded his spiritual children that "ye know" this absolutely foundational truth. Why did John deem it necessary to state this truth about Jesus that was so basic to Christian faith and that believers already knew? He deemed it necessary because of the dangerous influence of the early gnostics in the region. He labored persistently throughout his first epistle to render early gnostic error ineffective by stating and restating fundamental truths of the Christian faith.

Continuing in the same theme of sin and sinning in the next verse, John wrote,

"Whosoever abideth in him sinneth not..."

I John 3:6

John's concise statement in this verse was, once again, a direct assault on early gnostic error. The early gnostics claimed, "we have fellowship with him (God)," while they walked in darkness and transgressed God's law. John refuted their "saying" by stating that,

"Whosoever abideth in him (God) sinneth not." What John meant by his words was that any person who was a true believer did not willfully, carelessly, and happily live a lifestyle of sin in the dark with complete disregard for what God had instructed. The Amplified Bible confirms that this was what John intended to communicate, rendering his words this way,

> "No one who abides in Him (who remains united in fellowship with Him—deliberately, knowingly, and habitually) practices sin."
>
> I John 3:6 Amplified Bible

Continuing his thought in I John 3:6 by making a contrasting statement, John wrote,

> "...whosoever sinneth hath not seen him, neither known him."
>
> I John 3:6

The Amplified Bible renders John's words this way,

> "No one who habitually sins has seen Him or known Him."
>
> I John 3:6 Amplified Bible

John did not intend for his words in I John 3:6 to frighten or upset true believers who may have stumbled and sinned and were concerned about their standing with God. His words, rather, were part of his larger argument against early gnostic error concerning sin and sinning and were intended to enlighten believers to the important fact that no person who persistently and happily lived a lifestyle of sinning had seen God or knew Him. According to John, no matter what great things a person might claim about themselves, if they persisted in a lifestyle of sinning, they were testifying by their actions that they did not know God, had not seen Him, and were not abiding in Him. John wrote these words and others like them to help true believers recognize who was and who was not of God.

Continuing to expound on the subject of sin and sinning by issuing a strong warning to his spiritual children, John wrote,

"Little children, let no man deceive you: he that doeth righteousness is righteous, even as he (God) is righteous."

I John 3:7

The Amplified Bible clarifies John's warning, rendering his words this way,

"Little children (believers, dear ones), do not let anyone lead you astray. The one who practices righteousness (the one who strives to live a consistently honorable life—in private as well as in public—and to conform to God's precepts) is righteous, just as He is righteous."

I John 3:7 Amplified Bible

The early gnostics claimed to be in fellowship with God, claimed to be walking in the light, and claimed to be righteous while they lived carnal and unrighteous lives in the dark. Offering unabashed and bold disagreement with their claims, John stated simply and succinctly that those who were truly righteous lived righteous lives. The obvious implication of his words was that those who lived persistently unrighteous lives were unrighteous. In other words, they were not true believers.

John's words in this verse were both a warning to believers to not be led astray and a continuation of his argument against the errant teachings of the early gnostics. He wanted his spiritual children to be conscious of the fact that anyone who ignored God's teachings about sin and sinning and lived a blatantly unrighteous life was not righteous, no matter what they claimed. He wanted them to realize that some of the things they were hearing about sin and sinning were errant and they needed to be very cautious lest they be seduced into that error.

John continued his corrective teaching about sin and sinning in the next verse when he wrote,

"He that committeth sin is of the devil; for the devil sinneth from the beginning."

I John 3:8

The apostle John was so earnestly opposed to those who considered their beliefs about sin and sinning to be "enlightened" and so deeply concerned that true believers might fall prey to their error that he plainly stated, "He that committeth sin is of the devil." John did not mean by these words that any person who ever committed any sin was of the devil. He meant, rather, that any individuals who were happily and continually practicing a lifestyle of sinning in the dark with no concern for God's righteousness were not only not of God, but were "of the devil." John's words were harsh and pointed and they indicted the early gnostic liars.

The Amplified Bible renders John's words in I John 3:8 this way,

> "The one who practices sin [separating himself from God, and offending Him by acts of disobedience, indifference, or rebellion] is of the devil [and takes his inner character and moral values from him, not God]; for the devil has sinned and violated God's law from the beginning. The Son of God appeared for this purpose, to destroy the works of the devil."
>
> I John 3:8 Amplified Bible

John's words made explicit the fact that any person who practiced sin—one whose lifestyle was that of willfully "offending (God) by acts of disobedience, indifference, or rebellion"—took his inner character and moral values from the devil. He did not mince words when dealing with the dangerous error and false claims of the early gnostics concerning sin and sinning. He stated simply and clearly that those who lived righteous lives were of God and those who lived unrighteous lives were of the devil.

The next verse in John's extended dissertation on sin and sinning contained similar words. He wrote,

> "Whosoever is born of God doth not commit sin; for his (God's) seed remaineth in him: and he cannot sin, because he is born of God."
>
> I John 3:9

The Amplified Bible renders John's words this way,

"No one who is born of God (deliberately, knowingly, and habitually) practices sin, because God's seed (His principle of life, the essence of His righteous character) remains (permanently) in him (who is born again—who is reborn from above—spiritually transformed, renewed, and set apart for His purpose); and he (who is born again) cannot habitually (live a life characterized by) sin, because he is born of God and longs to please Him."

I John 3:9 Amplified Bible

John's words in this verse affirm once again that one of the primary reasons he wrote his first epistle was to expose errant teaching on the subject of sin and sinning and to correct that error through right teaching. In this passage, he made it abundantly clear that those who were born of God and had His seed in them did not persist in a lifestyle of sinning because their spiritual nature had been changed from a sin nature to a righteous nature. Being born of God had radically transformed them from sinners who were bound by sin and death and who, therefore, practiced sin, into saints who were born of God, who shared His righteous nature, and who, therefore, lived their lives righteously to please Him.

Some believers interpret John's words in I John 3:9 to mean that those who are born of God and have His seed in them are incapable of sinning. That was not, however, what John was communicating. His words in I John 3:9 were, rather, a continuation of his argument that any person who was a true believer did not willfully and happily persist in a lifestyle of sinning because their spiritual nature had been transformed, being born of God. Any person, on the other hand, who continued happily in the practice of sin revealed that they were not born of God and were not transformed in their spiritual nature. Again, the sharp contrast John drew between true believers and non-believers was intended to help his spiritual children correctly identify the errant early gnostics as "not of God."

Articulating truth with Spirit inspired sharpness at the conclusion of his short section of teaching on the subject of sin and sinning, John penned these plain words,

"In this the children of God are manifest, and the children of the devil: whosoever doeth not righteousness is not of God..."

I John 3:10

The English word "manifest" in this verse is translated from the Greek *phaneros* which means, "to make clear, to appear, or to reveal." With his words in this verse, John expressed that it could be known with certainty who were the children of God and who were the children of the devil. All one had to do was take note of how a person lived their life. Were they living a persistently righteous life in the light and in the love of God or were they living a persistently unrighteous life in the dark? Those who persisted in unrighteous living were not of God, according to John, but revealed themselves to be, "children of the devil." With his words in I John 3:10, John informed his spiritual children how to know with certainty whether individuals they were encountering who claimed to be in the light and professed fellowship with God were, in fact, born of God, in the light, and in fellowship with Him, or were not of God, but were children of the devil.

As he did other places in his first epistle, in I John 3:10, John created a sharp contrast between true believers and errant early gnostics. Leaving little room for doubt about who was of God and who was not of God, he drew a clear line of distinction, referring to those who persisted in a lifestyle of sin and unrighteousness as, "children of the devil," and referring to those who lived righteously as, "children of God." John was profoundly simple and perfectly clear in this message of truth he delivered to believers he loved.

Near the end of his first epistle, John wrote these words about sin and sinning,

"All unrighteousness is sin: and there is a sin not unto death. We know that whosoever is born of God sinneth not; but he that is begotten of God keepeth himself, and that wicked one toucheth him not."

I John 5:17-18

As he was concluding his first epistle, John returned once again to the theme of sin and sinning. And once again, he was concise in his words, stating simply that, "All unrighteousness is sin," and that, "whosoever is born of God sinneth not." As in other passages, John was not communicating in this passage that believers were incapable of sinning or that they never sinned. Rather, he was communicating that no one who was truly born of God happily engaged in a life-style of sinning, but, as he wrote, "he that is begotten of God keepeth himself." As with many of his other words, John penned these words so that true believers would not be misled by early gnostic sinners who claimed to be in relationship with God and claimed to be specially enlightened, but whose lifestyle of sinning proclaimed the opposite. Anyone who persisted in a lifestyle of sinning was not born of God, according to John, while those who were begotten of God kept them-selves from sin.

Our brief look at these many passages where John addressed the subject of sin and sinning makes it apparent that one of his main purposes for writing his first epistle was to deal with this very import-ant subject. Throughout his epistle, he warned his spiritual children of the dangerous error concerning sin and sinning being promulgated in the region, seeking to ensure that they would not be misled by indi-viduals who were masquerading as the spiritual elite while demon-strating by their lifestyle of sinning that they were not of God, but were "children of the devil."

What Was John's Purpose for Writing ?

Some think that the apostle John, often considered the apostle of love, wrote his first epistle for the purpose of expounding upon the excellent Christian virtue of love. Some think he wrote his first epistle to instruct believers in important, basic truths of the Christian faith. Some think he wrote his first epistle to caution believers against sinning. Although all of these elements can be found in John's first epistle, the main reason John wrote his first epistle was to warn believers he loved and that he was responsible for about the errant and dangerous teach-ings of the early gnostics who claimed to be in the light, who claimed to be in fellowship with God, and who often claimed to be spiritually superior, but were liars and seducers, were motivated by the spirit of antichrist, and, rather than being children of God, were children of the devil. He wrote to expose their error—including their dangerous error concerning sin and sinning—and to set forth a carefully crafted, intelligent, sometimes harsh argument against it. By warning believers about the dangerous early gnostic error being peddled in the region of Ephesus, John hoped to help them avoid the deception that some had already embraced.

Not unlike Jude in the writing of his epistle, it seems that the apostle John was compelled to write and to contend for the truth. Just as the Holy Spirit stirred Jude's heart, alerting him to the infiltration of false teachers into the church and inspiring him to address that issue in his epistle, so the Holy Spirit stirred John's heart to deal with the error that early gnostics were promoting in the region where he lived and inspired him to pen a strong, truth filled epistle in the hope of mitigating the effects of that error. The apostle John, a man called by Jesus to lead, to feed, and to protect the church, could not sit idly by while interlopers sought to undermine critical, first-order doctrines of the church, attempting to unsettle God's children and seduce them into an ungodly life in the dark.

Motivated by his deep concern for his spiritual children, John penned his first epistle, drawing a clear line of distinction between what was sound Christian doctrine and what was error and between what was righteous life in the light and what was unrighteous life in the dark. He wrote to expose and to argue against false teachings that could infiltrate the church, undermine fundamental truth, and unsettle believers; especially false teaching concerning who Jesus of Nazareth was and false teaching concerning sin and sinning. He wrote to make a defense of the truth, setting forth in clear terms the most foundational truths of the faith and exhorting believers to hold fast to those truths. He wrote in the hope of preventing believers from being seduced away from the truth, away from soundness in their life of faith, away from the sound body of Christ, and away from a righteous and joyful life of fellowship with God in the light.

In his first epistle, John reminded his spiritual children of the truths they knew and encouraged them to remain steadfast in Christ, to walk in the light, to walk in the truth, to keep the Word of God, to pay attention to the indwelling Holy Spirit, and to live righteously as God instructed. He reminded them that the anointing abiding in them was greater than the spirits of error operating in the world and speaking through false prophets, and reminded them that the anointing dwelling in them would teach them all things (I John 2:27; 4:4). The apostle John reminded his spiritual children of all these things to give them confidence concerning the truths they had already embraced so that they would not accept the errant doctrines of the "spiritually superior" early gnostics or join them in their "enlightened and free" lifestyle.

Why Is This View of I John 1:9 Important ?

In this chapter, we looked at I John 1:9 from our third point of view; from the point of view of John's purpose for writing his first epistle. A good understanding of his purpose for writing provides us with crucial context in which to view his words in I John 1:9. To really know "what" John meant by his words in I John 1:9, we need to know "why" he wrote them.

Too often, Scripture is viewed from a current century, native language, home country, preferred church affiliation context. Unfortunately, the context of current time, place, language, and church culture can distort the meanings of Scriptures that were written thousands of years ago in another time and place. The context that is appropriate to John's words in I John 1:9 and the context that will help us reach the best interpretation of his words in that verse is the context of the first century church in the region of Ephesus where John was living and ministering and where error that was dangerous to the church was being promoted.

In this chapter, we learned that one of John's primary purposes for writing his first epistle was to warn his spiritual children about early gnostic error concerning who Jesus of Nazareth was and early gnostic error on the subject of sin and sinning. Again and again, John addressed those errors, making it abundantly clear that they were prevalent in the region and dangerous for believers and for the church. Every statement he penned in his first epistle, including his important statement in I John 1:9, was intimately connected to this primary purpose for writing. In order to correctly interpret Johns words in I John 1:9, it is essential that we understand this fact because his words in I John 1:9 were part of his warning to believers about early gnostic error concerning sin and sinning that was being spread in the region.

John's words in I John 1:9 were some of the very important words he penned to his spiritual children concerning the error being spread in the region concerning sin and sinning. Many were saying, "we have no sin." Many were saying, "we have not sinned." Many were saying, "we are in fellowship with God," while they walked in darkness. John's words in I John 1:9 were intended to help reveal to his spiritual children the stark contrast in spiritual nature between those who were sin deniers and said, "we have no sin," and, "we have not sinned," and were not born of God and those who were sin confessors—those who "*homologeō* our sins"—and were born of God and righteous.

The message of John's first epistle was the response of a truly called and deeply concerned spiritual leader to what was going on spiritually in the region of Ephesus where he was living and ministering. If we are unaware of this fact and are not thoughtful in our consideration of these matters, we will view I John 1:9 from the context of our own time, our own traditions, or our own preferences and not see with the clarity of proper context what John was really saying. If we do not view John's words in I John 1:9 in the context of what was happening at the time he wrote them and do not examine his words in light of his purpose for writing his first epistle, then we might assign meanings to his words that do not fit the purpose for which he wrote them. Knowing why John wrote his first epistle is necessary to a correct understanding of what he was communicating in I John 1:9.

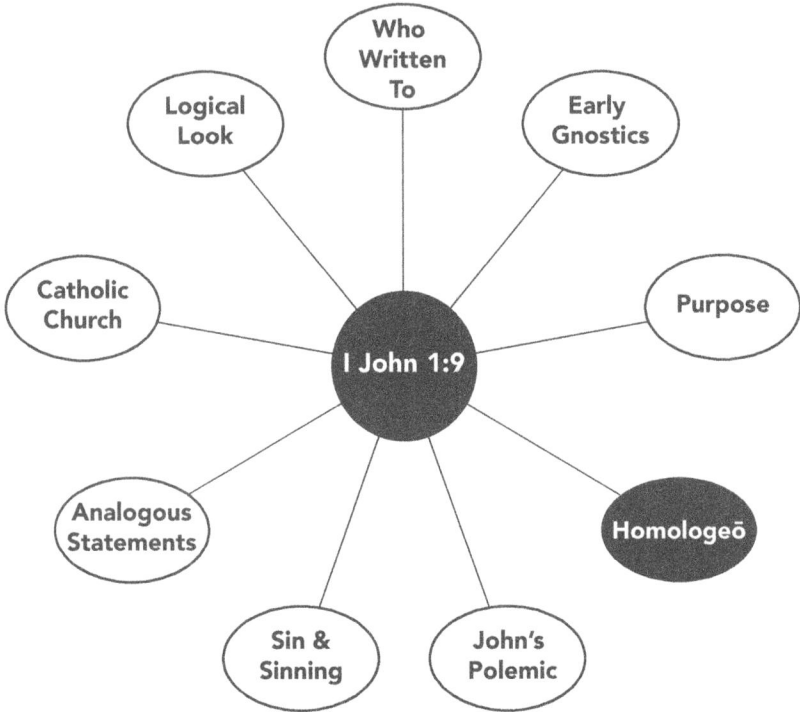

V

Homologeō

The meanings of individual words are very important to the meanings of sentences, which are very important to the meanings of paragraphs, which are very important to the messages of books. If the correct meanings of words in a sentence are not known, then an incorrect interpretation of that sentence is highly likely. And if sentences are misinterpreted, messages are misunderstood. This reality factors significantly into our consideration of John's words in I John 1:9 because the familiar and commonly accepted interpretation of I John 1:9—that believers must admit to God each and every sin they have committed in order to be forgiven and cleansed of those sins—is very much based upon the meaning and the common understanding of the English word "confess."

When John's words in I John 1:9 are interpreted with the strong influence of the English word "confess" in play and little or no consideration is given to the Greek verb *homologeō* that the English word "confess" is translated from, a wrong interpretation and a wrong understanding of I John 1:9 is very likely. When, on the other hand, the Greek verb *homologeō* John used in I John 1:9 is studied and carefully considered (including how it was conjugated in that verse) and when it is determined what *homologeō* would have meant to the first century believers John was writing to, then a correct interpretation of I John 1:9 is much more likely and a right understanding of what he meant to communicate by his words can be reached.

Because an accurate interpretation and a correct understanding of John's statement in I John 1:9 is dependent upon a good understanding of the Greek verb *homologeō*, in this chapter we will undertake the important task of learning about *homologeō*. Discovering the meaning of this important Greek verb, especially determining what it would have meant to the first century believers John wrote to, will aid us considerably as we seek to reach an accurate interpretation of I John 1:9.

The English Word "Confess"

Although the English verb "confess" can have a neutral meaning such as, "to acknowledge, to declare, or to affirm," it most often carries a negative connotation connected to the admission of guilt to another about wrongs that were done. To "confess" is commonly understood to be one person's verbal admission to another person, usually an authority, that they have done something bad, that they have done something wrong, that they have done something illegal, or that they have done something sinful. To "make a confession" is generally considered to be that action a person engages in when they disclose to another person that they have done something wrong, when they inform an authority that they have done something illegal, or when they admit to a priest or to God that they have sinned.

English dictionaries confirm that the word "confess" carries this negative connotation of admitting guilt or of disclosing wrong doing to another. The Merriam-Webster Dictionary, for example, defines "confess" this way: "To make an acknowledgment of something unpleasant one has done; to acknowledge something reluctantly, typically because one feels ashamed or embarrassed; to disclose one's faults; to unburden one's sin to God or to a priest; to admit that one did something wrong or illegal." The Oxford Dictionary defines "confess" this way: "To admit or to state that one has committed a crime or is at fault in some way; to admit or acknowledge something reluctantly, typically because one feels ashamed or embarrassed; to declare one's sins formally to a priest." To "make a confession" is defined by another dictionary as the acknowledgment of a sin or of sinfulness to another person in order to obtain absolution.

Because the English word "confess" carries the strong sense of acknowledging one's guilt to another, of admitting wrong doing to an authority, or of enumerating sins to God or to a priest in order to obtain absolution, it is understandable that when English speaking believers read I John 1:9, they suppose that John was informing his spiritual children that they must admit to God the sins they committed in order for their sins to be forgiven. Given the dictionary meanings of the English word "confess" and the common understanding of the English word "confess" it is easy to understand how the commonly accepted interpretation of I John 1:9 became the commonly accepted interpretation.

In order to determine the most accurate interpretation and truest meaning of John's words in I John 1:9, however, we must look deeper than the English word "confess." We must study the Greek word *homologeō* that the English word "confess" is translated from and discover what that word would have meant in John's day and in his epistle. Discovering what the Greek word *homologeō* would have meant to the first century believers John was addressing in his first epistle is absolutely essential to an accurate interpretation of I John 1:9.

What Is Homologeō?

The Greek verb *homologeō* is composed of two words: *homos*, which means, "together, or the same," and *lego*, which means, "to speak or to say; to say something that embodies an idea or concept." In John's day, the most basic meaning of *homologeō* was, "to openly agree with another, to not disagree with or deny what another had said, to assent to a thing, or to say the same thing another had said." In the classical Greek language, *homologeō* could mean, "to agree with, to make an agreement, to speak or to say something together, to speak one language, or to speak with one voice." Because the verb form of the word *homologeō* in I John 1:9 was the present tense, subjunctive mood, John's words, "If we confess," could be translated, "if we are same-wording."

From various Greek dictionaries of Bible words, we learn that *homologeō* could mean, "to concede that another is right, to not refuse to accept what another says, to not deny, to openly declare one's agree-

ment with another, to assent, to speak out one's agreement freely."
Homologeō had the sense of, "declaring something openly because
one was deeply convicted of facts that had been presented." It could
also mean, "to openly express one's allegiance to a proposition or a
person, or to make an emphatic declaration, often public." *Homologeō*
was sometimes used in a legal sense to mean, "to agree with someone
else's testimony in a court of law." It could mean, "to agree to the terms
of a contract in business." The Stoics used *homologeō* in their system of
philosophy to represent, "being a congruent person by living one's
external life in agreement with one's internal convictions." *Homologeō*
was sometimes used to describe the action of a defeated army when
they capitulated to the conquering army and "consented to" the terms
of surrender they were offered.

In the simplest terms, *homologeō* meant, "to agree with another
and to openly speak that agreement," or, "to agree with and to say
the same thing another person had said." It meant, "to not deny what
another had said; to concede that another was right; to openly express
allegiance to a proposition or a person; to speak the same thing as
another; to openly agree with another." One important aspect of *homologeō* was that it most often characterized an open saying or a public
statement rather than a private conversation. It rarely represented the
action of saying something privately to another person, but represented the action of, "openly saying the same thing someone else had
already said." The general nature of *homologeō*, then, was, "a person's
open expression of their inner conviction which was in alignment
with and in agreement with what another had said." In Scripture, to
homologeō most often meant for a person to openly express their heart
convictions which were in agreement with what God had said. The
sense of *homologeō* that these meanings express are critical to a right
interpretation of I John 1:9.

To recap, the primary sense of the English verb "confess" is, "to
admit to another, usually one in authority, that one has done something wrong, that one has committed a crime, or that one has committed a sin and is guilty." The primary sense of the Greek verb *homologeō*

was, "to agree with what another had said and to openly acknowledge that agreement; to speak with one voice with another." The most significant difference between to confess and to *homologeō* is that to confess means, "to admit wrong doing to another," while to *homologeō* meant, "to openly speak in agreement with what another person had said." In simple terms, to confess means, "to admit guilt to another person," while to *homologeō* meant, "to openly speak in agreement with another person." This difference between "admitting guilt to another" and "openly speaking in agreement with another" is very significant when it comes to interpreting I John 1:9 and determining the best meaning of John's words in that verse.

Because the Greek word *homologeō* is different enough from the English word "confess" to affect the meaning of John's words in I John 1:9, we must discover what *homologeō* would have meant to the believers he was writing to. To do that, we will study how *homologeō* was used in the gospels by Jesus and others, how it was used in the epistles by Paul and others, and, most importantly, how it was used by the apostle John in his first two epistles. Studying these uses of *homologeō*, especially giving attention to how the apostle John used *homologeō* in his first two epistles, will provide us with an accurate and rich sense of its meaning. This will, in turn, aid us significantly in reaching a correct interpretation and a right understanding of John's word in I John 1:9.

How Jesus Used Homologeō

In Matthew's gospel, we find these words that Jesus spoke,

> *"Whosoever therefore shall confess* (homologeō) *me before men, him will I confess* (homologeō) *also before my Father which is in heaven."*
>
> *Matthew 10:32*

In this passage, Jesus used the word *homologeō* to depict the action of those who would agree with God's message that He was the Son of God and the Christ and openly acknowledge their agreement before men and also to depict His own action of acknowledging before His Father in heaven that He embraced and certified that these agreeing individuals were His own.

This action of *homologeō* a person could engage in concerning Jesus was a verbal acknowledgment of the sort that said, "I believe God's message that Jesus of Nazareth is the Son of God, that He was sent from the Father, that He is the Christ and the promised Messiah of Scripture, and that He is the Savior of sinners and my Savior." This acknowledgment would be made "before men." In other words, it would be made openly before others. To *homologeō* in this context did not characterize a person speaking privately to God about their belief in Jesus and did not refer to a person's admission to God of sins they had committed. It referred, rather, to a person's open declaration before others of their heart persuasion that Jesus of Nazareth was the Son of God, the Messiah, and the Savior of the world, as God had said. The action Jesus described in Matthew 10:32 beautifully expresses this important meaning of *homologeō*: "to declare something openly because one was deeply convicted of facts that had been presented."

Jesus also used the word *homologeō* in Matthew 10:32 to describe His acknowledgment before His Father of those who had acknowledged Him on earth. He said that if a person confessed (*homologeō*) Him before men, He would confess (*homologeō*) them before His Father in heaven. The confession (*homologeō*) Jesus would make before His Father would be words like these: "I openly acknowledge that I know this person. They said openly that they believe the message declaring who I am and have openly expressed their faith in Me. Now I openly declare here in God's very presence that they are Mine."

Jesus continued His words in Matthew's gospel, saying,

> *"But whosoever shall deny me before men, him will I also deny before my Father which is in heaven."*
>
> *Matthew 10:33*

The English word "deny" in this verse comes from the Greek verb *arneomai* which means, "to not accept, to reject, to refuse something that is offered." When we consider Matthew 10:32 and Matthew 10:33 together, we can see that to confess (*homologeō*) and to deny (*arneomai*) were opposite actions. For a person to deny Jesus before men was for them to openly reject the truth about who He was; to not accept and to not say that He was the Christ, the Son of God, and the Savior. And for Jesus to then deny that person before His Father would be for Him to say, "I do not know this person. They do not believe who I am and have refused to acknowledge who I am. Therefore, I do not have a relationship with them and I do not acknowledge them as mine." Considering Matthew 10:32 and Matthew 10:33 together helps us understand that "to confess" and "to deny" were direct opposites and clarifies that one of the important Scriptural meanings of *homologeō* is, "to not deny and to not disagree with what God has said."

In Revelation 3:5, Jesus spoke these words about confessing men before His Father,

> "He that overcometh, the same shall be clothed in white raiment; and I will not blot out his name out of the book of life, but I will confess (homologeō) his name before my Father, and before his angels."
>
> Revelation 3:5

For Jesus to "confess" (*homologeō*) a person's name before His Father and before the angels was the opposite action of Him blotting their name out of the book of life. For Jesus to "confess" (*homologeō*) a person before His Father and before His angels was for Him to make an open verbal declaration before that heavenly audience that went something like this: "The way this person has lived their life is an obvious testimony to the fact that they believe who I am, that they know me, that they love me, and that they are in relationship with me. I openly profess before this heavenly gathering that I know this person and have accepted them. They are mine."

How John used Homologeō in His Gospel

The apostle John used the word *homologeō* several places in his gospel. In two places, he referred to a refusal to *homologeō* to depict the

action of certain Jewish individuals who would not openly acknowledge that Jesus of Nazareth was the promised Christ of Scripture.
They would not confess (*homologeō*) because the Jewish leadership had
warned that anyone who confessed (*homologeō*) that Jesus of Nazareth
was the Christ would be put out of the synagogue. There were many
Jews who would not confess (*homologeō*) that Jesus was the Christ
because they didn't want to lose their status in the synagogue or be
outcasts from the religious society of Judaism.

The Jewish parents of a blind man that Jesus healed faced this
dilemma of openly acknowledging Jesus as the Christ. In John nine,
we read this about them,

> *"His parents answered them* (the Jewish leaders) *and said, We
> know that this is our son, and that he was born blind: But by what
> means he now seeth, we know not; or who hath opened his eyes, we
> know not: he is of age; ask him: he shall speak for himself. These
> words spake his parents, because they feared the Jews: for the Jews
> had agreed already, that if any man did confess* (homologeō) *that he
> (Jesus) was Christ, he should be put out of the synagogue."*
>
> John 9:20-22

According to John, the parents of the man born blind did not
homologeō; they did not openly acknowledge that Jesus the Christ had
healed their son. Although they knew it was Jesus the Christ who had
healed their son, they twice said, "we know not," because they were
afraid of the Jewish leadership. They understood that if they *homologeō*—if they openly acknowledged that they believed that Jesus was
the Christ and that He had healed their son—they would be put out
of the synagogue. Therefore, they refused to *homologeō*. In this passage,
it is obvious that the word *homologeō* did not describe the action of
a person making a private, verbal admission to God of their sinful
condition or of specific sins they had committed. Rather, the refusal
to *homologeō* described these parents' refusal to openly acknowledge
God's truth that Jesus of Nazareth was the Christ and that He had
healed their son.

Later in his gospel, John revealed that although some of the chief religious leaders among the Jews believed that Jesus of Nazareth was the promised Messiah of Scripture, they refused to openly acknowledge their belief because of the negative consequences they would face. In John twelve, John wrote,

> *"Nevertheless among the chief rulers also many believed on him; but because of the Pharisees they did not confess* (homologeō) *him, lest they should be put out of the synagogue..."*
>
> *John 12:42*

Although many of the chief rulers believed that Jesus of Nazareth was the promised Christ of Scripture, "they did not confess (*homologeō*) him." In other words, they did not openly and publicly acknowledge what they believed. In this passage, John did not employ the word *homologeō* to describe the action of a person privately admitting their sins to God in order to be forgiven of those sins, but to describe the action of a person refusing to openly acknowledge their heart conviction that Jesus of Nazareth was the promised Christ of Scripture. John's use of *homologeō* in this passage reveals once again that the nature of the action of *homologeō* was the open expression of one's beliefs before others, not the private admission of one's of guilt to another.

Early in his gospel, the apostle John revealed that John the Baptist confessed (*homologeō*) when he answered those who were sent to enquire of him who he was. We read,

> *"And this is the record of John when the Jews sent priests and Levites from Jerusalem to ask him, Who art thou? And he confessed* (homologeō), *and denied not; but confessed* (homologeō), *I am not the Christ. And they asked him, What then? Art thou Elias? And he saith, I am not. Art thou that prophet? And he answered, No. Then said they unto him, Who art thou? that we may give an answer to them that sent us. What sayest thou of thyself? He said, I am the voice of one crying in the wilderness, Make straight the way of the Lord, as said the prophet Esaias."*
>
> *John 1:19-23*

When questioned about who he was, John the Baptist, "confessed (*homologeō*), and denied not; but confessed (*homologeō*)." In other words, he acknowledged openly before others his agreement with what God had said about him. He stated that he was not the Christ, was not Elijah, and was not "that prophet," but was, "the voice of one crying in the wilderness...as said the prophet Esaias." John the Baptist openly testified in agreement with what God had said about him, including what God had foretold about him through the prophet Isaiah as recorded in Scripture. He openly expressed his agreement with God that he was, "the voice of one crying in the wilderness." When John the Baptist confessed (*homologeō*), he "spoke with one voice with God."

In this passage of Scripture, as in the other passages we examined from John's gospel, the word *homologeō* did not describe the action of a person admitting their sins to God in a private time of prayer so that they could be forgiven. Rather, the word *homologeō* described a person's alignment with God and with His truth, their agreement with what He had said in Scripture, and their open expression before others of that agreement. John the Baptist *homologeō*—he openly and publicly acknowledged his agreement with what God had said.

Homologeō in Matthew's Gospel

There was one place in the gospels that the word *homologeō* may have been used differently than the primary way it was used throughout the New Testament. In Matthew 14:7, it was used to describe king Herod's action of promising the daughter of Herodias, his brother's wife, whatever she asked for because she had danced before him in a way that pleased him. Matthew recorded Herod's action with these words,

> *"Whereupon he* (Herod) *promised* (homologeō) *with an oath to give her whatsoever she would ask."*
>
> *Matthew 14:7*

In this context, we can't determine if Herod made his oath—if he *homologeō*—privately to Herodias or openly before others at the party. Based on the meaning of *homologeō*, it seems more likely that he spoke out his oath openly at the party. Verse 9 strongly suggests that he spoke openly before others mentioning, "them which sat with him at meat." We cannot say for certain, however, that this was how Matthew used *homologeō* in this context. The use of *homologeō* in Matthew's gospel to characterize Herod making an oath is the only place in the gospels where it may have been used to characterize one person saying something privately to another person. It is abundantly clear, however, that *homologeō* was not used in this passage to characterize a person privately admitting their sins to God in order to be forgiven of those sins.

Homologeō in the Book of Acts

The word *homologeō* was used two places in the book of Acts. In Acts 23:8, we find these words,

"For the Sadducees say that there is no resurrection, neither angel, nor spirit: but the Pharisees confess (homologeō) *both."*

Acts 23:8

In this passage, both the Sadducees and the Pharisees said something. Both of their "sayings" were a declaration of what they believed and what doctrine they were aligned with. Concerning angels, spirits, and the resurrection, the Sadducees did not agree with the teaching of others who said that there were angels or spirits or a coming resurrection. The Pharisees, on the other hand, *homologeō* concerning angels and spirits and the coming resurrection. In other words, they openly professed their agreement with the teaching that there were angels and spirits and a future resurrection.

The Amplified Bible accurately expresses the meaning of *homologeō* as it was used in this passage, rendering Acts 23:8 this way,

"For the Sadducees say that there is no (such thing as a) resurrection, nor an angel, nor a spirit, but the Pharisees (speak out freely and) acknowledge (their belief in) them all."

Acts 23:8 Amplified Bible

According to the Amplified Bible, to *homologeō* in this passage meant to agree with beliefs that had been previously set out and to "speak out freely" and acknowledge that agreement. The Sadducees in this passage were "deniers." They openly disagreed with what others had said about the resurrection, angels, and spirits. The Pharisees, on the other hand, were "confessors." They openly agreed with what others had said about the resurrection, angels, and spirits. When the Pharisees *homologeō* in this passage, they were not privately admitting their sins to God so that they could be forgiven of those sins, but were openly acknowledging their convictions which were in agreement with what others had already set forth as truth. When they *homologeō*, they were not speaking privately to God about sins they had committed, but were speaking openly before others about what they believed.

One chapter later in the book of Acts, we find the story of the apostle Paul being accused before Felix. When given a chance to defend himself concerning the accusations made against him, Paul "confessed" (*homologeō*). We read,

> *"Then Paul...answered, Forasmuch as I know that thou hast been of many years a judge unto this nation, I do the more cheerfully answer for myself...But this I confess* (homologeō) *unto thee, that after the way which they call heresy, so worship I the God of my fathers, believing all things which are written in the law and in the prophets: And have hope toward God, which they themselves also allow, that there shall be a resurrection of the dead, both of the just and unjust. And herein do I exercise myself, to have always a conscience void to offence toward God, and toward men."*
>
> *Acts 24:10, 14-16*

What did Paul do when he was given the opportunity to defend himself? He "confessed" (*homologeō*). He openly spoke the core convictions of his own heart which were aligned with God's truth as set out in Scripture. He said, "(I) worship the God of my fathers." He publicly stated, "(I believe) all things which are written in the law and in the prophets." He said, "(I) have hope toward God...that there shall be a resurrection of the dead, both of the just and unjust." Paul was aligned with and openly assented to what God had spoken. He acknowledged that he believed God's words as they were recorded "in the law and in the prophets." What Paul did when he openly expressed his heart convictions which were in agreement with what God had revealed in Scripture could be briefly summarized as, "Paul *homologeō*."

When Paul confessed *(homologeō)* in this situation, he was making a declaration of what he believed, which beliefs were in agreement with what God had said in the Scriptures. He aligned himself with, agreed with, and spoke with one voice with God. It is obvious that in this passage from Acts, the word *homologeō* did not characterize the action of Paul privately admitting his sins to God so that he could be forgiven, but characterized his action of speaking openly before others about the core convictions of his heart which were in agreement with what God had said in Scripture. What Paul did in this passage from the book of Acts beautifully characterizes the essence of the Greek word *homologeō*.

Homologeō in the Epistles

The apostle Paul employed the word *homologeō* in his epistle to the Romans when he stated that men were saved by believing God's message that He had raised Jesus from the dead and by confessing *(homologeō)* with their mouths the truth that Jesus was Lord. He wrote,

> *"That if thou shalt confess* (homologeō) *with thy mouth the Lord Jesus, and shalt believe in thine heart that God hath raised him from the dead, thou shalt be saved."*
>
> *Romans 10:9*

The action of, "confess *(homologeō)* with thy mouth," in Paul's words described a person's open declaration that they believed the message they heard from God concerning Jesus; that He was the Son of God and Savior of the world, that He had died for their sins, and that God had raised Him again from the dead. To "confess" *(homologeō)* in this passage did not refer to a believer's private admission to God of sins they had committed so that they could be forgiven of those sins, but referred to a sinner's open acknowledgment that they believed God's message that He had raised Jesus from the dead so that they could be saved.

In the epistle to the Hebrews, we find a use of the word *homologeō* which confirms again that throughout the New Testament it depicted the action of agreeing with what God had said and openly acknowledging that agreement. In Hebrews eleven, we read,

> *"These all died in faith, not having received the promises, but having seen them afar off, and were persuaded of them, and embraced them, and confessed* (homologeō) *that they were strangers and pilgrims on the earth."*
>
> *Hebrews 11:13*

Referring to Old Testament saints who had died in faith, not having received the promises that would later accompany salvation through faith in Jesus Christ, the author of Hebrews stated that they "saw" those promises, were "persuaded" of those promises, "embraced" those promises, and "confessed" (*homologeō*) that earth was not their home. What was it that these Old Testament saints did when they confessed (*homologeō*)? They openly acknowledged their conviction about what they were persuaded of and what they had embraced in their hearts. When they, "confessed (*homologeō*) that they were strangers and pilgrims on the earth," they were speaking in concert with God; with what He had said. They were openly agreeing with His promises as prophesied by His prophets and as recorded in Scripture.

As with the other New Testament passages we examined where the word *homologeō* was used, in this passage from Hebrews eleven *homologeō* did not characterize believers privately admitting their sins to God so they could be forgiven of those sins, but characterized the action of God's saints openly verbalizing their core convictions which were in alignment with and in agreement with what had been spoken by Him.

There is another place the word *homologeō* was used in the book of Hebrews. In chapter thirteen, we find these words,

*"By him therefore let us offer the sacrifice of praise to God continu-
ally, that is, the fruit of our lips giving thanks* (homologeō) *to his
name."*

Hebrews 13:15

In this passage, *homologeō* characterized believers speaking words
of praise and thanks to God for the many marvelous things He had
done. It is very likely that this praise was being offered in a corporate
and public manner, but it is also possible that this speaking of praise
and thanks to God could be done in a private manner. This passage
in Hebrews is the only place in the epistles where the word *homologeō*
may have been employed to characterize a person saying something
privately to God. That being said, it is obvious that in this passage the
word *homologeō* was not used to characterize a person's private admission to God of sins they had committed so that they could be forgiven
of those sins.

Homologeō in the Pastoral Letters

The word *homologeō* was used once by Paul in his first letter to
Timothy and once in his letter to Titus. Concerning Timothy's open
profession of faith before many witnesses, Paul wrote,

*"Fight the good fight of faith, lay hold on eternal life, whereunto thou
art also called, and hast professed* (homologeō) *a good profession*
(homologia) *before many witnesses."*

I Timothy 6:12

In this context, the verb *homologeō* characterized Timothy's open
acknowledgment before others of his personal conviction that God's
message was true and that he was called by Him to eternal life. His
words were not spoken privately to God or privately to another individual, but were spoken openly before others; "before many witnesses."
When Timothy *homologeō*, he gave a public testimony that he believed,
that he had embraced, and that he was living in agreement with the
new life God had called him to through the gospel of His Son, Jesus

Christ. Timothy's *homologeō*, according to Paul, was a *kalos homologia*. The Greek word *kalos* can mean, "beautiful, or excellent in nature." The open expression of heart faith in Jesus Christ that Timothy rendered before others was beautiful and excellent. Clearly, Paul's use of the word *homologeō* in this passage did not characterize Timothy personally admitting his sins to God so that he could be forgiven of those sins, but characterized Timothy's open expression before others of what he believed, which belief was in agreement with the message of truth God had spoken.

The word *homologia* Paul used in this passage, which is very closely related to *homologeō*, was used other places in the New Testament to characterize people's open expression of their faith in God and their devotion to what He had revealed through the gospel and through His Son. *Homologia* was used by Paul in II Corinthians 9:13 to characterize the public profession of faith the Corinthian believers made which others recognized and thanked God for. *Homologia* was used by Paul in I Timothy 6:13 to characterize the public witness Jesus gave before Pontius Pilate. *Homologia* was used by the author of Hebrews in both Hebrews 3:1 and Hebrews 4:14 to characterize the New Covenant that Hebrew believers had entered into through faith in Jesus Christ. In those two passages, *homologia* was translated to the English, "our profession." In Hebrews 10:23, *homologia* was used as part of an exhortation where believers were encouraged to, "hold fast the profession *(homologia)* of our faith." In all these places, the word *homologia*, closely related to *homologeō*, was used to characterize the open expression of heart convictions which were in agreement with God's revealed truth.

In his letter to Titus, Paul wrote these words characterizing those individuals who made public claims about what they believed which were actually false claims,

> *"They profess* (homologeō) *that they know God; but in works they deny him, being abominable, and disobedient, and unto every good work reprobate."*
>
> *Titus 1:16*

In this passage, the word *homologeō* characterized the public declaration of individuals who were claiming that they knew God. These
individuals that Paul had already warned Titus about and charged
him to rebuke sharply may have been early gnostics. He had referred
to them as those who gave "heed to Jewish fables" and as those who,
being false prophets, had subverted whole houses (Titus 1:11-12, 14).
Paul's characterizing words concerning these individuals were similar
to the apostle John's words in I John 1:6 where he described individuals who claimed that they were in fellowship with God, but walked in
darkness. According to Paul's words to Titus, these individuals who
made public claims (*homologeō*) that they knew God proved by their
lifestyle that they did not know God at all. In fact, Paul said, "in works
they deny him." This clear conflict between a person's public claims
of knowing God and their contrary personal lifestyle which revealed
that they did not know God at all was characteristic of the early gnostics. In any case, in Titus 1:16 it is perfectly clear that the word *homologeō* characterized the action of speaking out publicly, not the action of
privately admitting one's sins to God in order to be forgiven of those
sins.

John's Use of Homologeō in His Epistles

Learning the various dictionary definitions of *homologeō* and
learning how *homologeō* was used by Jesus, how it was used by John in
his gospel, how it was used in the book of Acts, and how it was used
in the epistles and pastoral letters is very helpful in determining what
homologeō would have meant to first century Christians. Even more
helpful, however, in determining what *homologeō* would have meant
to those who read or heard the apostle John's words in I John 1:9 is
becoming acquainted with how John used *homologeō* in his epistles.
Discovering what he intended to communicate by the word *homologeō*
in the various places he employed it in his epistles will aid us considerably in determining what he meant to communicate by *homologeō* in
I John 1:9.

The word *homologeō* was an especially significant word in John's first two epistles. It was a word he employed to characterize true believers and also to aid him in revealing the stark contrast between true believers and errant early gnostics. Throughout his first two epistles, he repeatedly characterized true believers as those who *homologeō* with God, with God's Word and with His truth, and repeatedly characterized errant early gnostics as those who did not *homologeō* with God, with God's Word and with His truth. This important insight into how John employed *homologeō* in his first two epistles is crucial to an accurate understanding of what he intended to communicate by his words in I John 1:9. For that reason, we will study all the passages from his first two epistles where he used the word *homologeō* and discover what he was communicating by its use in those places.

I John 2:21-23

In chapter two of his first epistle, John used the word *homologeō* to characterize true believers' open agreement with God's truth that Jesus of Nazareth was the Christ and the Son of God. He wrote,

> *"I have not written unto you because ye know not the truth, but because ye know it, and that no lie is of the truth. Who is a liar but he that denieth that Jesus is the Christ? He is antichrist, that denieth the Father and the Son. Whosoever denieth the Son, the same hath not the Father: he that acknowledgeth* (homologeō) *the Son hath the Father also."*
>
> I John 2:21-23

Earlier in this chapter, we learned that *homologeō* could mean, "to not deny." In this passage, John not only referred to individuals who *homologeō*, but also referred three times to individuals who denied. These individuals denied that Jesus was the Christ, denied the Father and the Son, and denied the Son. The English word "denieth" in this passage comes from the Greek verb *arneomai* which means, "to speak or to utter one's disagreement, to refuse, or to not accept." The only other place in the New Testament this Greek word was used was in Luke 12:9 where Jesus said, "But he that denieth *(arneomai)* me before men shall be denied before the angels of God." The word "denieth" in this passage from Luke refers to a public denial.

John employed the opposite words "denieth" *(arneomai)* and "acknowledgeth" *(homologeō)* in I John 2:21-23 to help him distinguish between two completely opposite groups of individuals. Those who denied what God had said about Jesus of Nazareth were characterized as liars and antichrists who had no relationship with the Father. On the opposite end of the spectrum were those who, "acknowledgeth *(homologeō)* the Son," and that, "hath the Father." John used the word *homologeō* to characterize those who openly acknowledged their agreement with God's testimony about His Son. They did exactly what we learned about *homologeō* earlier in this chapter; they, "declared something openly because they were deeply convicted of facts that had been presented to them." The individuals who *homologeō* that Jesus of Nazareth was the Christ and the Son of God were true believers. The individuals who did not *homologeō* that Jesus of Nazareth was the Christ and the Son of God, but denied God's truth were the errant early gnostics.

John's words in I John 2:21-23 reveal one of the strongest identifying characteristics of the errant early gnostics; they denied *(arneomai)* that what God had said was true—in other words, they refused to *homologeō* with God. John's words in I John 2:21-23 also reveal one of the strongest identifying characteristics of true believers; they *homologeō* with God—in other words, they align with God, agree with His testimony, and say the same things He said. The way John employed the words *arneomai* (denieth) and *homologeō* (confess) as direct opposites in this passage helps us to better understand what he intended to communicate by his use of the word *homologeō*. One thing that is abundantly clear from John's words in I John 2:21-23 is that he did not use *homologeō* to characterize believers privately admitting their sins to God so that they could be forgiven of those sins. He used *homologeō*, rather, to express the action of not disagreeing with God and not denying what He had said about His Son, but of aligning with Him, of agreeing with His testimony, and of openly saying the same things He had said.

I John 4:1-3

Later in his first epistle, John used the word *homologeō* in his instruction to believers about how to determine whether a person was speaking by the inspiration of the Spirit of God and could be trusted or was speaking by the inspiration of some other spirit and should be considered suspect. He wrote,

> *"Beloved, believe not every spirit, but try the spirits whether they are of God: because many false prophets are gone out into the world. Hereby know ye the Spirit of God: Every spirit that confesseth (homologeō) that Jesus Christ is come in the flesh is of God: And every spirit that confesseth (homologeō) not that Jesus Christ is come in the flesh is not of God: and this is that spirit of antichrist, whereof ye have heard that it should come; and even now already is it in the world."*
>
> I John 4:1-3

According to John, one of the ways his spiritual children could determine if a person was speaking by the Spirit of God was that person would *homologeō*—would align with and speak in agreement with God—that, "Jesus Christ is come in the flesh." A person who did not *homologeō*—who did not align with and speak in agreement with God—that, "Jesus Christ is come in the flesh," was, "not of God," but was speaking by, "that spirit of antichrist." John offered this crucial information to his spiritual children about how to determine who was speaking by the Spirit of God because they were encountering individuals who claimed to be of God, but were, at the same time, denying that Jesus of Nazareth was God incarnate in flesh. According to John, those who did not *homologeō* were, "not of God," but were false prophets speaking by the spirit of antichrist. He was warning his spiritual children not to embrace or follow those individuals no matter how spiritual they sounded or how persuasive they were. John did not use *homologeō* in this passage to characterize the action of believers verbally admitting sins they had committed to God, but to characterize those who spoke in agreement with God that Jesus Christ had come in the flesh as "of God," to characterize those who did not speak in agreement with God that Jesus Christ had come in the flesh as "not of God," and to express the stark contrast between these two groups of individuals.

I John 4:14-15

Just a few verses later, John penned these words,

> "And we have seen and do testify (martyreō) that the Father sent the Son to be the Saviour of the world. Whosoever shall confess (homologeō) that Jesus is the Son of God, God dwelleth in him, and he in God."
>
> I John 4:14-15

In this passage, John stated that he and others testified (*martyreō*—verbally bore witness) to what they had seen and knew to be true; that the Father had sent His Son, Jesus Christ, to be the Savior of the world. He also stated that, "Whosoever shall confess (*homologeō*) that Jesus is the Son of God, God dwelleth in him, and he in God." Again, John used *homologeō* to describe the action of a person openly acknowledging their agreement with God's testimony that Jesus of Nazareth was the Son of God and that He, the Father, had sent His Son to be the Savior of the world. In this passage, those who *homologeō* were those who agreed with and spoke in unison with God concerning who Jesus of Nazareth was. It is clear that John did not use the word *homologeō* in this passage to characterize the action of believers privately admitting to God the sins they had committed so they could be forgiven of those sins or, in fact, to characterize the action of believers speaking to God about anything.

I John 5:10-11

Near the end of his first epistle, John again described individuals who refused to align with God and to agree with the record He gave of His Son. Although he did not use the word *homologeō* in this passage to describe these individuals, he was communicating the same essential message he had communicated other places in his epistles, clearly distinguishing between those who did *homologeō* with God and those who did not *homologeō* with God. He wrote,

> "He that believeth on the Son of God hath the witness in himself: he that believeth not God hath made him a liar; because he believeth not the record that God gave of his Son. And this is the record, that God hath given to us eternal life, and this life is in his Son."
>
> *I John 5:10-11*

In this passage, the English word "record" comes from the Greek noun *martyria* and means, "the testimony given, the witness given before a judge, or evidence in a legal or historical sense." The companion verb *martyreō* means, "to bear witness, to testify of what someone has seen and knows, or to utter honorable testimony." The bearing record God did concerning His Son has the sense of, "speaking truth as evidence," or, "giving a truthful and historically accurate testimony." John had used the verb *martyreō* earlier when he wrote, "For there are three that bear record *(martyreō)* in heaven, the Father, the Word, and the Holy Ghost" (I John 5:7). He also used both *martyreō* and *martyria* in his third epistle when he wrote, "...yea, and we also bear record *(martyreō)*; and ye know that our record *(martyria)* is true" (III John 1:12).

According to John's words in I John 5:10-11, God had born honest testimony and had offered a true and historically accurate witness about His Son. In other words, God was on the record with solid, truthful, and historically accurate evidence about His Son. The truthful testimony He offered was that Jesus of Nazareth was His Son and that He, the Father, had given eternal life to men through Him. There were individuals, however, who did not believe, "the record that God gave of his Son." According to John's stout words, by refusing to agree with God's testimony, they had, "made (God) a liar." In other words, they had accused God of speaking lies and of giving false testimony about who Jesus of Nazareth was and what He had done.

Although John did not employ the word *homologeō* in I John 5:10-11, his point was consistent with the point he made other places in his first two epistles. His point was that in the region where his spiritual children were residing, there were two groups of individuals who stood in stark contrast to one another. One group of individuals *homologeō* with God—they aligned with God, agreed with His testimony and with His Word, and openly acknowledged their alignment and agreement. Those individuals were true believers. The other group of individuals did not *homologeō* with God—they did not align with God, they disagreed with His testimony and with His Word, they denied that what He had said was true, and they basically accused Him of being a liar. Those individuals were the errant early gnostics.

II John 1:7

John echoed words from his first epistle when he penned these words in his second epistle,

> *"For many deceivers are entered into the world, who confess* (homologeō) *not that Jesus Christ is come in the flesh. This is a deceiver and an antichrist."*
>
> *II John 1:7*

In this passage from his second epistle, John once again characterized certain individuals as those who did not *homologeō* that Jesus Christ had come in the flesh. In other words, they did not agree and speak in agreement with God's testimony about Jesus of Nazareth. John labeled these individuals as "a deceiver" and "an antichrist." The deceivers and antichrists he identified in this passage who did not *homologeō* with God were the same errant early gnostics he identified in his first epistle. John was passionate and strident in his language concerning these individuals. He did not characterize them as people with a different point of view or as people expressing their own rightful opinions, but as, "a deceiver and an antichrist." As with all the passages we examined from his first epistle, in this passage from his second epistle, John did not use the word *homologeō* to characterize the action of believers admitting to God the sins they had committed so they could be forgiven of those sins, but to characterize the action of individuals either openly agreeing with God's testimony or openly disagreeing with God's testimony.

What Does Homologeō Mean?

At the beginning of this chapter, we learned that the fundamental meaning of the Greek verb *homologeō* was, "to agree with another person, to assent to a thing, to not deny, to not refuse, to say the same thing another had said, to freely speak out one's agreement with another." We learned that in the classical Greek language, *homologeō* could mean, "to assent to something, to agree with another, to speak or to say together, to speak with one voice." We learned that *homologeō* could be used in a legal sense to mean, "to agree with someone else's testimony in a court of law." We learned that *homologeō* was sometimes used to describe the action of a defeated army when they submitted to the terms of surrender presented by a victorious army. Very importantly, then, to *homologeō* was not, "to speak privately to another person," but was, "to openly agree with another person."

Throughout this chapter, we investigated how *homologeō* was used in the New Testament and learned how the apostle John used *homologeō* in his first and second epistles. In nearly every New Testament Scripture where *homologeō* was used and in all the passages we studied from John's first two epistles where he used the word *homologeō*, it was used to describe the action of, "not denying and not disagreeing, but aligning with, assenting to, and agreeing with another person—that person usually being God—and openly acknowledging that agreement." Most importantly, in none of the passages we studied from the gospels, from Acts, from the epistles, from the pastoral letters, or from John's first two epistles, did the word *homologeō* refer to the action of a believer privately admitting their sins to God in order to be forgiven of those sins. Having carefully considered all this critical information about *homologeō*, we can confidently say that throughout the whole New Testament, including John's first and second epistles, *homologeō* meant, "to not deny and to not disagree with God and with what He had said, but to align with God, to assent that He was right, to agree from the heart with what He had said, and to openly acknowledge that agreement." It meant, "to agree with and to say the same things God had said, speaking with one voice with Him."

In order to reach a correct interpretation of I John 1:9, we must acknowledge the fact that nowhere in the New Testament was the word *homologeō* used to characterize a person privately admitting their sins to God. We must also acknowledge the fact that nowhere in his first two epistles did the apostle John use the word *homologeō* to depict the action of believers privately admitting their sins to God. Rather, John always used *homologeō* to depict the action of persons aligning with God, openly agreeing with His truth and with His testimony, and saying the same things He had said.

In order to reach a correct interpretation of I John 1:9, we must also be aware of the important fact that John strategically employed the word *homologeō* in his first two epistles for the purpose of creating a stark contrast between those individuals who refused to agree with God, with His Word, and with His testimony, and those individuals who agreed with God, with His Word, and with His testimony. According to John, the individuals who did not *homologeō* with God were not born of God, were not in fellowship with God, were not in the light, did not do righteousness, were liars, were deceivers, were antichrists, were false prophets, and were children of the devil—those individuals were the errant early gnostics. The individuals who did *homologeō* with God, on the other hand, were born of God, had entered into eternal life, dwelt in God, were in fellowship with God, walked in the light, did righteousness, had the Holy Spirit dwelling in them, and were the children of God—those individuals were true New Covenant believers.

Homologeō in I John 1:9

Now that we are familiar with the various meanings *homologeō* had in the first century, are familiar with how *homologeō* was used in various places in the New Testament, and are familiar with how the apostle John employed *homologeō* in his first and second epistles, we are ready to examine how John used *homologeō* in I John 1:9. Let's begin by substituting the Greek word *homologeō* for the English word "confess" and read John's words. He wrote,

> *"If we* (homologeō) *our sins, he is faithful and just to forgive us our sins, and to cleanse us from all unrighteousness."*
>
> I John 1:9

In I John 1:9, John used *homologeō* in the present tense, active voice, and subjunctive mood. The present tense in the Greek language represents a reality that is occurring presently; not something that happened in the past or something that might happen in the future. The active voice in the Greek language reveals that the subject of the sentence was the one who would, as an act of their own volition, perform the action of the verb *homologeō*. In I John 1:9, the subject who would perform the action of *homologeō* was "we." The "we" in I John 1:9 could be any individual who read or heard John's epistle, but primarily referred to the believers he knew and loved and was addressing. The subjunctive mood in the Greek language is the mood of possibility and potentiality. In I John 1:9, the subjunctive mood reveals that by his words, "If we *homologeō*," John was referring to an action that depended upon the choice that "we" (believers) would make. The subjunctive mood also suggests that John was not referring to a specific believer, but to any believer who would choose to *homologeō*.

The specific action described by the verb *homologeō* in I John 1:9 was the action "we" could take of aligning with God and speaking in agreement with Him on the subject of "our sins." The action of, "*homologeō* our sins," that John expressed in I John 1:9 was opposite of the actions he had expressed in I John 1:8 and I John 1:10; the actions of openly speaking in disagreement with God on the subject of sin and sinning by saying, "we have no sin," and, "we have not sinned."

Greek scholars reveal that in I John 1:9, John used the verb *homologeō* in the present tense, but even more specifically in the gnomic present tense. This is important information for us to consider because whereas the customary present tense would have suggested a regularly recurring and habitual action and the iterative present tense would have suggested an action that continued to be repeated at various intervals, the gnomic present tense suggested a more general and timeless action that was connected to fellowship with God. The fact that John used *homologeō* in the gnomic present tense in a conditional statement reveals that he was not communicating an instruction to believers that they must admit their sins repeatedly or habitually or that they must continually admit each and every sin to God in order for their sins to be forgiven, but was communicating the more general and eternal spiritual principle that any individual who aligned with God and agreed with God about sin and about their own sins and openly acknowledged their agreement revealed that they were not a "denier of sin and of sinning" who was not in fellowship with God, but were a "confessor of sin and of sinning" who was in true fellowship with God. The "confessor-believer" John characterized in I John 1:9 by his use of *homologeō* was that true believer in relationship with God through Jesus Christ who would continually experience the New Covenant benefit of the forgiveness of sins they might commit by their faithful and just God.

If, in I John 1:9, John had used the word *homologeō* in the iterative present tense—a tense which depicts an action repeated at various intervals rather than a statement of universal truth as the gnomic tense does—it may have indicated that John was informing believers that only if they repeatedly admitted to God each and every sin they committed would they be forgiven and cleansed. Or if, in I John 1:9, John had used the word *homologeō* in the customary present tense—a tense that refers to a regularly recurring action—it might have indicated that John was instructing believers about something they needed to do regularly. But because John used *homologeō* in the gnomic present tense in I John 1:9, it indicates that he was stating the timeless principle that if any person was a "confessor"—if they were a person who agreed with God about sin and sinning—that person was a true believer and would continually enjoy the consequence of being a confessor/believer—the consequence of being forgiven of sins they committed and of being cleansed from all unrighteousness.

The way John conjugated *homologeō* in I John 1:9, including how he used it in the gnomic present tense, lends strong support to the view that by his words, "If we confess our sins," John was not informing believers that only if they admitted each and every sin they had committed to God would He forgive those sins, but was revealing that those individuals who aligned with God's truth on the matter of sin and sinning and agreed with Him about their own sins—those who *homologeō* and were, therefore, confessors—were true believers in relationship with God through faith in Jesus Christ and were, therefore, qualified to experience the privilege of being forgiven of sins they would commit and to experience being cleansed from all unrighteousness by their faithful and just God.

In I John 1:9, John was not instructing his spiritual children that they must continually engage in the admission of their sins to God or they wouldn't be forgiven and cleansed by Him, but was expressing the timeless spiritual principle that those who openly agreed with God concerning the matter of sin and sinning and concerning their own sins confirmed by so doing that they were, indeed, true believers in an authentic relationship with God through faith in Jesus Christ. Because they were true believers, they would continually be forgiven of sins they committed and be cleansed from all unrighteousness by their faithful and just God.

What Does It Mean to Homologeō Our Sins?

What the word *homologeō* characterized in nearly all the places it was used in the New Testament and what the word *homologeō* characterized in every place John used it in his first two epistles is exactly what the word *homologeō* characterized in I John 1:9. In other words, the action characterized by *homologeō* in I John 1:9 was the same action *homologeō* characterized throughout John's first two epistles and the same action *homologeō* characterized throughout the New Testament. The apostle John employed the word *homologeō* in I John 1:9 to represent the action of individuals aligning with God, submitting to His truth, agreeing with Him and with what He had said, and openly acknowledging their agreement with Him on the matter of sin and sinning and concerning their own sins. Unlike the action of denying sin and sinning that John expressed in I John 1:8 and in I John 1:10—the action of unsaved early gnostic sinners—the action of *homologeō* our sins was the action of true believers.

It is essential to a right interpretation of I John 1:9 to realize and to acknowledge the fact that the word *homologeō* was never used anywhere in the New Testament, including by the apostle John in his first two epistles, to characterize the action of a person privately admitting their sins to God. As well, the word *homologeō* was never used anywhere in the New Testament, including by the apostle John in his first two epistles, to characterize the action of a person asking forgiveness from God. The word *homologeō* was used, rather, to describe the action of a person not denying or disagreeing with what another person had already said—that person usually being God—but of aligning with, openly agreeing with, and saying the same thing that another person had already said—that person usually being God. The word *homologeō* was never used in the New Testament to characterize a person, "admitting their sins privately to God so they could be forgiven of those sins," but was used almost exclusively to refer to a person, "openly expressing their alignment with, their allegiance to, and their agreement with God and with whatever He had said."

In light of all we have learned up to this point, we can say that John's words, "If we *homologeō* our sins," found in I John 1:9 characterized the response that believers who were being exposed to errant teaching about sin and sinning could choose to make to God's revealed truth about sin and sinning and about their own sins. If believers chose to, "*homologeō* (their) sins," they would be openly acknowledging their belief that what God had said was true. That would include agreeing with Him that they had sinned themselves if they had done anything He said was a sin.

The choice presented to believers by John's conditional statement in I John 1:9 was not a choice about whether or not they would regularly admit each and every sin they had committed to God in order to qualify themselves to be forgiven of those sins. The choice presented by John's conditional statement in I John 1:9 was, rather, a choice about whether or not they would to continue to align with God and to remain in agreement with Him on the subject of sin and sinning and concerning their own sins. Would they continue to, "homologeō our sins," or would they go the way of the errant early gnostics, claiming that they had no sin and claiming that they had not sinned? If John's spiritual children chose to not, "homologeō our sins," it would mean that they no longer agreed with God's truth on the subject of sin and sinning and no longer agreed with His truth about their sins, but, like the early gnostics, were denying sin and denying that they had sinned (I John 1:8, 10).

Considered in their immediate context, John's words, "If we homologeō our sins," meant to do the direct opposite of saying, "we have no sin," and, "we have not sinned" (I John 1:8, 10). The action depicted by his words, "homologeō our sins," was not for a believer to sorrowfully admit to God each and every sin they had committed in a private time of prayer in order to qualify themselves to be forgiven, but was to choose to agree with God and with His Word on the subject of sin and concerning their own sins and to openly speak their agreement. By so doing, they would reveal themselves to be confessors-believers and not deniers-sinners. In their fundamental essence, then, John's words, "If we homologeō our sins," meant, "If we do not deny and do not disagree with what God has already said on the subject of sin and sinning, either on a theological level or on a personal level, but openly agree with Him about sin and about our own sins." According to the apostle John, those who homologeō their sins—those who were confessors-believers—could be confident that God would forgive them and cleanse them, not because they had admitted every sin to Him in a private time of confession, but because they were true believers in relationship with Him through faith in Jesus Christ and because He was faithful and just.

To homologeō one's sins in I John 1:9 did not describe believers fulfilling a mandated Christian requirement of admitting each and every sin to God in order to initiate the process of Him forgiving their sins and cleansing them. To *homologeō* one's sins in I John 1:9 described, rather, the action of true believers aligning with and speaking in agreement with what God had said about sin and sinning and speaking in agreement with Him about their own sins. To *homologeō* one's sins in I John 1:9 was not about believers privately lifting up their voice to God with a sense of guilt, beseeching Him to extend mercy and forgive their sins, but was about believers lifting up their voice in unison with God, speaking in agreement with His revealed truth about sin and sinning and agreeing with Him about their sins. To *homologeō* one's sins was the action of true believers openly acknowledging their agreement with God's truth about sin and sinning and openly agreeing with God that they had sinned if, indeed, they had done something He had characterized as sin. To *homologeō* one's sins was to stand in unity with God's truth on the subject of sin and sinning and to speak with one voice with God concerning one's own sins.

If John's words in I John 1:9 were a revelation that believers must verbally admit to God every sin they had committed in order to be forgiven of those sins, then I John 1:9 was the only place in the whole New Testament and the only place in John's first two epistles where the word *homologeō* was used to describe the action of a believer privately admitting their sins to God. If John's words in I John 1:9 actually mean, "If believers admit to God the sins they have committed, then He will forgive them of those sins," then John's use of *homologeō* to describe the action of believers admitting their sins to God was a "one time only in the whole New Testament" occurrence.

Why Is This View of I John 1:9 Important?

In this chapter, we looked at I John 1:9 from the point of view of an accurate and comprehensive understanding of the Greek word *homologeō*. As I stated at the beginning of this chapter, in order for us to reach a correct interpretation of I John 1:9 and come to a right understanding of John's words in that verse, we must know what the Greek verb *homologeō* would have meant to the first century believers he was writing to. Without this important information, we cannot discover the best interpretation and the truest meaning of his words in I John 1:9. Too many have made the mistake of depending completely upon the common meaning of the English word "confess" to interpret John's words in I John 1:9. That mistake has led to misinterpretations and wrong applications of his important words.

I also stated at the beginning of this chapter that in order to reach a correct interpretation of I John 1:9, we had to be aware of the important fact that the apostle John strategically employed the word *homologeō* throughout his first two epistles to reveal the stark contrast and clear distinction between two groups of people—the errant early gnostics and true believers. Throughout his first two epistles, he characterized errant early gnostic sinners as those who did not *homologeō* with God and with His truth, but were deniers, were deceived, were not in fellowship with the Father, did not have God's Word in them, and were void of truth. And throughout his first two epistles, John characterized true believers as those who did *homologeō* with God and with His truth and were born of Him, were His children, were in fellowship with Him, and were continually being forgiven. That is precisely what John was doing in I John 1:9. He was characterizing those who, in stark contrast to the errant early gnostics deniers he characterized in I John 1:8 and I John 1:10, aligned with and openly agreed with God about sin and sinning and about their own sins. Those who *homologeō* their sins were true believers.

The Greek word *homologeō* was a very significant word in the apostle John's writings. He employed it often to characterize the action of true believers agreeing with God, assenting to His truth, saying the same things He had said, and speaking with one voice with Him. And he employed it often to draw a clear line of demarcation between true believers—those who aligned with God and openly agreed with what He had said—and errant early gnostics—those who did not align with God and did not agree with what He had said.

Having learned what the Greek verb *homologeō* meant at the time John wrote his first epistle and having given careful attention to how *homologeō* was used throughout the New Testament and by John in his first two epistles, we now realize that John's words in I John 1:9 might mean something quite different than the commonly accepted meaning. Looking at I John 1:9 through the essential lens of a comprehensive understanding of the Greek verb *homologeō* has shined a bright light on John's words and will aid us considerably in our goal of reaching a correct interpretation and right understanding of what I John 1:9 really means.

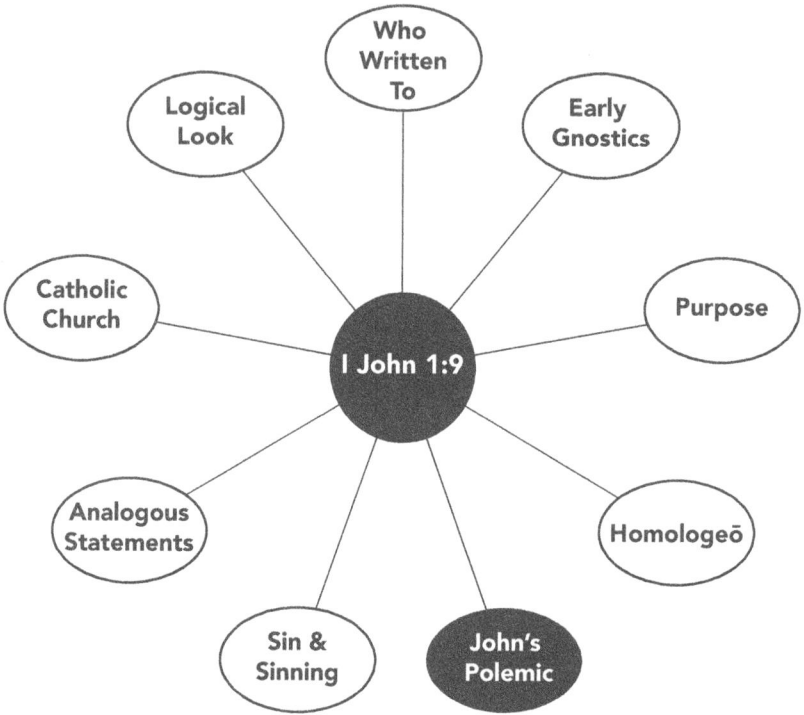

VI

John's Polemic

It is plainly evident from the apostle John's first epistle that he was not only a man who loved God and God's people passionately, but was also an intelligent spiritual leader who was passionate about truth. He had a deep knowledge of God's truth and a comprehensive understanding of the past and present work of Jesus Christ. He understood that Jesus was not only the propitiation for sinners' sins, but was also the propitiation for believers' sins and their advocate with the Father. He knew the witness of the Holy Spirit and understood His important role in teaching, guiding, and warning believers. John was not only a loving and kind apostle; he was also a mature, intelligent, passionate, and strong apostle. He was not only an apostle of love; he was also an apostle of truth.

As we have been learning in our study, one of the primary reasons the apostle John wrote his first epistle was to alert believers to the errant doctrines and ungodly lifestyle of the early gnostics. Deeply concerned that his little children might be seduced by their error and follow their dark lifestyle, he wrote to warn them concerning, "them that seduce you," and to exhort them, "that ye sin not" (I John 2:26; 2:1). To aid in the accomplishment of this important task, John set forth an exquisitely crafted, potent, and lawyerly argument near the beginning of his epistle. This argument, found in I John 1:5 through I John 2:11, was a compelling discourse against the error of the early gnostics on the subject of sin and sinning, a refutation of their ungodly lifestyle, and a robust defense of Christian truth and godly life in the light. In one sense, John's whole epistle was an argument against error. But the specific argument against early gnostic error concerning sin and sinning that he set forth in I John 1:5 through I John 2:11 should be considered a polemic.

A polemic is a written or spoken attack against the opinions, beliefs, or practices of another person or group. It is a pithy argument against and a robust refutation of the philosophies, principles, or beliefs of others. The word "polemic" comes from the Greek word *polemikos* which means, "warlike or hostile." This meaning reveals that a polemic is more than a light-hearted disagreement with someone over a non-essential matter. In fact, the art of polemics is sometimes referred to as, "the practice of using language to strongly defend or to harshly criticize something or someone." A polemic is a strong and logical assault upon and argument against the positions, the ideas, and the beliefs espoused by another person or group.

John set forth his robust polemic in I John 1:5 through I John 2:11 for the purpose of exposing and refuting the errant teachings of the early gnostics on the subject of sin and sinning and to strongly confirm God's truth on that subject. Deeply concerned that his spiritual children might be seduced into error rather than continuing in the truth they had embraced, he felt compelled to deliver a strong and alerting message. With his pen and by the impulse of the Holy Spirit, he harshly condemned early gnostic error and set it in stark contrast with eternal Christian truth. His Holy Spirit inspired, intelligent, and skillfully written polemic, like a legal brief crafted by a formidable lawyer, leaves no doubt that he was in complete disagreement with the teachings of the early gnostics on the subject of sin and sinning and was passionately opposed to the lifestyle that accompanied their teaching. The polemic he penned in opposition to their errant teaching and sinful lifestyle in the dark and in support of foundational Christian truth and a godly lifestyle in the light was both harsh and beautiful.

This chapter where we will examine I John 1:9 from the point of view of John's polemic is the most in-depth chapter in our study. As we delve into this chapter, you might ask, "Is it really necessary to get into this much detail when we are simply trying to understand I John 1:9?" The answer to that query is, "Yes, it is necessary because it is in the immediate context of John's polemic that I John 1:9 sits." If we are unaware that John's writing in I John 1:5 through I John 2:11 was a polemic against early gnostic error on the subject of sin and sinning and do not appreciate the fact that I John 1:9 was one of the very important statements he penned in that polemic, we will lack the contextual awareness necessary to an accurate interpretation of I John 1:9.

I Was There

The apostle John didn't preface his polemic with careful formality or social niceties. Rather, he prefaced his polemic with a strong declaration about who Jesus of Nazareth was and with a confident statement about his own qualifications as an eye, ear, and touch witness of Him. He declared,

> "That which was from the beginning, which we have heard, which we have seen with our eyes, which we have looked upon, and our hands have handled, of the Word of life; (For the life was manifested, and we have seen it, and bear witness, and shew unto you that eternal life, which was with the Father, and was manifested unto us;) That which we have seen and heard declare we unto you, that ye also may have fellowship with us: and truly our fellowship is with the Father, and with his Son Jesus Christ. And these things write we unto you, that your joy may be full."
>
> I John 1:1-4

By opening his epistle and prefacing his polemic with this potent prose, John not only leveled the first attack of his epistle against early gnostic error on the critical subject of who Jesus of Nazareth was; he also authorized himself as an expert witness on the person of Jesus Christ and a qualified spiritual leader. By so doing, he created a powerful backdrop for the argument he would make throughout his polemic in I John 1:5 through I John 2:11. Citing his credentials as one who had seen, heard, and touched Jesus of Nazareth, he presented himself as an expert witness on the subject of who Jesus was, what He taught, and what was truth.

The apostle John was not some distant reporter who had minor contact with Jesus of Nazareth and decided to write a letter to friends to mention a few things he was concerned about. John was an eye, ear, and touch witness of Him who, "was from the beginning...the Word of life." He had been called and trained by Jesus Himself to be a leading apostle in the first century church. This leading apostle opened his epistle and prefaced his polemic with a robust assertion that Jesus of Nazareth was the eternal God and the Word of life who had come to earth in the flesh and with a claim of authority to speak about Him and about truth. All who would read or hear the opening words of John's epistle—the pretext to his polemic—would hear him saying,

> "To all who will read or hear my words; I want you to know that I heard the eternal Word of life myself. I walked with Him who was from the beginning; the eternal God. I touched Him. I sat with Him, ate with Him, learned from Him, and ministered with Him. I am an eyewitness and earwitness of Him Who is eternal life. I am in relationship with God the Father and with His Son, Jesus Christ. And my words are true!"

The Style of John's Polemic

Throughout his polemic, John set the errant beliefs and the ungodly lifestyle of the early gnostics in stark contrast with sound Christian doctrine and the godly lifestyle of true believers. He did this by making alternating statements in a back and forth presentation. He used six say statements—three "If we say" statements and three "He that saith" statements—to characterize what the early gnostics believed, what they said, and how they lived. These "say" statements are found in I John 1:6, 8, and 10 and I John 2:4, 6, and 9. In the alternating statements, John characterized Christian truth and the godly lifestyle of true believers. These alternating statements are found in I John 1:7 and 9 and I John 2:1-3, 5-6, and 10.

John employed this back and forth, alternating statements style, throughout his polemic to highlight the stark contrast between early gnostic error and their ungodly lifestyle in the dark and Christian truth and the godly lifestyle of true believers in the light. Being aware of his alternating, back and forth style is critical to following his argument. Below is a simplified view of John's polemic, verse by verse:

I John 1:5   The truth-foundation for John's polemic: "God is light, and in him is no darkness at all."

I John 1:6   Early gnostic saying/error, their ungodly lifestyle, and what was true of them.

I John 1:7   Christian truth and the godly lifestyle of true believers and what was true of them.

I John 1:8   Early gnostic saying/error, their ungodly lifestyle, and what was true of them.

I John 1:9   Christian truth and the godly lifestyle of true believers and what was true of them.

I John 1:10   Early gnostic saying/error, their ungodly lifestyle, and what was true of them.

I John 2:1-3 Christian truth and the godly lifestyle of true believers and what was true of them.

I John 2:4   Early gnostic saying/error, their ungodly lifestyle, and what was true of them.

I John 2:5   Christian truth and the godly lifestyle of true believers and what was true of them.

I John 2:6   Early gnostic saying/error, their ungodly lifestyle, and what was true of them.

I John 2:7-8 Christian truth and the godly lifestyle of true believers and what was true of them.

I John 2:9   Early gnostic saying/error, their ungodly lifestyle, and what was true of them.

I John 2:10   Christian truth and the godly lifestyle of true believers and what was true of them.

I John 2:11   Early gnostic error, their ungodly lifestyle, and what
was true of them.

Also important to our understanding of John's polemic and to
our interpretation of his words in I John 1:9 is to know that each of
his six "If" statements in I John 1:6-2:1 were what Greek scholars refer
to as fifth class conditional statements. A conditional statement is an
"if-then" statement, comprised of a cause clause and an effect clause. A
conditional statement expresses that if something happens first or if
something is true first, then something else will happen or will be true.
In the Greek language, fifth class conditional statements express eternal spiritual principles, especially in regards to fellowship with God.
In each of the six fifth class conditional statements John penned in I
John 1:6-2:1, he revealed in the effect clause what would be true of any
person if they did what he represented in the cause clause of that statement.

John's statement in I John 1:9 was the fourth of five fifth class conditional statements he penned in I John 1:6-10. Three of those conditional
statements were negative statements in the cause clause—I John 1:6, 8,
10—and two of those conditional statements were positive statements
in the cause clause—I John 1:7, 9. The negative conditional statements
in 1 John 1:6, 8 and 10 characterized the actions of the errant early gnostics and what was, therefore, true of them whereas the positive conditional statements in I John 1:7 and 9 characterized the action of true
believers and what was, therefore, true of them. John's statement in I
John 1:9 was one of the positive fifth class conditional statements he
penned in his polemic.

As we study John's polemic, pay close attention to the six say
statements he penned which expressed early gnostic error and what
was true of them and to the alternating statements he penned which
expressed Christian truth and what was true of believers. Remember
that the style he employed in his polemic was to alternate back and
forth between statements that characterized early gnostics and their
error and statements that characterized believers and New Covenant
truth. Remember that his six statements in I John 1:6-2:1 were fifth

class conditional statements, revealing in the effect clause what would be true of anyone who did what he wrote in the cause clause. Keep in mind, as well, the very important fact that his statement in I John 1:9 was one of his fifth class conditional statements and that it was positioned in the middle of his polemic against early gnostic error on the subject of sin and sinning.

I John 1:5

After creating the backdrop for his polemic and qualifying himself as an expert witness of Jesus Christ and a qualified spiritual leader in I John 1:1-4, John laid the truth foundation upon which he would construct his argument against early gnostic error on the subject of sin and sinning. The truth foundation for his polemic was the message that he and others had heard from Jesus. He wrote,

"This then is the message which we have heard of him (Jesus), *and declare unto you, that God is light, and in him is no darkness at all."*
I John 1:5

Firmly founded upon the truth foundation that, "God is light, and in him is no darkness at all," John was ready to commence his polemic against the errant beliefs of the early gnostics on the subject of sin and sinning and to argue against their claims that they were in fellowship with God and did not sin. The whole body of John's polemic against early gnostic error was intimately connected to the foundational truth he stated that, "God is light and in him is no darkness at all." According to him, if God was light and there was no darkness in Him at all, then anyone walking in darkness was not in fellowship with God. Let's proceed now to examine John's first "If we say" conditional statement.

I John 1:6

Immediately after laying the foundation for his polemic, John penned his first "If we say" fifth class conditional statement. He wrote,

"If we say that we have fellowship with him, and walk in darkness, we lie, and do not the truth."

I John 1:6

John's words following, "If we say," in this verse characterized what the early gnostics believed, what they were saying, how they were living, and what was, therefore, true of them. The early gnostics claimed that they were in fellowship with God, saying, "we have fellowship with him," but they were, "walk(ing) in darkness." According to John, any person who said, "(I) have fellowship with (God)," but was habitually walking in darkness was lying and not doing the truth. After all, if God was light and there was no darkness in Him, then anyone who was walking in darkness could not be living in true fellowship with Him.

What John wrote in I John 1:6 accurately characterized both the claim the early gnostics made and the way they actually lived. What they said and how they lived were not in agreement. They claimed to be specially enlightened, claimed to know God, and said that they had fellowship with Him. The truth of the matter, however, was that they were living in sin and walking in darkness. They were not in fellowship with God no matter what they claimed. John was adamant with his words in I John 1:6 that any person who said they were in fellowship with God, but was walking in darkness was lying and not doing the truth.

In his first "If we say" conditional statement, John enlightened his spiritual children concerning what the early gnostics were saying, how they were living, and what was true of them and warned them that if they made claims of being in fellowship with God while they were walking in darkness, they would also be lying and not doing the truth. John was not implicating his spiritual children in I John 1:6 or accusing them of having already joined the early gnostics in their error. He was, however, making sure they understood that if they chose to identify with the early gnostics, saying what they said and living how they lived, then they would also be lying and not doing the truth. With his bold "If we say" conditional statement in I John 1:6, he not only characterized the early gnostics as errant, as walking in darkness, and as liars who were not doing the truth; he also made it clear that any believer who joined them would also be errant, would also be walking in darkness, and would also be a liar who was not doing the truth.

I John 1:7

Continuing his polemic in I John 1:7, John alternated to pen his second fifth class conditional statement; a statement that characterized Christian truth and the godly lifestyle of true believers in the light, expressing what was true of them. His words in verse seven were a counter statement to his statement in verse six where he had characterized early gnostic error and their ungodly lifestyle in the dark. In I John 1:7, John wrote,

"But if we walk in the light, as he is in the light, we have fellowship one with another, and the blood of Jesus Christ his Son cleanseth us from all sin."

I John 1:7

John began his conditional statement in I John 1:7 with the words, "But if." "But" is a contrasting conjunction that connects two contrasting statements. "But" can mean, "on the contrary," or, "on the other hand," or, "the opposite would be." By using the word "But" to open verse seven, John notified his readers that what he was about to write would be in contrast to what he had written in verse six. His use of the word "if" revealed that his statement in I John 1:7 was another conditional statement which presented another choice for his spiritual children to consider.

In contrast to his words in I John 1:6 where he described a person who said they were in fellowship with God, but were actually walking in darkness and lying, in I John 1:7, John described a person who truly walked in the light, who was in fellowship with God and with others, and who was experiencing the continual cleansing of their sin by the blood of Jesus Christ. The person he characterized in verse seven was a true believer. According to John's previous words in I John 1:6, the claims the early gnostics made of being enlightened and in fellowship with God were nothing more than empty talk and lies because their walk was not a walk in the light, but a walk in the dark. On the other hand, those who truly walked in the light, as John described in I John 1:7, experienced the wonderful consequences of walking in the light. They enjoyed true fellowship with God and with others and continued to experience the cleansing of sin by the blood of Jesus.

As in I John 1:6, John used the word "if" in I John 1:7, indicating that he was not stating what was actually happening or was necessarily true, but was revealing what could happen and what could be true depending on the choice his spiritual children would make about what they believed and said and about how they lived. They could choose to join the early gnostics, making false claims about being in fellowship with God while walking in darkness (I John 1:6) or they could choose to continue to walk in the light as God was in the light and, as a result of that choice, continue to experience the ongoing cleansing of their sin by the blood of Jesus Christ (I John 1:7).

In the second part of his statement in I John 1:7, John expressed a powerful and beautiful reality of the New Testament. He wrote,

> *"...the blood of Jesus Christ his Son cleanseth us from all sin."*
>
> *I John 1:7*

The English word "cleanseth" in I John 1:7 comes from the Greek word *katharizei*. In this passage, John used *katharizei* in the third person, present tense, active voice, and indicative mood. The way he conjugated *katharizei* reveals that the cleansing he was referring to was being accomplished by a third person—in this case, Jesus' blood—and was presently, continually, and truly occurring. This cleansing of sin was not the initial, complete cleansing of sin that had occurred when these believers were first saved. This cleansing of sin was also not a cleansing that could happen in the future. The cleansing of sin John was referring to in I John 1:7 was that effectual, ongoing cleansing of sin by the blood of Jesus that true believers—those who were walking with God in the light—continued to experience if they sinned.

Completely contrary to what the early gnostics believed—that there was no sin, that they did not have a sin nature, and that they did not sin—John revealed in I John 1:7 that sin existed and that sin was being committed. According to him, even true believers who were walking in the light might sin; they might stumble in their walk, miss the mark, and do things contrary to the will of God. Because they were true believers, however, the same blood of Jesus Christ that had cleansed them from all the sins they committed as sinners would cleanse them from whatever sin they might commit as believers.

John's declaration that, "the blood of Jesus Christ, his Son, cleanseth us from all sin," was not just a powerful truth-statement of the Christian faith. It was also a pointed attack of the sword of truth against early gnostic teaching that Jesus of Nazareth was not the Son of God and the Savior who had come to earth to save men from their sins and a pointed attack of the sword of truth against early gnostic teaching that men did not have a sin nature and did not sin. Although modern day believers may take no special note of John's words in I John 1:7, to the believers of John's day the fundamental truth expressed in I John 1:7 was a critical truth that needed to be stated again and again.

John's fifth class conditional statement in I John 1:7 was one of many important statements he penned in his polemic for the purpose of warning and instructing believers he loved. The fundamental truth he set forth in I John 1:7 was completely opposite to the teaching of the early gnostics who said that man did not have a sin nature, said that there was no sin, and said that they had not sinned. With his statement of Christian truth in I John 1:7, John hit hard against early gnostic error on the subject of sin and sinning and reassured the hearts of true believers with a powerful and beautiful New Covenant truth— the truth that if they chose to continue living in the light and chose to continue walking in true fellowship with God, any sin they committed would be cleansed by Jesus' blood. In I John 1:7, John was essentially saying this:

> "But if, on the other hand, you choose to continue to believe
> God's truth and continue to walk in the light with Him, then

as true believers, you will continue to experience true fellowship with Him and with each other and the blood of Jesus
Christ, God's Son, will continue to cleanse you of any sin you
commit."

I John 1:8

John continued his polemic in I John 1:8, penning his third fifth
class conditional statement and his second "If we say" statement, alternating back to his characterization of the early gnostics and their error.
Like his statement in I John 1:6, John's words in I John 1:8 expressed an
errant belief and a familiar saying of the early gnostics and revealed
what was true of them. He wrote,

> *"If we say that we have no sin, we deceive ourselves, and the truth
> is not in us."*
>
> I John 1:8

John's words in this verse characterized one of the primary beliefs
and teachings of the early gnostics; their belief and teaching that, "we
have no sin." The early gnostics believed that man's spirit was good
and pure because it came from God, while the body was evil. They
believed that because the spirit of man was pure, man did not have
a sin nature and did not need to be saved from his sins. Many early
gnostics believed that because the spirit and the body were essentially
separate, nothing they did in their body could affect their spirit or
their spiritual life. It was this early gnostic error that John characterized and was alerting believers to in I John 1:8. He was alerting them
because he did not want them to embrace this gross error and begin to
say, "we have no sin."

John was direct with his words in I John 1:8, stating that anyone
who said, "we have no sin," was deceiving themselves. The English
word "deceive" in this passage comes from the Greek *planaō* which
means, "to lead astray, to wander, to be led into error, to fall away from
the truth." John used the word *planaō* two other places in his first epis-

tle. He used it to inform his spiritual children of why he had written to them when he said,

> *"These things have I written unto you concerning them that seduce* (planaō) *you."*
>
> I John 2:26

He also used it when he offered this warning to his spiritual children,

> *"Little children, let no man deceive* (planaō) *you."*
>
> I John 3:7

John's statement in I John 1:8 that anyone who said, "we have no sin," was self deceived and the truth was not in them was a confrontational declaration about early gnostic error and a full indictment of their belief. The self deception of the early gnostics he characterized by the word *planaō* was not a minor mistake in thinking or a slight error in judgment that could be easily rectified. Their deception was a serious self-delusion, a falling away from the truth, and a journey into error. According to John, those who said, "we have no sin," were void of the truth.

As he had done in his first two conditional statements in I John 1:6 and I John 1:7, John set up a hypothetical situation for his spiritual children to consider in his conditional statement in I John 1:8. He was not accusing his spiritual children of having already embraced early gnostic error, but was revealing to them what their condition would be if they embraced that error and began to believe and say what the early gnostics believed and said. According to John, if they said, "we have no sin," they would be deceiving themselves and would be void of the truth just as the early gnostics deceived themselves and were void of the truth. There is no doubt the apostle John was deeply concerned that believers he loved might be deceived, might depart from the truth, and might embrace dangerous early gnostic error. Hence, the strong statements and stark warnings of his polemic.

I John 1:9

John continued his polemic against early gnostic error in I John 1:9, alternating once again to make a statement that characterized Christian truth and the action and saying of true believers. Like his words in I John 1:7, his words in I John 1:9 represented what true believers believed, what they said and did, and what was, therefore, true of them. He wrote,

> *"If we confess our sins, he is faithful and just to forgive us our sins, and to cleanse us from all unrighteousness."*
>
> I John 1:9

In I John 1:9, John alternated from his statement in I John 1:8 which characterized early gnostic belief and saying and what was, therefore, true of them to pen another fifth class conditional statement that characterized the beliefs and actions of believers and what was true of them. His statement in I John 1:9 was a counter statement to his statement in I John 1:8 just as his statement in I John 1:7 was a counter statement to his statement in I John 1:6. Although John did not begin his counter statement in I John 1:9 with the contrasting conjunction "But" as he had done in I John 1:7, the word "But" was implied in his statement. In fact, according to some Greek scholars, the English rendering of I John 1:9 may have more accurately followed the Greek language if it had been written this way, "If, however, we confess our sins."

In I John 1:9, John continued his pattern of alternating back and forth between statements that characterized the early gnostics, their error, and what was true of them and statements that characterized true believers, the truth they believed and walked in, and what was, therefore, true of them. His alternating statements in I John 1:8 and I John 1:9 highlighted the profound contrast between those who said, "we have no sin," but were self-deceived and void of the truth and those who, "confess (*homologeō*) our sins," and were forgiven and cleansed of their sins by their faithful and just God.

Unlike the early gnostics who denied God's truth about sin and sinning and said, "we have no sin," true believers, "confess *(homologeō)* our sins." In other words, true believers aligned with God and agreed with His truth concerning sin and sinning and openly acknowledged their agreement. They agreed with God that sin existed. They agreed with Him that all men were sinners and needed to be saved from their sins. And if they sinned, they did not deny that they had sinned, but agreed with God and His Word and acknowledged that they had sinned. Unlike the early gnostics John characterized in I John 1:8 who said, "we have no sin," true believers did not deny that sin existed and did not deny that they had sinned when they had sinned. Rather, they, "confess *(homologeō)* our sins."

John's statement in I John 1:9 stood in contrast to his statements in both I John 1:8 and I John 1:10 in that to, "confess *(homologeō)* our sins," was the direct opposite of claiming, "we have no sin," and saying, "we have not sinned." John's statement in I John 1:9 was not a teaching about what believers were required to do in order to be forgiven of the sins they had committed, but was one of several important conditional statements he penned in his polemic to highlight the stark contrast between early gnostic error and Christian truth on the subject of sin and sinning and to notify his spiritual children that they had choices to make.

Like his previous three statements, John's statement in I John 1:9 was a fifth class conditional statement containing a cause clause and an effect clause. The effect clause of his statement, the second part, revealed what would be true of his spiritual children if they chose to do what was written in the cause clause; the first part of his statement. The cause clause in I John 1:9 was, "If any of us do confess *(homologeō)* our sins." The effect clause was, "He (God) is faithful and just to forgive us our sins." Just as John's three fifth class conditional statements in I John 1:6, 7, and 8 revealed what would be true of his spiritual children if they chose to do what he presented in the cause clause of those statements, so his conditional statement in I John 1:9 revealed what would be true of his spiritual children if they chose to do what he presented in the cause clause of that statement.

John's fifth class conditional statement in 1 John 1:9 asserted a universal truth concerning fellowship with God. That truth was that if any person did at any time confess *(homologeō)* their sins and was, therefore, a "confessor of sins" and not a "denier of sin and sins," they revealed themselves to be a true believer in relationship with God through faith in Jesus Christ. Because they were a true believer, as evidenced by the fact that they *"homologeō* our sins," then God, who was faithful and just, would continue to forgive their sins and cleanse them. Why would God continue to forgive and cleanse them? He would continue to forgive and cleanse them, not because they obediently admitted every one of their sins to Him in a time of confession, but because forgiving sins and cleansing from all unrighteousness is what the faithful and just God does for true New Covenant believers. In his powerful conditional statement in I John 1:9, John characterized those who "confess *(homologeō)* our sins" as true believers who were aligned with and spoke in agreement with God concerning sin and sinning and whose sins, therefore, God was faithful and just to forgive.

Like his previous conditional statements in I John 1:6, 7, and 8, John's conditional statement in I John 1:9 presented a hypothetical situation for his spiritual children to consider. Due to the dangerous error being peddled in the region, they had choices to make about what they were going to believe, about who they were going to agree with, and about how they were going to live. John's words in the effect clause of his statement revealed what would be true of them if they chose to do what he stated in the cause clause of his statement. By means of his conditional statement in I John 1:9, he hoped to persuade his spiritual children to remain steadfast in the truth they had already embraced and not be deceived by the error of the early gnostics and begin to say, "we have no sin," and, "we have not sinned" (I John 1:8 and 10).

The apostle John wanted his spiritual children to remain sound in God's truth and to, "confess *(homologeō)* our sins." In other words, he wanted them to continue to agree with God's truth that sin existed and, if they missed the mark of His will and sinned, to not deny that they had sinned, but agree with God, acknowledging that they had sinned.

By making the choice to, "confess *(homologeō)* our sins," rather than denying God's truth and saying, "we have no sin," and, "we have not sinned," John's spiritual children would remain steadfast in their relationship with God and continue to experience one of the most beautiful provisions of the New Covenant—the forgiveness of sins they had committed and a cleansing from all unrighteousness by their faithful and just God.

John's words in I John 1:9 revealed that contrary to the belief and the saying of the early gnostics, people can sin and, in fact, even true believers can sin. John did not, however, want his spiritual children to be afraid or over anxious if they had sinned. To ensure that they were securely grounded in their salvation and confident in their new life in Christ, he penned the powerful New Covenant reality that those who confess *(homologeō)* their sins—in other words, those who were true believers—were continually being forgiven of sins they committed and were continually being cleansed from all unrighteousness because their covenant God was faithful and just. Just as he revealed in I John 1:7 that the blood of Jesus Christ was presently and continuously cleansing those who walked in the light of any sin they might commit, John revealed in I John 1:9 that God was faithful and just to forgive the sins and to cleanse from all unrighteousness those who were agreers with God concerning sin and sinning; in other words, those who were true believers. John's spiritual children need not be over anxious or fearful if they had stumbled and sinned. Because they were walking in the light and were "confessors of sins"—because they were New Covenant believers—they would continually be forgiven of their sins and cleansed from all unrighteousness.

John revealed in I John 1:9 that God forgives believers' sins because He is faithful and just. The fact that God is faithful means that He keeps His word. It means that He follows through on what He has promised. It means that He acts in agreement with the New Covenant He designed and which was put into effect through the suffering, the shedding of blood, and the death of His Son, Jesus Christ. The fact that God is just means that He does what is legally right. It means that He doesn't violate spiritual laws or violate any terms of the better New Covenant. It is because of His word, His oath, His promise, and the legalities of the New Covenant that God forgives believers' sins. He is faithful to keep His Word and acts justly, according to the terms of the New Covenant that He ordained and established. That is what it means that God is, "faithful and just to forgive us our sins, and to cleanse us from all unrighteousness."

Essential to a correct interpretation and a right understanding of John's words in I John 1:9 is a keen awareness of the important fact that John's statement in I John 1:9 was not disconnected from the flow of the argument he began in I John 1:5. His words in I John 1:9 were not an instruction about what believers needed to do, but were part and parcel of his polemic against early gnostic error on the subject of sin and sinning. Although I John 1:9 has often been singled out and popularized above other verses in the same context, John's statement in I John 1:9 was not a stand alone statement, but was one of many important statements he penned as he set errant early gnostics and true believers in stark contrast throughout his polemic.

I John 1:9 was one of six important fifth class conditional statements John penned in his polemic to reveal to his spiritual children what would be true of them if they did what he presented in the cause clause of that statement. His words should not be interpreted outside the context of his polemic in I John 1:5 through I John 2:11, outside the more specific context of his five conditional statements in I John 1:6-10, or outside the narrow context of his contrasting statements in I John 1:8-10. If John's words in I John 1:9 are interpreted outside of these important contexts, a faulty interpretation is highly likely.

I John 1:10

In I John 1:10, John continued his polemic, alternating once again to make a statement that characterized the errant early gnostics and their error and to reveal what was true of them. Penning his fifth fifth class conditional statement and his third "If we say" statement, he wrote,

"If we say that we have not sinned, we make him (God) a liar, and his (God's) word is not in us."

I John 1:10

In I John 1:10, John again characterized the early gnostics and their error. His third "If we say" statement strengthened and expanded his second "If we say" statement in I John 1:8. In I John 1:8, John's words, "If we say that we have no sin," characterized what the early gnostics believed and said about their own internal spiritual condition. Because they believed that their spirit came from God and was pure, they did not believe they had a sin nature. In I John 1:10, John's words, "If we say that we have not sinned," characterized what the early gnostics believed and said about their lifestyle. Because they believed that no carnal deed done in the body was a sin, they confidently claimed, "we have not sinned," while they were sinning and walking in darkness. The way John used his two statements in I John 1:8 and in I John 1:10 in a repeating fashion was similar to a style of Hebrew poetry where a second written statement embellished and affirmed the first statement. According to John's stout words in I John 1:10, any person who said, "we have not sinned," was calling God a liar; asserting that what He said in His Word was not true and revealing that His truth had no place in their lives.

Regardless of what the errant early gnostics believed or said about sin and sinning, the fact of the matter was that throughout His written Word, God revealed that men were sinners and needed a Savior and revealed with clarity that some things were, indeed, sin and unrighteousness. The apostle Paul made it clear, for example, that every person was a sinner and every person sinned when he wrote,

"As it is written, There is none righteous, no, not one...Now we know that what things soever the law saith, it saith to them who are under the law: that every mouth may be stopped, and all the world may become guilty before God."

Romans 3:10, 19

Not unlike the serpent himself, the early gnostics called into question the veracity of what God said through His prophets, through His Son, through his apostles, and through His written Word. They had no respect for His words and certainly did not *homologeō*—align and speak in agreement—with Him. They denied that what He said was true and refused to concede that He was right. They did not believe the record He gave of His Son and did not agree with His testimony that men needed a Savior. They did not agree with Him that they were sinners, did not agree with His Word about what things were sin, and did not agree with Him when they had sinned themselves. According to John, the truth of God was not in their hearts and lies were in their mouths. In I John 1:8 and I John 1:10, John revealed that anyone who said they had no sin and said they had not sinned was deceived, was lying, had made God a liar, was void of the truth, and did not have God's Word in them.

As he did in both I John 1:6 and I John 1:8, John used his "If we say" conditional statement in I John 1:10 both to characterize what the early gnostics believed and were saying and to alert believers to the fact that they had choices to make. If they joined with the errant early gnostics, said, "we have not sinned," and followed them in their dark lifestyle, then like the errant early gnostics, they would be calling God a liar and revealing that His Word had no place in their lives. No doubt, John hoped that his stout words would awaken his spiritual children to the dangers they were facing and persuade them to not be seduced by early gnostic error, but to remain steadfast in the truth they had already embraced.

I John 2:1-2

In I John 2:1-2, John alternated again and penned his final fifth class conditional statement, characterizing Christian truth and what was true of New Covenant believers. The truth he expressed in these two verses was not a new or a different truth, but was the same essential truth he had expressed in both I John 1:7 and in I John 1:9. He wrote,

"My little children, these things write I unto you, that ye sin not. And if any man sin, we have an advocate with the Father, Jesus Christ the righteous: And he is the propitiation for our sins: and not for ours only, but also for the sins of the whole world."

I John 2:1-2

John briefly punctuated the flow of his polemic with personal words in I John 2:1, informing his little children that one of the primary reasons he had written to them was, "that ye sin not." His words about not sinning transmitted a much deeper concern for his little children than that they might occasionally stumble and commit a few sins, however. His deeper concern was that his little children might embrace early gnostic error and follow them in a dark lifestyle of sinning while claiming, "We are in fellowship with God; we have no sin; we have not sinned." John wrote to his little children to warn them because he did not want them to be misled by the seductive early gnostics, fall into their error, and follow them in their dark lifestyle of sinning.

John revealed in his conditional statement in I John 2:1-2 that, "if any man sin, (then) we have an advocate with the Father, Jesus Christ… And he is the propitiation for our sins." John wanted his spiritual children to know that if they stumbled and sinned, they need not panic or be in fear thinking that God would reject them or thinking that they had become unclean or unrighteous and that their fellowship with Him was broken. He wanted them to be aware of the fact that their all wise Father God had already put in place for them a divine remedy for any sins they might commit. That divine remedy was Jesus Christ the righteous, their advocate with the Father and the propitiation for their sins.

In I John 2:1-2, John revealed to his spiritual children that Jesus Christ was their advocate with the Father if they sinned. The English word "advocate" is translated from the Greek word *paraklētos*. In Bible times, the *paraklētos* was a person who pled the case of another before a judge; who was a legal assistant, an intercessor, a lawyer. The role of the *paraklētos* was to defend his client by proving to the judge that his client was not guilty. In order to effectively defend his client, the *paraklētos* had to know all the facts of his client's case and be an expert on all the laws that pertained to his client's case. The *paraklētos* would present all the pertinent facts of his client's case before the judge and argue for a decision of "Not guilty." If, in the end, his client was found to be guilty, the *paraklētos* would do everything in his power to ensure that no penalty was imposed that was illegal or inappropriate.

The truth John presented to believers in I John 2:1-2—that Jesus was their advocate with the Father—raises this obvious question: "Why do believers need an advocate with the Father?" If it was true that everything was made perfect in believers' lives the moment they believed, and if it was true that every past, present, and future sin was forgiven and that nothing more needed to be said, needed to be done, or needed to be dealt with, then why would believers need an advocate with the Father?

The simple answer to this question is that believers need an advocate with the Father because after they are saved, they will sin; they will break God's commandments and do unrighteous things. And after believers sin, they need to be forgiven and cleansed of their sins. That is why the Father designed the New Covenant the way He did. That is why He planned and put in place a divine remedy for the sins believers would commit. That is why He ordained that Jesus Christ the righteous would be believers' advocate with the Father, always present with Him to plead their cases.

In His role as advocate with the Father, Jesus defends believers when they sin by presenting all the facts of their case; including all the legal realities of the New Testament. When Jesus pleads before the Father on the behalf of believers, He doesn't plead on the basis of their good intentions or on the basis of any good works they may have done. He also doesn't plead on the basis of the Father's mercy, compassion, or kindness. Jesus pleads, rather, on the basis of the legalities and realities of the New Covenant. He pleads on the basis of the complete efficacy of His own shed blood to cleanse all sins, including the sins of believers. He presents these essential matters to the Father and reminds Him to be "faithful and just" as I John 1:9 says He is and to forgive believers' sins according to the New Covenant that He put in place. As advocate with the Father, Jesus argues for justice, undertaking to ensure that believers are not punished for sins they commit after they are saved because He, Jesus Christ the righteous, already paid the full penalty for those sins and provided for the complete forgiveness of those sins.

John also revealed in I John 2:1-2 that Jesus is, "the propitiation for our sins." The English word "propitation" comes from the Greek *hilasmos* which means, "the atonement, the expiation; the means of appeasing." The scriptural conception of the effect of the propitiation is that it moves out of the way any sins that might separate a person from God. As the *hilasmos*, Jesus propitiates the sins believers commit, moving them out of the way so that no sin will stand between them and the Father. The fact that Jesus is the propitiation for the sins of believers reveals that believers will sin and also reveals that their sins must be dealt with. If believers did not sin or if every one of their future sins was already forgiven, there would be no need for Jesus to be the propitiation for believers' sins.

Most believers are aware that Jesus is the propitiation for the sins of sinners. Many are not aware of the significant truth, however, that Jesus is also the propitiation for their sins. God assigned Jesus this important role because He knew that believers would sin after they were saved. Those sins would have to be forgiven and cleansed and moved out of the way so that believers' right standing with God and their access to Him would be safeguarded. Thanks to the keen foresight and great wisdom of God, Jesus' work as the propitiation for believers' sins is part of the glorious New Covenant.

John wrote his words in I John 1:1-2 because he wanted his spiritual children to understand that the same powerful blood of Jesus Christ that had cleansed them from all their past sins when they first believed was sufficient to cleanse them of every sin they might commit as believers. He wanted them to know that Jesus not only "was" the propitiation for all their past sins, but that He "is" the propitiation for any present or future sins. As the, "propitiation for our sins," Jesus propitiates the sins of every believer, ensuring that no sin they commit will alter their legal righteous status with God or be an impediment to their personal fellowship with Him. This truth is a fundamental and strikingly beautiful New Covenant truth.

In I John 2:1-2, John informed his little children that he had written to them because he did not want them to turn back from the truth they had embraced and turn back to a lifestyle of sinning. He wanted them to continue to walk in the light and to live righteous lives according to God's will and His commandments. He made it clear, however, that if they did sin, there was a divine remedy in place to deal with those sins. Jesus Christ the righteous was their advocate with the Father and the propitiation for their sins.

I John 2:3

John followed his statement in I John 2:1-2 with another statement that characterized true believers. In I John 2:3, he wrote,

"And hereby we do know that we know him, if we keep his commandments."

I John 2:3

Although believers can know they are saved, know they are born of God, and know they are cleansed from past sins on the basis of what Scripture says and by the witness of the Holy Spirit in their own spirit, John revealed in I John 2:3 that believers could know that they knew God if they, "keep his commandments." In other words, those who embrace God's Word and are endeavoring to live in agreement with His righteous instructions can know on that basis that they know Him. The reason John included this important statement in his polemic against early gnostic error was because of the disconnect the early gnostics exhibited between their saying and their living. They said, "We are in fellowship with Him," but they walked in darkness. They said, "We know Him," but they did not keep His commandments. John wanted his spiritual children to understand that no matter what kinds of claims anyone made, if they did not live a life of endeavoring to keep God's commandments and did not walk in the light of His revealed will concerning righteous living, they did not know God. On the other hand, as John said, those who truly know God, "keep his commandments."

The early gnostics said, "we know God," and, "we are in fellowship with Him," and, "we have not sinned," while they walked in darkness, refused to submit to His Word, and did not keep His commandments. What they said about themselves was not the truth about themselves. Rather, how they lived was the truth about themselves. If a believer "listened to their living," they could know with confidence that those individuals did not know God. True believers, on the other hand, walked in the light, agreed with God (*homologeō*), embraced His Word, and kept His commandments. They lived this way because they knew God and were born of Him. According to the apostle John, the fact that believers kept God's commandments was one of the proofs that they truly knew Him.

Throughout his polemic and, in fact, throughout his whole first epistle, the apostle John revealed again and again that the true Christian life was not a life where one's words and one's lifestyle were incongruent, but was a life where one's words and one's lifestyle were harmonious. He offered the accurate indicator of how a person lived their life as one way his spiritual children could determine who was a true believer and living in the truth and who was a liar, a deceiver, and a sinner living in the dark. He wanted them to understand that they could determine who was and who was not of God by whether or not a person was living in agreement with God's commandments. Having this insight about how to accurately judge others would keep his spiritual children from being seduced by those who talked a good talk, but did not live a godly life and were not of God.

I John 2:4

In I John 2:4, John penned the first "He that saith" statement of his polemic. The three "He that saith" statements he penned in chapter two of his epistle, like the three "If we say" statements he penned in chapter one of his epistle, characterized the beliefs and saying and life-style of the early gnostics and presented hypothetical situations for his spiritual children to consider as they made choices about what they were going to believe, who they were going to follow, what they were going to say, and how they were going to live.

John's words in his "He that saith" statement in I John 2:4 characterized the errant early gnostics—what they believed and said and what was true of them. He wrote,

> "He that saith, I know him, and keepeth not his commandments, is a
> liar, and the truth is not in him."
>
> I John 2:4

In contrast to those John characterized in I John 2:3 who truly knew God and kept His commandments, the individuals he characterized in I John 2:4 said, "I know (God)," but did not keep His commandments. These individuals, according to John, were liars, and, "the truth is not in (them)." Interestingly, this is exactly how John characterized the early gnostics in his three "If we say" statements in I John 1:6, 8, and 10. In those verses, he stated that they were liars who were lying and not doing the truth, that they were deceived, and that God's Word and His truth was not in them.

If the individuals John characterized in I John 2:4 were liars, what was the lie they were telling? The lie they were telling was, "I know (God)." It was obvious, however, that they did not know God because if they knew God, they would keep His commandments, as John had stated in I John 2:3. John's statement in I John 2:4 declaring that those who said, "I know him," but did not keep God's commandments were liars who did not have the truth in them was an accurate assessment of both the "talk" and the "contrary to their talk lifestyle" of the early gnostics. With his words in I John 2:4, John again highlighted the serious disconnect between what the early gnostics said and how they lived. The message of their living was completely incongruent with the message of their speaking and contrary to what God had said. According to John, the fact that the early gnostics did not keep God's commandments was sufficient proof that they did not know God.

John had made it clear in his statement in I John 2:3 that those who kept God's commandments were those who knew Him; in other words, they were true believers. In his "He that saith" statement in I John 2:4, he made it clear that those who said they knew God, but did not keep His commandments did not know God; in other words, they were not true believers. Making use of contrasting statements in I John 2:3 and I John 2:4, John once again set the beliefs, the sayings, and the lifestyle of errant early gnostics and true believers in stark contrast and endeavored to alert believers so that they would not be misled. He wanted to be sure his spiritual children were cognizant of the fact that if any of them joined the early gnostics, saying what they said while living how they lived, they would be in the same spiritual condition as the early gnostics; they would be liars who did not possess the truth and did not know God.

I John 2:5

John's next statement in I John 2:5 was a counter statement to his "He that saith" statement in I John 2:4 where he had characterized the errant early gnostics. He made it clear that his statement in I John 2:5 was a contrasting statement by opening it with the contrasting word "But." He wrote,

> "But whoso keepeth his word, in him verily is the love of God perfected: hereby know we that we are in him."
>
> I John 2:5

John's statement in this verse was essentially a restatement of his words in I John 2:3. Just as he had stated in I John 2:3 that a person could know they knew God because they kept His commandments, he stated in this verse that a person could know that they were "in him (God)" because they "keepeth his (God's) word." According to John, those who kept God's Word were growing to maturity in the love of God and, on the basis of that reality, could be certain that they were in a true relationship with God.

John's statement in I John 2:4 where he had characterized the early gnostics was neatly sandwiched between his nearly identical statements in I John 2:3 and I John 2:5 where he characterized true believers. In I John 2:4, John characterized those who did not keep God's commandments and His Word as those who were not in Him, but were liars who did not have the truth in them. In both I John 2:3 and I John 2:5, John characterized those who kept God's commandments and kept His Word as those who were in relationship with God and growing in love. The contrast between the errant early gnostics and true believers could not be clearer. The early gnostics talked about how they were spiritually elite, about how they were walking in the light, and about how they knew God, but their lives did not match their rhetoric; they were walking in darkness and not living in agreement with God's commandments. True believers, on the other hand, kept God's Word, were growing in their life of love, and, because of that, could know with certainty that they knew God and were in Him.

Throughout his polemic, John made it clear that the true Christian life was not just one of making wonderful claims about one's self and about spiritual posturing, but was a life lived in agreement with God and with His Word; with His commandments. The true Christian life was a life lived in alignment and agreement with God on all matters; including the matter of sin and sinning. It was regarding this essential reality of true Christianity where the early gnostics erred and exposed themselves as not true believers, but as liars who were void of truth and did not know God.

I John 2:6

In I John 2:6, John alternated and penned his second "He that saith" statement, again characterizing the errant early gnostics. As with his other say statements, his words, "He that saith," in I John 2:6 prefaced his characterization of the early gnostics and set up another hypothetical situation for his spiritual children to consider. He wrote,

"He that saith he abideth in him (in Jesus) *ought himself also so to walk, even as he walked."*

I John 2:6

John's words in I John 2:6 expressed once again that the true Christian life was characterized by an essential agreement between what one said and how one lived. A person who said they were abiding in Jesus ought to be walking the way Jesus walked. Their saying and their living should be congruent. The early gnostics did not demonstrate that essential congruence. They said they abided in Jesus, but they did not walk as He walked. Their saying and their living was not in agreement. John's second "He that saith" statement in I John 2:6 again expressed this major flaw of the early gnostics and alerted his spiritual children to that flaw so that they did not follow their example. He did not want believers that he was responsible for making claims of an authentic relationship with God and with His Son, Jesus Christ, while they walked a walk that was not like Jesus' walk. If they did so, they would be thinking, speaking, and living just like the early gnostics.

I John 2:7-8

In his next two statements, John alternated again and directly addressed his spiritual children, similar to the way he had addressed them in I John 2:1-2. He wrote,

"Brethren, I write no new commandment unto you, but an old commandment which ye had from the beginning. The old commandment is the word which ye have heard from the beginning. Again, a new commandment I write unto you, which thing is true in him and in you: because the darkness is past, and the true light now shineth."

I John 2:7-8

With these words, John bridged between God's Old Covenant commandments to His people about living a righteous life and

Jesus' new commandment to His disciples about walking in love. He exhorted his spiritual children to walk in agreement with God's commandments that they had heard from the beginning, but then pressed forward to reveal that a true life in Christ and in the light was more than living in agreement with God's Old Testament commandments. This new life in Christ included the new commandment that Jesus, the true light, had delivered to them. This new life in the light was about more than not sinning against God's moral code; it included living by the new commandment of love that came from Jesus Christ.

As John neared the end of his polemic, it seems that he wanted to be sure his brethren understood that living their new life in Christ included living by God's moral code which they already knew—"the old commandment...which ye have heard from the beginning"—but that it was also about living in the light of the truth that had been delivered to them through Jesus Christ, God's Son; specifically His new commandment to, "love one another." John's words in I John 2:7-8 bridged between the commandments of both testaments and introduced the important subject of love; a subject he would take up in his next statement and refer to throughout the rest of his epistle.

I John 2:9

In I John 2:9, John alternated again to pen his third "He that saith" statement; the sixth and final say statement of his polemic. His final say statement again characterized the errant early gnostics and set up a hypothetical situation for his spiritual children to consider. As he neared the end of his polemic, John shifted his focus from what the early gnostics said and how they lived in respect to God's moral code as recorded in the Scriptures and touched on what would be one of the important themes of his first epistle; the theme of love. He wrote,

> "He that saith he is in the light, and hateth his brother, is in darkness even until now."
>
> *I John 2:9*

Throughout his polemic, the apostle John made it clear that walking in the light referred to living a life of true fellowship with God and leading a righteous life—a life that was in agreement with God's Word and a life of keeping His commandments. As he now made clear with his statement in I John 2:9, walking in the light included a true love for one's brethren. In fact, since loving one another was the singular commandment Jesus gave to His disciples, there could be no greater sin and no darker deed than to hate one's brother while claiming to be in the light.

As John was concluding his polemic and finishing his work of setting errant early gnostics and true believers in stark contrast, he addressed the essential New Covenant lifestyle of loving the brethren. According to John, those who said, "we are in the light," but hated their brethren were yet in darkness. They were not born of God or in fellowship with Him; they were not true believers. Any person who claimed, "I am in the light," but hated his brother was lying and was bound in darkness, "even until now."

In his sixth and final say statement, John again alerted his spiritual children to the fact that they were going to encounter individuals whose "saying" and "living" were not in agreement. These individuals would make wonderful claims about themselves, but their lives would not harmonize with their claims. These individuals were the same errant early gnostics he had characterized in his previous five say statements. John not only wanted his spiritual children to recognize these individuals for who they truly were, however; he also wanted them to realize that if they joined with these individuals and began to say that they were in the light while they hated their brethren, they would also not be in the light, but would be in darkness.

I John 2:10

Following his final say statement in I John 2:9, John alternated once again and penned a final counter statement in I John 2:10, characterizing Christian truth and the godly lifestyle of true believers and what was true of them. His contrasting statements in I John 2:9 and I John 2:10 served again to highlight the stark contrast between the errant early gnostics and true believers. In I John 2:10, he wrote,

"He that loveth his brother abideth in the light, and there is none occasion of stumbling in him."

I John 2:10

In stark contrast to the individuals John characterized in I John 2:9 who said that they were in the light, but hated their brethren, revealing that they had never come into the light, but were still in darkness, the individuals John characterized in I John 2:10 loved their brethren and abided in the light. These individuals were true believers. According to John, for those who loved their brothers and abided in the light, there was, "none occasion of stumbling." The phrase, "occasion of stumbling," comes from the Greek word *scandalon* which refers to a trap or snare or, "an impediment that causes one to stumble." For true believers—those who loved their brothers and abided in the light—there would be nothing to trap them or to get in their way, causing them to stumble.

To hate one's brother, according to John's words in I John 2:9, was proof that one was yet in darkness. Conversely, according to his words in I John 2:10, there was no greater proof that a person was abiding in the light than that they loved their brother. The individuals John had characterized in I John 2:9 who hated their brethren and were yet in the dark were the same early gnostic sinners he had been exposing throughout his polemic. The individuals he characterized in I John 2:10 who loved their brethren and were walking safely in the light were his spiritual children and his brethren; they were true New Covenant believers who were born of God and in fellowship with Him and with His Son, Jesus Christ.

I John 2:11

Concluding his polemic in I John 2:11, John alternated one last time to make a statement about the errant early gnostics, characterizing them as individuals who hated their brethren, who had never come out of the darkness, and who were not in relationship with God. Although his last statement was not a say statement, like the six say statements he had already penned, it was a statement that character-ized the errant early gnostics. He wrote,

> *"But he that hateth his brother is in darkness, and walks in dark-ness, and knoweth not wither he goeth, because that darkness hath blinded his eyes."*
>
> I John 2:11

John began the final statement of his polemic with the contrast-ing word "But," revealing that his words in I John 2:11 would be in contrast to his statement in I John 2:10 where he had characterized true believers. His words in the final statement of his polemic were a repetition and a slight expansion of the negative characterization of the errant early gnostics he had presented in I John 2:9. In I John 2:11, John characterized the early gnostics as those who hated their breth-ren, who were in darkness, who were walking in darkness, and who did not know where they were going, "because that darkness hath blinded (their) eyes." The spiritual condition of the individuals John characterized in I John 2:11 was in complete contrast to the spiritual condition of those he had characterized in I John 2:10 who abided in the light and of whom he said that nothing could get in their way and cause them to stumble.

John could not have created a more stark contrast between the errant early gnostics and true believers than the contrast he created in the final three statements of his polemic (I John 2:9-11). The early gnos-tics hated their brothers, were in darkness, walked in darkness, were blinded by darkness, and did not know where they were going. True believers, on the other hand, loved their brothers, were abiding in the light, and would experience no stumbling at all as they lived their new lives in Christ.

Another View of John's Polemic

Although John's polemic is a beautifully organized, skillful, and well set forth argument and should be read exactly as he wrote it, we can, for the sake of additional clarity, rearrange his statements, separating them into two categories: his statements that characterized the early gnostics and their error and his statements that characterized true believers and New Covenant truth. Laying out John's polemic in this unique way presents us with a very clear view of what he was expressing.

Here are the statements from John's polemic that characterize the early gnostics and their error. These statements express what they believed, what they said, how they lived, and what was, therefore, true of them:

I John 1:6   They say, "We have fellowship with God," but they walk in darkness, they lie, and they do not do the truth.

I John 1:8   They say, "We have no sin"—no sin nature—but they have deceived themselves, and the truth is not in them.

I John 1:10   They say, "We have not sinned," but by saying this, they make God a liar and reveal that His Word is not in them.

I John 2:4   They say, "I know Him," but they do not keep His commandments. They are liars and the truth is not in them.

I John 2:6   They say, "I abide in Him," but they don't walk as He walked.

I John 2:9   They say, "I am in the light," but they hate their brothers. They are in darkness even until now.

I John 2:11   They hate their brothers, are walking in darkness, and don't even know where they are going.

Now let's look at the alternating statements from John's polemic which represent the New Covenant truths believers embraced and lived in and which characterized them. These statements express what true believers believed, what they said, and what was, therefore, true of them:

I John 1:7   They walk in the light as God is in the light. Because they do, they have fellowship with God and with one with another and the blood of Jesus Christ, God's Son, cleanses them from all sin.

I John 1:9   They confess *(homologeō)* their sins—they agree with God about what sin is and if they sin themselves, they don't deny that they have sinned, but openly acknowledge that they have sinned. God forgives their sins and cleanses them from all unrightcousness because He is faithful and just.

I John 2:1-2 They should not sin, but if they do sin, they have an advocate with the Father, Jesus Christ the righteous. That same Jesus is the propitiation for any sins they commit and for the sins of the whole world.

I John 2:3   They know God and they keep His commandments.

I John 2:5-6 They keep God's Word and the love of God is perfected in them. That is how they know they are in Him. They say that they abide in Him and that is how they walk; even as He walked.

I John 2:10   They love their brothers and abide in the light. There is no occasion of stumbling in them.

Laying out the contrasting statements of John's polemic in this fashion makes even more apparent the stark contrast between the beliefs, the sayings, the lifestyle, and the spiritual condition of the errant early gnostics and the beliefs, the sayings, the lifestyle, and the spiritual condition of true believers. Laying out the contrasting statements of John's polemic in this way also helps to reveal the intent of his polemic; to expose the early gnostics and their error so that his spiritual children would not be seduced by them and abandon the truth of God they had embraced.

Conclusion

We have learned several important things in this chapter that will guide our interpretation of John's words in I John 1:9, helping us to determine what he really meant by his words. First, we learned that John's words in I John 1:5 through I John 2:11 constituted a powerful polemic against early gnostic error on the subject of sin and sinning. Second, we learned that throughout his polemic, John employed an alternating-statement style, going back and forth between say statements that characterized the early gnostics and their error and contrasting statements that characterized true believers and New Covenant truth. Third, we learned that John used six say statements to identify what the early gnostics believed and said and what was, therefore, true of them. Fourth, we learned that John's statement in I John 1:9 was one of six fifth class conditional statements he penned in I John 1:6-2:2. His statement in I John 1:9 characterized true believers and, like his other conditional statements, presented a choice for his spiritual children to consider. Fifth, we learned that John's contrasting statement in I John 1:9 answered to both his "If we say" statement in I John 1:8 and his "If we say" statement in I John 1:10 where he characterized the errant early gnostics as those who said, "we have no sin," and, "we have not sinned." John's words in I John 1:9 must be considered and interpreted with these important facts in mind.

Throughout his polemic, John methodically laid out his case against early gnostic error and revealed to his spiritual children two very different choices they were facing that would take them down two very different paths and result in two very different lives. His statement in I John 1:9 revealed one of those choices as he set the "in agreement with God about sin and sinning" posture and speaking of true believers in stark contrast to the "disagreeing with God about sin and sinning" posture and speaking of the errant early gnostics.

How would John's spiritual children respond to his words? Would they allow themselves to be seduced by the errant early gnostics, embrace what they taught, say what they said, and live how they lived? Or would they remain firm and steadfast in the faith, hold fast to the truths they had embraced from the beginning, and continue to agree with God about everything He had said; including what He had said about sin and sinning? Would they make claims of being in fellowship with God while they walked in darkness and said things like, "we have no sin," and, "we have not sinned," or would they walk in the light and, "confess (homologeō) our sins?"

Why Is This View of I John 1:9 Important?

In this chapter, we looked at I John 1:9 from the point of view that John's words in I John 1:5 through I John 2:11 constituted a written polemic against the error of the early gnostics concerning sin and sinning and that his statement in I John 1:9 was an integral part of that polemic. This critical point of view has provided us with excellent insight into John's purpose for writing his words in I John 1:9 and furnished us with important general and immediate contexts for those words. This view has enlightened us greatly as to the true purpose of his words in I John 1:9 and helped us significantly in our endeavor to discover what he intended to communicate to his spiritual children.

It was the rise of dangerous early gnostic error in the region of Ephesus where John was living and ministering that gave rise to his first epistle and his powerful polemic. And it was in the context of his powerful polemic that he penned his familiar words in I John 1:9. His words in I John 1:9 must be viewed, studied, and interpreted in their appropriate contexts—in the larger context of his polemic against early gnostic error concerning sin and sinning, in the more specific context of his six fifth class conditional statements found in I John 1:6 through I John 2:1-2, and in the immediate context of his three fifth class conditional statements in I John 1:8-10. As we search for the best interpretation of John's words in I John 1:9, we must take care not to lift them out of these appropriate and crucial contexts and assign them meanings that are not harmonious with the purpose for which they were written or that are divorced from the contexts in which they are located.

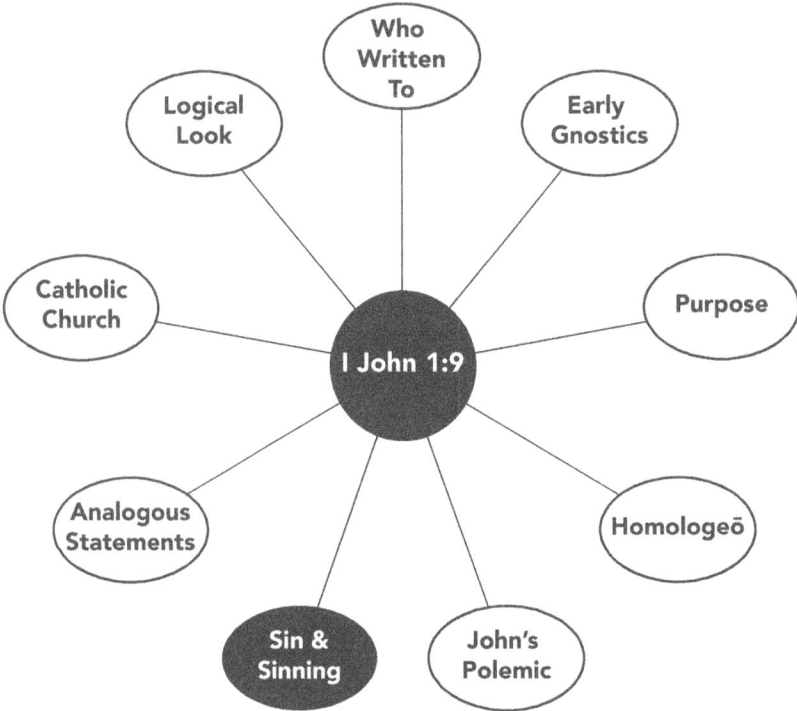

VII

Sin And Sinning

One of the most serious spiritual problems developing in the region of Ephesus where the apostle John was living and ministering at the time he wrote his first epistle was being perpetrated by the early gnostics. These individuals rejected God's truth about His Son and God's truth about sin and sinning and were endeavoring to peddle their error into the church. As we learned earlier in our study, many early gnostics believed that they had no sin nature and believed that they did not sin. They believed, rather, that their spirit was good and pure and because it had no effective contact with their evil body, it didn't matter what they did in their body; it would not affect their spirit or their spiritual life. They believed they could indulge in whatever kind of carnality and fleshliness they wanted and would not be sinning.

Throughout his first epistle, the apostle John exposed and contended against this early gnostic error and set forth sound and accurate New Covenant truth for his spiritual children to lay hold of and live in the light of. Again and again, he characterized the early gnostics as those who, although they claimed to be in fellowship with God, claimed to be righteous, and claimed to be in the light, lived contrary to God's truth concerning sin and sinning and were walking in darkness. Again and again, he set the errant early gnostics in stark contrast with true believers who agreed with God about sin and sinning, who walked in the light, who kept God's law, and who lived righteously. The amount of attention the apostle John gave to the subject of sin and sinning in his first epistle and the force of his writing against early gnostic error on this subject reveals that he was deeply concerned about the negative influence this dark error could have on his spiritual children and on the church. If his spiritual children embraced early gnostic error concerning sin and sinning, it would erode the richness of their relationship with God, would negatively impact their spiritual life, and could undermine the very foundation of their faith.

In this chapter, we will study passages from John's first epistle where he exposed and brought correction to errant teaching on the subject of sin and sinning. Studying the many things he wrote on this subject will create important context and provide another valuable point of view from which to view I John 1:9. As we proceed in this chapter, it will become evident that John's statement in I John 1:9 was not an off topic statement or a one verse instruction, but was part and parcel of the important corrective teaching he offered throughout his epistle on the subject of sin and sinning. In fact, his statement in I John 1:9 was positioned in the middle of seven consecutive statements he made addressing the subject of sin and sinning and was a counter statement to both I John 1:8 and I John 1:10; two statements that characterized early gnostic error on the subject of sin and sinning. Let's proceed now to examine some important things the apostle John wrote in his first epistle about sin and sinning.

I John 1:6

Early in his first epistle, John delved into the subject of sin and sinning, stating clearly that any person who claimed to be living in fellowship with God was nothing more than a liar if their lifestyle was one of sinning in the dark. He wrote,

> *"If we say that we have fellowship with him, and walk in darkness, we lie, and do not the truth..."*
>
> I John 1:6

John's words in this conditional statement did not describe an unlikely situation, but described what was actually occurring where he was living and ministering. Many early gnostics living in the region of Ephesus considered themselves to be specially enlightened and made claims of being in true fellowship with God while they walked in darkness and lived carnal, sinful lives. John stated with harsh clarity that for any person to say that they were in fellowship with God while they walked in darkness was to, "lie, and do not the truth." After all, if it was true that God was light and that there was no darkness in Him at all, as he had stated in I John 1:5, then any person who was walking in darkness was not living in true fellowship with God. John was adamant that any claim a person made of being in fellowship with God was nothing more than empty talk and lies if they were walking in darkness.

To "walk in darkness" was to live a life that was unenlightened by the truth of God's Word, to live a life that disregarded God's instructions about how to conduct one's self righteously, and to live a life of persistent sinning. It meant to live without concern for God's standards of holiness as revealed in the commandments of His Word and to indulge in carnal passions, yielding to base impulses and pleasures of the flesh. It meant to live a low life below God's high standards and a dark life away from His light. It meant to live a life characterized by immorality, selfishness, and foolishness helped along by the temptations of the world and Satan. Jesus remarked about darkness, connecting it to evil deeds, when He said,

> "And this is the condemnation, that light is come into the world, and men loved darkness rather than light, because their deeds were evil."
> John 3:19

John's words in I John 1:6 made it clear that any person who claimed, "I am in fellowship with God," while they walked in darkness was lying about their relationship with God and not doing the truth. His words not only accurately characterized the errant early gnostics; they also served as a warning to his spiritual children. They should not believe what the early gnostics believed, should not say what they said, and should not live how they lived. John's words revealed that his spiritual children had a choice to make. Would they continue to walk in the light in true fellowship with God, or would they embrace the error they were hearing, wander back into darkness, and return to sinful living while claiming to be in fellowship with God?

I John 1:7

In I John 1:7, John continued addressing the subject of sin and sinning, revealing what was true of those who walked in the light with God. He wrote,

> *"But if we walk in the light, as he is in the light, we have fellowship one with another, and the blood of Jesus Christ his Son cleanseth us from all sin."*
>
> I John 1:7

John began his conditional statement in I John 1:7 with the contrasting words, "But if," signifying that the choice he would present to believers in this verse would be in contrast to the choice he had presented in I John 1:6. In this verse, he presented to believers that if they chose to continue walking in the light as God was in the light, living in true fellowship with Him and with others, they would continue to experience the cleansing from all sin by the blood of Jesus Christ. By his conditional words, "But if we walk in the light as he is in the light," John was not indicating that only if a person lived as fully in the light as God Himself was in the light would their sins be forgiven. By, "walk(ing) in the light," John was referring, rather, to living in an authentic New Covenant relationship with God through faith in Jesus Christ. John was essentially saying, "If we are living in true fellowship with God through faith in Jesus Christ and are living righteously as He has instructed, then as true believers living in the light, we will continue to experience the forgiveness of any sin we commit."

In I John 1:7, John revealed that believers who chose to remain in the faith, walking in the light in authentic relationship with God, would continue to experience that, "the blood of Jesus Christ his Son cleanseth us from all sin." The English word "cleanseth" in this passage is translated from the Greek word *katharizei*. John used *katharizei* in I John 1:7 in the third person, present tense, active voice, and indicative mood. By conjugating *katharizei* this way, he revealed that Jesus' blood was presently, truly, and continually cleansing the sin of those who were walking in the light; namely, true believers. The third person, causative active voice of *katharizō* indicated that it was the blood of Jesus that caused those who walked in the light with God to be purified from every sin. John's words in I John 1:7 were not referring to the original cleansing from sin that occurred when a person was first saved, but were referring to the ongoing cleansing of sin by the blood of Jesus that those who walked in the light with God—true believers—would continually experience.

Contrary to what the early gnostics believed and taught, John revealed in I John 1:7 that sin existed and that sins were being committed. Even those who walked in the light and lived in true fellowship with God might sin; they might miss the mark and think, say, or do things contrary to God's instructions. They might yield to the passions of their flesh, follow the impulses of their emotions, bend to the temptations of the world, and sin. As John made clear, however, the same precious and powerful blood of Jesus Christ that had been completely effective in cleansing them of all their past sins when they first believed was equally effective to cleanse them of any sin they might commit as believers.

With his bold statement in I John 1:7, John not only hit hard against early gnostic error on the subject of sin and sinning; he also reassured the hearts of true believers by making it clear that if they stumbled and sinned, their sin would be cleansed by Jesus' blood. In I John 1:7, John was essentially saying this:

"If, on the other hand, we choose to hold fast to God's truth and continue to walk in the light as He is in the light—living as He has called us—then we demonstrate that we are true believers in fellowship with God through faith in Jesus Christ. Because we are true believers, the blood of Jesus Christ, His Son, will continue to cleanse us of any sin we might commit. This is one of the great redemptive realities of the New Covenant."

I John 1:8

Continuing to address the subject of sin and sinning in his next statement, again penning words that characterized the early gnostics and their error, John wrote,

"If we say that we have no sin, we deceive ourselves, and the truth is not in us."

I John 1:8

For many modern day believers, John's "If we say" statement in I John 1:8 might seem like a unlikely saying. What kind of persons, after all, would ever think, or actually say, "we have no sin?" The words John wrote, however, accurately described what errant early gnostics believed and said. Because they did not believe they had a sin nature and did not believe that they were sinners, they said, "we have no sin." Their belief and their saying was, of course, completely contrary to the truth God had revealed throughout Scripture, through His Son, and through the preaching of the gospel; the truth that men were sinners and needed a Savior. Nevertheless, the early gnostics did not believe the gospel and the Scriptures; they did not believe they were sinners who needed a Savior. John's deep concern that his spiritual children would be influenced by this dark error caused him to boldly state that anyone who said they had no sin had deceived themselves and, "the truth is not in (them)."

To ensure that his spiritual children understood how dangerous the early gnostics were, John characterized them as those who were self deceived and void of the truth. With his strong words, he not only exposed their error; he also delivered a strong word of caution to his spiritual children about embracing their error. He made it clear that if they embraced their error and began to believe and to say, "we have no sin," then, like the errant early gnostics, they would also be deceived and the truth would no longer be abiding in them.

If the early gnostics of John's day had just been a group of people living their lives in the way that ordinary sinners live, they would not have been a serious threat to the church or a serious concern to the apostle John. But the early gnostics claimed to be enlightened, even to be specially enlightened Christians, and some of them had once fellowshipped as if they were part of the church, but then had, "(gone) out from us" (I John 2:19). Some of those who had gone out from the church were endeavoring to extend their influence back into the church, presenting themselves as teachers of truth and spiritually enlightened. The active proselytizing of these individuals who had once behaved as if they were part of the sound body of Christ made them a unique threat to the well being of the churches in the region and to John's spiritual children. That is why John was so deeply concerned and that is why he repeatedly and strongly addressed their error and the lifestyle that accompanied it, warning his spiritual children to avoid those deceived deceivers.

I John 1:9

In I John 1:9, John continued the flow of his writing, still dealing with the subject of sin and sinning, and penned the words we are focusing on in our study. His words in I John 1:9 comprised the middle statement of seven consecutive statements he penned on the subject of sin and sinning. He wrote,

> "If we confess our sins, he is faithful and just to forgive us our sins, and to cleanse us from all unrighteousness."
>
> I John 1:9

It is important to understand that John's statement in I John 1:9 was not an isolated statement, but was part and parcel of his systematic and extended argument against early gnostic error on the subject of sin and sinning. He had just used conditional "If we" statements in I John 1:6 and I John 1:7 to create a clear contrast between those who said they had fellowship with God, but walked in darkness and were lying and those who truly walked in the light whose sin was continually being cleansed by Jesus' blood. Now he used conditional "If we" statements in both I John 1:8 and I John 1:10 and a conditional "If we" statement in I John 1:9 to create a clear contrast between those who disagreed with God, saying, "we have no sin," and, "we have not sinned," and were deceived, were void of truth, and made God a liar and those who, "*homologeō* our sins," and were forgiven and cleansed of their sins by their faithful and just God.

John situated his conditional statement in I John 1:9 between his two conditional statements in I John 1:8 and I John 1:10 to highlight the extreme contrast between those who denied sin and denied that they had sinned and those who agreed (*homologeō*) with God about sin and about their own sins. It was this significant contrast between early gnostic sinners and true believers in belief and speaking and in what was, therefore, true of them that John was expressing in his three conditional statements in I John 1:8-10. The errant early gnostics, characterized in I John 1:8 and I John 1:10, did not believe that they were sinners, did not believe that they sinned, and openly spoke their disagreement with God. They were contrary to God, His Word was not in them, they were void of truth, and they remained unclean, yet in their sins. True believers, on the other hand, characterized in I John 1:9, agreed with God that sin was a reality and that men were sinners, agreed with God when they sinned, and openly spoke their agreement; they, "*homologeō* our sins." The "confessors" John characterized in I John 1:9 had already been cleansed from all their past sins by faith in Jesus Christ and they continued to be forgiven and cleansed of any sins they committed after they were saved. It was this stark contrast between "disagreers" and "agreers," between "deniers" and "confessors," between the errant early gnostics and true believers that John was expressing with his important statements in I John 1:8, I John 1:9, and I John 1:10.

John never intended his words in I John 1:9 to be understood as a teaching to believers that, "only if you admit to God every one of the sins you have committed will He forgive you of those sins." His words, rather, were intended to enlighten his spiritual children to the profound difference between being a person who disagreed with God, saying, "I have no sin," and, "I have not sinned," and being a person who agreed with God and acknowledged that agreement concerning sin and concerning their own sins. Those who disagreed with God about sin and sinning were not true believers. Those who agreed with God about sin and sinning were true believers.

John penned his conditional statement in I John 1:9 as part of his warning about and argument against early gnostic error because he did not want his spiritual children to abandon their place of alignment and agreement with God on the matter of sin and sinning. Rather, he wanted them to continue to *homologeō* their sins. In other words, he wanted them to remain aligned with God, remain submitted to His truth, and continue speaking in agreement with Him concerning the matter of sin and sinning. He wanted them to continue to speak with one voice with God on the subject of sin and sinning and to agree with Him that they had sinned if, indeed, they had sinned.

Like his other four conditional statements in I John 1:6-10, John introduced his conditional statement in I John 1:9 with the word "If" revealing to his spiritual children that they had a choice to make. Would they embrace the error they were hearing and become deniers of sin and deny when they had sinned themselves? Would they join the early gnostics who were deceived and void of truth and who were calling God a liar? Or would they remain steadfast in their agreement with God and His Word and continue to *homologeō* their sins? Those who chose to remain steadfast and unmoved in their alignment and agreement with God's truth and continued to *homologeō* their sins were true believers, born of God and in covenant with Him through faith in Jesus Christ. Because they chose to remain unmoved from that place of sound faith in God and agreement with His truth, they would continue to be forgiven of any sins they committed and cleansed from all unrighteousness by their faithful and just God.

The word "forgive" in I John 1:9 comes from the Greek verb *aphiemi* which means, "to send away, to hurl away, to put away." The basic idea of *aphiemi* is that it is an action which causes a complete separation and a total detachment. When God forgives believers of their sins, He lets go of anything and everything that might be owed Him by one who has sinned against Him. He cancels any debt and releases the one who has sinned from any obligation. John's use of *aphiemi* is very important, expressing a complete release from any legal bond or legal consequence.

In I John 1:9, the word "cleanse" describes how God deals with those who *homologeō* their sins—true New Covenant believers—just as the word "cleanse" in I John 1:7 described how the blood of Jesus dealt with the sin of those who walked with God in the light—true New Covenant believers. John used the same Greek word in I John 1:9 that he had used in I John 1:7 to refer to the cleansing of sin, but used it in a slightly different tense. In I John 1:9, he used *katharisē* in the aorist, active, subjunctive tense. The aorist tense of the verb *katharizō* is a culminative or consummative aorist and represented the fullness of God's action in purifying believers from all unrighteousness. The active voice of *katharizō* indicated that God was the one who would perform the action of cleansing believers from all unrighteousness. The subjunctive mood of *katharizō* identified that the cleansing of sins would be facilitated by God in the present or in the future for every person who was part of that group of individuals who *homologeō* their sins; namely, true New Covenant believers.

John's words in I John 1:9 reveal three vital truths concerning sin and sinning. First, his words reveal that true believers are capable of sinning and that they sometimes sin. After all, there would be no "our sins" for believers to agree with God about and no "our sins" for God to forgive if believers could not sin. Second, his words reveal that true believers, unlike the individuals he characterized in I John 1:8 and I John 1:10, do not deny the reality of sin and do not deny that they have sinned when, in fact, they have sinned. Rather, they agree with God's truth about sin and sinning and agree with Him that they have sinned if they have thought, said, or done anything that He characterized as sin. In other words, they do not say, "I have not sinned," if they have sinned, but they, "*homologeō* our sins." Third, his words reveal the beautiful, powerful, and praiseworthy truth that true believers' faithful and just God is continually forgiving and cleansing them of sins they commit.

I John 1:10

Not only did the early gnostics believe and say that there was no sin and that they were not sinners; they also believed and said that they had not sinned. John was referring to this gross error and false saying in his conditional statement in I John 1:10 when he wrote,

"If we say that we have not sinned, we make him (God) a liar, and his (God's) word is not in us."

I John 1:10

Many early gnostics believed that no fleshly thing they did in their physical bodies, no matter how carnal or perverse, was sin or in any way affected their spiritual life or their relationship with God. They believed that because their pure spirit and their evil body had no essential contact, nothing they did in their body could touch their spirit, alter their spiritual life, or affect their relationship with God. They could live as carnally as they pleased and with firm conviction say, "I have done nothing wrong; I have not sinned." Their belief system set them free from moral restraint and from a bothersome conscience.

This early gnostic "revelation" about sin and sinning may have been attractive to some believers. After all, if they embraced this "more enlightened revelation," they could live by the baser impulses of their flesh and say, "I have not really sinned because my pure spirit, the real me, didn't do anything. My physical body did something, but what my body did has no connection to my pure spirit and has no bearing on my relationship with God." Perhaps some believers of John's day had an inclination to sin, but needed the validation of some "truth" or "special enlightenment" to justify their actions and to prevent any conviction from alerting their conscience that they were doing wrong.

As in his other conditional statements, John began I John 1:10 with the word "If." He was notifying his spiritual children once again that they had serious things to consider and significant choices to make. Would they embrace the error about sin and sinning they were being exposed to or would they refuse that error? John informed his spiritual children that "If" they embraced that error and said, "we have not sinned," they would be calling God a liar and making it evident that His Word was not in them. The way they would "make (God) a liar" was by saying that the words He had spoken about sin and sinning throughout His written Scriptures, through the mouths of His Old Testament prophets, through His own Son, and through His New Testament ministers was not the truth. John was alerting believers to the serious error of the early gnostics concerning sin and sinning because he did not want them to be deceived and embrace that error. If they did, they would no longer be, "*homologeō* our sins," and their spiritual future could be in jeopardy.

The seductive nature of early gnostic error concerning sin and sinning motivated John to be strong and explicit in his writing, revealing their error to be completely opposed to God's Word and His truth. To catch the attention of his spiritual children, he explicitly stated in I John 1:8 and I John 1:10 that anyone who said, "we have no sin," and said, "we have not sinned," was self deceived, did not have the truth in them, did not have God's Word in them, and was basically calling God a liar. The apostle John did not want his spiritual children to be seduced by early gnostic error and was doing everything he could do to prevent that from happening.

I John 2:1-2

Throughout his first epistle, the apostle John wrote as if sin existed, as if believers were capable of sinning, and as if believers did sin. He also wrote as if the subject of sin and sinning needed to be addressed. In fact, he informed his spiritual children that one of the main reasons he had written was, "that ye sin not." He said,

> *"My little children, these things write I unto you, that ye sin not. And if any man sin, we have an advocate with the Father, Jesus Christ the righteous: And he is the propitiation for our sins: and not for ours only, but also for the sins of the whole world."*
>
> I John 2:1-2

What were the "these things" the apostle John was referring to when he said, "My little children, these things write I unto you, that ye sin not?" He was referring both to the things he had already written in chapter one about sin and sinning and to the things he would write later about sin and sinning. John wrote about "these things" in his first epistle because he did not want his spiritual children to embrace dangerous error about sin and sinning and engage in a sinful lifestyle that would not only be displeasing to their Father, but would ruin their own lives and negatively effect the lives of others. He wanted them to stand firm in the truth they had already embraced, remain in alignment and agreement with God concerning sin and sinning, resist the error they were hearing, and refuse to yield to any temptation to sin that was confronting them.

If we were unaware of the spiritual climate of John's day and read his words in I John 2:1-2 with a twenty first century Christian mind set, we might conclude that like any good spiritual leader, he was exhorting believers to not sin. But knowing something about the spiritual climate of John's day sheds fuller light on his words and illuminates their meaning more completely. More than simply informing believers that he didn't want them to sin, John was warning his beloved children about the dangerous error concerning sin and sinning that was spreading in the region and endeavoring to ensure that they did not abandon God's Word and His truth, embrace that dangerous error, and join those who were promoting it. In effect, John was saying this:

> "My little children that I love, I do not want you to be seduced
> by the errant teaching concerning sin and sinning that you
> are hearing and then, swayed by that error, engage in a life-
> style of sinning, thinking that sinning doesn't affect you, that
> it doesn't affect others, that it doesn't hurt the church, and
> that it doesn't matter to God. It is not God's will for you to
> live a lifestyle of sinning. That is why He delivered you from
> the power of sin and cleansed you! I am writing to warn you,
> hoping to prevent you from abandoning God's truth, hoping
> to keep you from leaving your walk in the light and in truth,

and hoping to prevent you from entering into error, into darkness, and into a sinful lifestyle."

John followed his exhortation to his spiritual children that, "ye sin not," with New Covenant truth that was essential for them to understand in the event that they did stumble and sin. He informed them of the divine remedy already in place to deal with their sins. Not only was the blood of Jesus continually cleansing them as he had expressed in I John 1:7, and not only was God faithful and just to forgive and cleanse them as he had expressed in I John 1:9; Jesus was also their advocate with the Father and the propitiation for any sins they might commit (I John 2:2). John assured his spiritual children with this foundational and beautiful New Testament truth so that if they did stumble and sin, they would not fret anxiously or become fearful, but would be confident that their covenant God had already made provision for their sins to be forgiven.

John's well known words in I John 2:1-2 were more than a general exhortation to not sin that any good spiritual leader would offer to believers under their care. His words were part of his warning to his spiritual children about dangerous early gnostic error concerning sin and sinning being propagated in the region. His words also revealed that if his spiritual children would hold their place in the truth and continue to walk with God in the light, any sins they might commit would be forgiven and cleansed because God had already put a divine remedy in place. Jesus the righteous was their advocate with the Father and the propitiation for their sins.

I John 2:12

A few verses later, John again addressed the subject of sin and sinning, revealing once more that one of the main reasons he had written his first epistle was because he felt compelled to deal with this subject. He wrote,

> "I write unto you, little children, because your sins are forgiven you for his name's sake."
>
> I John 2:12

With these words, John again assured his spiritual children of the fundamental and significant New Testament truth that because of God's provision—both the finished work of Christ Jesus and His current work in His present day ministry—their past sins were forgiven and any sins they might commit in the future would also be forgiven. Considered in the context of his epistle and in light of his words in other passages like I John 1:7, I John 1:9, and I John 2:1-2, it seems that John was not only reminding believers that all the sins they had committed before they were saved were forgiven, but was confirming to them that God had made provision to forgive them of any sins they might commit as believers.

John wrote, "My little children, your sins are forgiven for his (Jesus') name's sake." This is a powerful statement to consider. Many Christians suppose that God forgives their sins for their benefit. But John revealed in this passage that it is also for, "(Jesus') name's sake," that believers' sins are forgiven. Believers are not the only persons who have a vested interest in the forgiveness of their sins. God Himself and Jesus, His Son, also have a vested interest in believers' sins being forgiven. Not only does the forgiveness of believers' sins keep God's sons and daughters in righteous standing and good fellowship with Him; it also proves over and over again that God's love and His wisdom and His greatness are matchless and that His plans and purposes in the glorious New Covenant cannot be sabotaged; not even by the failure of His own children. God's name and the name of Jesus will be eternally glorified for all they have done for every lost sinner and for all they continue to do for their own sons and daughters!

I John 2:29

Just a few verses later, in the style typical to his first epistle, the apostle John circled back again to the subject of sin, stating that those who were truly born of a righteous God lived righteous lives. He wrote,

> "If ye know that he (God) is righteous, ye know that every one that doeth righteousness is born of him."
>
> *I John 2:29*

By his words in this verse, John did not intend to convey that any person who ever did anything righteous was born of God. Even atheists, after all, can do some righteous things. John's words in this verse were part of the larger argument and teaching he was offering throughout his first epistle where, again and again, he set the error of the early gnostics and their unrighteous lifestyle in stark contrast to Christian truth and the righteous lifestyle of true believers. What John was saying by his words in I John 2:29 was something like this:

> "Because you know that God is righteous, you know that those who are living consistently righteous lives are born of Him. They are living consistently righteous lives because their Father is righteous in nature and they, being born of Him, share His righteous nature."

As we have learned throughout our study, many of the early gnostics claimed to be specially enlightened and professed to be in fellowship with God while they lived persistently unrighteous lives. But according to John, any person who claimed that they were in fellowship with God, that they were in the light, and that they were righteous while they walked in darkness and lived unrighteous lives were not born of God no matter what claims they made. John wanted his spiritual children to understand that it was those individuals who lived consistently righteous lives who were truly born of God, not those who claimed wonderful things about themselves.

The simple and fundamental truth John expressed in I John 2:29 was in direct opposition to the early gnostic claim that because their spirit was pure, they could live as they wished and it didn't really matter. According him, those who were truly born of God did not live unrighteous lives, but, "(did) righteousness." Once again, John refuted the early gnostic claim that they were in fellowship with God by pointing out their sinful lifestyle in the dark.

The Amplified Bible renders John's words in I John 2:29 this way,

> *"If you know that He is absolutely righteous, you know (for certain)*

that everyone who practices righteousness (doing what is right and conforming to God's will) has been born of Him."

I John 2:29 Amplified Bible

The Amplified Bible's rendering of John's words in I John 2:29 makes a powerful statement. It says that, "everyone who practices righteousness (doing what is right and conforming to God's will) has been born of Him." The obvious implication of John's words was that those who did not practice righteousness and conform to God's will were not born of Him. By his words in I John 2:29, John again revealed the error of the early gnostics while setting forth important truth for his spiritual children to read, to understand, and to live by.

I John 3:4

John returned once again to the subject of sin and sinning in chapter three of his first epistle, writing these words,

"Whosoever committeth sin transgresseth also the law: for sin is the transgression of the law."

I John 3:4

In this short and succinct statement, John set forth simple, fundamental truth for the benefit of believers he loved and again took a strong stand against the errant teaching of the early gnostics who said that when they sinned, they hadn't done anything against God, against His law, or against His truth, and had not sinned (I John 1:10). John was blunt and clear with his words in I John 3:4, revealing that some deeds were sin and a transgression of the law. In other words, some deeds were a missing of the mark, a disagreement with God by action, and a violation of the clear instructions set forth in His Word. Those deeds, according to John, were, indeed, sin.

John wanted believers to accept and to agree with God that if He had stated in His written Word—in "the law"—that a particular thought, word, or deed was contrary to His will and a sin, then that thought, word, or deed was a sin. He also wanted them to recognize that anyone who lived contrary to God's law, but said, "No, I have not sinned," was making God a liar and revealing that His Word was not in them.

I John 3:5-10

In the next few verses of his epistle, John penned a substantial portion of teaching on the subject of sin and sinning. In this extended teaching found in I John 3:5-10, he articulated many significant truths and again created a sharp contrast between early gnostic error and sound New Covenant truth. At the beginning of this extended portion of teaching, he wrote,

> *"And ye know that he* (Jesus) *was manifested to take away our sins."*
> I John 3:5

John began his statement with the words, "And ye know," revealing that what he was about to write was not new information, but was truth that his spiritual children had already embraced and understood. His short statement, "And ye know that he (Jesus) was manifested to take away our sins," contained the obvious implications that sin existed in the world, that sin existed in men's nature, and that sins had to be dealt with. After all, Jesus would not have manifested to "take away our sins" if there were no "our sins" to be taken away. John's succinct words in this passage completely contradicted the doctrine of the early gnostics who taught that men did not have a sin nature and did not sin and taught that Jesus of Nazareth was not the Son of God who had been sent to earth to save men from their sins, but was one of several heavenly messengers sent to earth to guide people into enlightenment. His short, but powerful statement in I John 3:5 declared Jesus of Nazareth to be the Savior of the world who was, "manifested to take away our sins." Although his spiritual children had already embraced this absolutely essential truth and were born of God, John labored tirelessly throughout his epistle to ensure that they would remain firmly grounded in that truth and not be seduced by error.

Continuing in the next verse, John wrote,

"Whosoever abideth in him sinneth not..."

I John 3:6

John's simple statement of truth in this verse was, once again, a direct assault on early gnostic teaching and lifestyle. Many of the early gnostics said, "We are abiding in God," while they lived carnal lives with no regard for what God had instructed. John refuted their error and confronted their living by stating that, "Whosoever abideth in him (God) sinneth not." He was not asserting by these words that true believers were incapable of sinning, but was revealing that a person who was truly abiding in God—in other words, a true believer—did not willfully and persistently live a lifestyle of sinning with complete disregard for what God had instructed. The Amplified Bible confirms this meaning of John's words, rendering them this way,

"No one who abides in Him (who remains united in fellowship with Him—deliberately, knowingly, and habitually) practices sin."

I John 3:6 Amplified Bible

This rendering of John's words confirms that he was not suggesting that believers were incapable of sinning, but was communicating that any person who deliberately and habitually practiced a lifestyle of sinning was not abiding in God, regardless of any claims they made. The truth, rather, was that, "No one who abides in Him...practices sin." Again, his words exposed the errant early gnostics as "not of God."

Continuing this same thought in the second part of I John 3:6 by making a contrasting statement, John wrote,

"...whosoever sinneth hath not seen him, neither known him."

I John 3:6

The Amplified Bible renders John's words this way,

"No one who habitually sins has seen Him or known Him."

I John 3:6 Amplified Bible

With these words, John revealed that any person who habitually sinned had not seen God and did not know God. In other words, they were not a true believer. John penned these words and others like them because he did not want his spiritual children to be misled by individuals who made lofty claims about being spiritually enlightened and about knowing God and about being in fellowship with Him while they persisted in a sinful lifestyle. He clearly identified habitual sinners as those who did not know God, revealing that how a person conducted their life was a far more accurate representation of who they were than any verbal claims they might make about themselves.

John's words in I John 3:6 were not intended to frighten true believers who had stumbled and sinned and might be condemning themselves, worried about their relationship with God because their conscience was guilty. His words, rather, were part of his warning and the argument he made throughout his first epistle as he sought to educate believers concerning the very important truth that no person who sinned persistently and happily with no concern for their actions and without any remorse had seen God or knew God. Those who happily and habitually sinned, rather, did not know God and were not abiding in Him; they were not true believers.

Continuing in this same theme, John warned believers not to allow themselves to be deceived on the crucial matter of sin and sinning. He wrote,

> *"Little children, let no man deceive you: he that doeth righteousness*
> *is righteous, even as he is righteous."*
>
> *I John 3:7*

John's deep concern about the deceptive and negative influence of the errant early gnostics was in plain view all throughout his first epistle. In I John 3:7, he warned his spiritual children not to allow any person to deceive them on the matter of who was truly righteous with God's nature and who was not. According to him, it was those who lived righteous lives who were righteous in God's kind of righteousness. The obvious implication of his words was that those who lived unrighteous lives were unrighteous; in other words, they did not have

God's righteous nature, not being born of Him. John expressed with simplicity that any person who lived a righteous life was righteous and that any person who lived an unrighteous life was unrighteous. He wanted to be sure that his spiritual children had perfect clarity on this matter so they would not be deceived and misled by those who claimed to be righteous, but were not.

The Amplified Bible clarifies John's warning in I John 3:7, rendering his words this way,

> *"Little children (believers, dear ones), do not let anyone lead you astray. The one who practices righteousness (the one who strives to live a consistently honorable life—in private as well as in public— and to conform to God's precepts) is righteous, just as He is righteous."*
>
> I John 3:7 Amplified Bible

John wrote with loving passion when he said, "Little children... do not let anyone lead you astray." But he wrote with raw straightforward clarity when he stated that it was the person who practiced righteousness who was truly righteous. The obvious implication of his words was that those who did not practice righteousness were not righteous. He was not ambiguous on this matter because he did not want his spiritual children to be confused.

John sharpened his corrective words about sin and sinning and about who was of God and who was not of God in the next verse when he wrote,

> *"He that committeth sin is of the devil; for the devil sinneth from the beginning. For this purpose the Son of God was manifested, that he might destroy the works of the devil."*
>
> I John 3:8

John was not suggesting by these words that any person in any place who had ever committed any sin was "of the devil." He was revealing, rather, in a somewhat abrasive manner, that any person who happily and habitually practiced a lifestyle of sinning not only did not know God, but was "of the devil." John's words were harsh and pointed and clear.

The Amplified Bible renders John's words this way,

> "The one who practices sin (separating himself from God, and offend-ing Him by acts of disobedience, indifference, or rebellion) is of the devil (and takes his inner character and moral values from him, not God..."
>
> I John 3:8 Amplified Bible

John stated that, "The one who practices sin...is of the devil... and takes his inner character and moral values from him." He could not have been more explicit. And he could not have created a sharper contrast between the errant early gnostics and true believers. Simply put, the errant early gnostics who practiced sin were of the devil while true believers who lived righteously were of God. It was that elementary.

With his biting words in I John 3:8, John left no room for doubt about who the errant early gnostics were and whether or not their "truth" was true. He had previously labeled them as liars and pronounced them to be self deceived. He had revealed that they did not know God. He had identified them as void of truth and stated that God's Word was not in them. Now he went even further and boldly declared that they were, "of the devil." John did not spare his words, soften the truth, or err on the side of diplomacy. He made it abundantly clear that the errant early gnostics and anyone else who embraced their doctrine and followed their sinful lifestyle were not born of God, were not in fellowship with God, were not in the light, and were not righteous, but were "of the devil." Undoubtedly, John hoped that his blunt and explicit language would catch the attention of believers and put them in a defensive posture.

In the next verse, John reiterated the same basic truth he had penned earlier in I John 3:6. He wrote,

> "Whosoever is born of God does not commit sin; for his (God's) seed remaineth in him: and he cannot sin, because he is born of God."
>
> I John 3:9

Contrary to what some believe, John's words in this verse were not intended to convey that those who were born of God and had His seed in them were incapable of sinning. His words, rather, were one more statement in his ongoing argument against the errant early gnostic teaching concerning sin and sinning that was proliferating in the region. His statement in I John 3:9 must not be lifted out of its proper context and interpreted to mean that true believers cannot sin. We know that true believers can sin because John stated many times in his first epistle that they could. The apostle Paul also revealed in his writings that believers can sin. The apostle Peter did the same, as did James and Jude. And we know from our own experience that believers can sin because every believer we know, including ourselves, has sinned.

In I John 3:9, John was communicating that anyone who was truly born of God and had His seed abiding in them did not happily persist in a lifestyle of sinning. They did not imagine ways to sin or manufacture teachings to support a lifestyle of sinning. Rather, because they were born of God, they desired to please God. Because they desired to please Him, they made efforts to govern their lives in righteous ways, in His ways, and kept themselves under control. John intended for his words in I John 3:9 to make it abundantly clear to believers that the errant early gnostics active in the region who claimed to be children of God and claimed to be living in fellowship with God proved by their own persistent, sinful lifestyle that they were not, in fact, born of God and that they did not, in fact, have God's seed in them.

The Amplified Bible confirms this interpretation of I John 3:9 with this rich, beautiful, and clear rendering of John's words,

> "No one who is born of God (deliberately, knowingly, and habitually) practices sin, because God's seed (His principle of life, the essence of His righteous character) remains (permanently) in him (who is born again—who is reborn from above—spiritually transformed, renewed, and set apart for His purpose); and he (who is born again) cannot habitually (live a life characterized by) sin, because he is born of God and longs to please Him."
>
> I John 3:9 Amplified Bible

John concluded his pithy, extended warning and teaching about sin and sinning in I John 3:5-10 with these sharp, descriptive words in verse 10,

> "In this the children of God are manifest, and the children of the devil: whosoever doeth not righteousness is not of God, neither he that loveth not his brother."
>
> I John 3:10

The English word "manifest" in this verse is translated from the Greek word *phaneros* which means, "evident, plainly recognized, outward, visible, or open to sight." *Phaneros* comes from the root verb *phaino* which means, "to bring into the light, to shed light upon, to make evident, to expose to view." John was informing his spiritual children that the way to identify with certainty and to know with confidence who were the children of God and who were the children of the devil was this way: "Whosoever doeth not righteousness is not of God, neither he that loveth not his brother."

The Amplified Bible renders John's words in I John 3:10 this way,

> "By this the children of God and the children of the devil are clearly identified: anyone who does not practice righteousness (who does not seek God's will in thought, action, and purpose) is not of God..."
>
> I John 3:10 Amplified Bible

John informed his spiritual children that they could know with certainty whether a person was a child of God or was a child of the devil by observing their life and noting whether or not they practiced righteousness. Those who did not practice righteousness were not God's children, but were, "children of the devil."

With his concise and harsh words in I John 3:10, John again created a sharp contrast between true believers and early gnostic sinners, revealing to his spiritual children how they could know with certainty whether individuals they encountered were of God or not. According to John, it was not the claims a person might make about themselves that made manifest whether they were a child of God or not. It was, rather, how a person lived their life that made manifest whether they were a child of God or not. Those who did not live righteous lives were not of God, but were of the devil; in other words, they were not true believers. It is wholly evident from John's words that he was determined to make sure his spiritual children were able to discern who was and who was not of God so that they would not be deceived by seducers who were peddling error.

It is unambiguous from John's extended teaching in I John 3:5-10 that he greatly desired for his spiritual children to have right thinking concerning sin and sinning—thinking that was in agreement with God's truth and His Word. It is also abundantly clear that he greatly desired for his spiritual children to be able to discern between who was and who was not of God and between who should and who should not be listened to and followed. He upheld in his important teaching in I John 3:5-10 that being a true believer was not about making claims of enlightenment or of being in fellowship with God, but was about living a life of true righteousness in Christ. John devoted much of his first epistle to the subject of sin and sinning and to the education of his spiritual children about how to know with certainty who was and who was not of God because the errant teachings of the early gnostics and their dark spiritual influence was potentially dangerous to the spiritual life of the church.

I John 5:16-18

Near the end of his first epistle, John returned once more to the important subject of sin and sinning when he wrote,

> "If any man see his brother sin a sin which is not unto death, he shall ask, and he shall give him life for them that sin not unto death. There is a sin unto death: I do not say that he shall pray for it. All unrighteousness is sin: and there is a sin not unto death."
>
> *I John 5:16-17*

John was explicit with his words about sin and sinning in this passage just as he had been explicit with his words about sin and sinning other places in his first epistle. He revealed that sin was a reality and that true believers could sin. After all, if a brother could, "sin a sin which is not unto death," then clearly a brother could sin. He also stated with raw brevity that, "All unrighteousness is sin." His succinct statements of truth in this verse were, once again, completely contrary to the errant teachings of the early gnostics who believed that nothing carnal they did in their body was unrighteous or sin.

John's final statement about sin and sinning in his first epistle was strong and clear. Opening that statement with the confident words, "We know," he wrote,

> *"We know that whosoever is born of God sinneth not; but he that is begotten of God keepeth himself, and that wicked one toucheth him not."*
>
> *I John 5:18*

As in previous passages, John was not communicating in this passage that a person who was born of God never sinned or was incapable of sinning. Rather, he was continuing to enlighten his spiritual children to the fact that any person who was truly born of God did not willfully and happily persist in a lifestyle of sinning. That is what he meant when he stated, "We know that whosoever is born of God sinneth not." It would also be true, then, that any person who happily persisted in sin was not born of God, was not in fellowship with Him, and had not come into His light, regardless of any lofty claims they made.

The Amplified Bible clarifies John's words in I John 5:18, rendering them this way,

> *"We know (with confidence) that anyone born of God does not habitually sin..."*
>
> *I John 5:18 Amplified Bible*

John also wrote in I John 5:18 that,

> *"...he that is begotten of God keepeth himself, and that wicked one toucheth him not."*
>
> *I John 5:18*

The English word "keepeth" in this verse is translated from the Greek word *tēreō* which means, "to attend to, to take care of, or to guard." According to John, those who were truly born of God attended to their lives, guarded themselves from temptation, and made efforts to keep themselves free from sin. Rather than looking for opportunities to indulge the flesh and fulfill sensual passions with no concern for God's instructions, true believers endeavored to keep themselves safe from thinking any thoughts, saying any words, or doing any deeds that God said were sin.

John also said concerning those who were born of God that, "that wicked one toucheth him not." The English word "toucheth" in this passage comes from the Greek verb *haptomai* which can mean, "to fasten one's self to, adhere to, or cling to." *Haptomai* was sometimes used to refer to carnal intercourse or to the act of fastening fire to an object to set it on fire. For the wicked one to "touch" someone was for him to do something much more substantial than tap them on the shoulder or a pat them on the back. To "touch" someone suggested that the wicked one would make an effort to connect with a person or be granted permission by a person to make a connection with them; even to cling to them.

John stated that those who were born of God did not permit the wicked one to connect with them in such a way that they entered into any kind of fellowship with him. The wicked one might tempt, of course, and may introduce himself, but true believers would not consort with him or permit a connection to develop. Others, however, who were not born of God might happily consort with the wicked one. Jesus revealed, in fact, in His words to the churches in Revelation that some individuals had connected so completely with the wicked one that they, "know the depths of Satan." Those who were truly born of God, however, would not permit this kind of connection with the wicked one. They not only did not make a practice of looking for ways to sin; they made a practice of keeping watch over their lives lest being in contact with sin or with the wicked one would become a regular part of their lives.

John's final words about sin in I John 5:18 would undoubtedly have been an affront to the early gnostics who, in their deceived and arrogant state, claimed to be in fellowship with God and to be greatly enlightened while, in fact, they were living in darkness and under the influence of the wicked one. Although they presented themselves as spiritually enlightened and in fellowship with God, he characterized them as liars, seducers, and children of the devil. Rather than treating the early gnostics with a measure of respect for their beliefs and actions, John exposed them with strong and contentious language. According to him, they were not nice people who accidentally got things wrong. Rather, they were errant, they were antichrists, they were liars, they were self deceived, they were seducers and false prophets, they were children of the devil, and some of them consorted with the wicked one himself!

Conclusion

Due to the errant and dangerous teaching about sin and sinning that was spreading in the region of Ephesus, John felt compelled to write to his spiritual children, warning them of that error and reminding them of basic truths they had already embraced. In I John 2:1, he told them that he had written to them, "that ye sin not." John did not want his spiritual children to abandon God's truth, be led astray by deceivers, and join those deceivers in their unrighteous lifestyle of sinning in the dark.

Throughout his first epistle, John repeatedly addressed the issue of sin and sinning. He revealed to his spiritual children that sin was a reality, that men were sinners with a sin nature, and that Jesus of Nazareth, God's Son, had come to earth, had shed His blood, and had died to be the Savior of sinners. He informed them that any person who transgressed God's commandments and lived contrary to what He had instructed in His Word was living unrighteously and was sinning. He told them that any person who claimed to be in fellowship with God, but was persisting in a lifestyle of sinning was a liar, was deceived, was not born of God, was living contrary to God and

His truth, was unrighteous, and was a child of the devil. He expressed clearly that anyone who said, "we have no sin," or, "we have not sinned," was deceived and did not have God's Word or His truth in them. He also expressed that those who, "*homologeō* our sins," and conducted their lives in accord with God's will by walking in the light and living righteously were true believers, were righteous, were born of God, and were God's true children. He also shared with his spiritual children the beautiful truth that their Father God had put in place all the provision and arrangements necessary to deal with any sins they might commit after they were saved. Every true believer could be completely confident, due to God's full and perfect provision, that they would be forgiven and cleansed of any sins they committed.

John dealt extensively with the subject of sin and sinning in his first epistle because he did not want his spiritual children to follow after the dangerous error of the early gnostics—to believe what they believed, to say what they were saying, and to live how they were living. Rather, he wanted them to stay home in the truth, to continue walking in the light, to live righteously, to agree with God's truth and with His word, and, as he specifically expressed in I John 1:9, to, "*homologeō* our sins." He wanted them to remain aligned with God's truth and to speak in agreement with Him about sin and about their own sins. And he wanted to be sure that his spiritual children, the true believers who *homologeō* our sins, were completely confident that any sins they committed would be forgiven and cleansed by their faithful and just God.

Why Is This View of I John 1:9 Important ?

In this chapter, we looked at I John 1:9 from the point of view of John's many warnings, teachings, and insights concerning sin and sinning in his first epistle. The many passages we examined provided us with excellent context and an invaluable point of view from which to consider his words in I John 1:9. What we learned in this chapter makes it very apparent that John's statement in I John 1:9 was not just a one sentence, stand alone, off topic comment, but was one of many important statements he made in his first epistle to warn his spiritual children about the error concerning sin and sinning that was being promoted in the region where they lived. Looking at I John 1:9 from the point of view of John's many statements about sin and sinning helps us see more clearly what he intended to communicate by his important words in that verse.

The early gnostic error concerning sin and sinning that John was warning his spiritual children about and correcting by teaching is summarized well by his statements in I John 1:8 and I John 1:10. The early gnostics believed and said, "we have no sin," refusing to acknowledge that they had a sin nature and denying that they needed to be saved from their sins. And they believed and said, "we have not sinned," refusing to acknowledge that they had sinned when they had thought, spoken, or acted in ways that were contrary to God's commandments. John did not want his spiritual children to join the early gnostics in their error, saying what they said and living the way they lived. Rather, he wanted them to do what he wrote in I John 1:9. He wanted them to agree with God and acknowledge that sin existed, agree with God and acknowledge that sin and sinning was a violation of His instructions, and agree with God and acknowledge when they had sinned themselves. In other words, the apostle John wanted his spiritual children to refuse to embrace the error of the early gnostics and choose to *"homologeō* our sins."

In order for us to understand what John intended to communicate by his words in I John 1:9, we must pay close attention to the general and immediate contexts of his words. We must pay attention to the fact that his statement in I John 1:9 was an important part of his first epistle where he dealt extensively with the subject of sin and sinning. We must pay attention to the fact that his statement in I John 1:9 was positioned in the middle of seven consecutive verses he penned on the important subject of sin and sinning. And we must pay attention to the important fact that his statement in I John 1:9, a contrasting statement that characterized the action, the speaking, and the spiritual condition of true believers, was sandwiched between two statements in I

John 1:8 and I John 1:10 where he characterized the actions, the speaking, and the spiritual condition of errant early gnostics. John's statement in I John 1:9 expressed the exact opposite action of the actions he expressed by his words in I John 1:8 and I John 1:10. To *"homologeō our sins"* meant to not disagree with God by denying sin and denying that one had sinned, but to align with and to agree with God about sin and sinning and about one's own sins and to openly acknowledge that agreement.

When considered in light of the fact that throughout his first epistle, John was exposing early gnostic error on the subject of sin and sinning and endeavoring to confirm his spiritual children in God's truth on this important subject, it becomes even more clear that in I John 1:9, he was not informing believers of an action they must repeatedly perform in order to be forgiven of sins they had committed, but was revealing what true believers believed, who they were aligned with, what they said, and what was, therefore, true of them. True believers, according to John, did not deny sin or sinning and did not deny that they had sinned if they had sinned. True believers, rather, agreed with God, acknowledging the reality of sin and acknowledging when they had sinned. In other words, true believers *"homologeō our sins."*

Contrary to the common interpretation of I John 1:9, John's words in I John 1:9 were not an instruction to believers about a required, repeated admission of sins to God that they must engage in so that God could forgive and cleanse them of those sins. John's words in I John 1:9 were, rather, a statement revealing that true believers agreed with God's truth concerning sin and sinning, agreed with God's truth concerning their own sins, openly acknowledged their agreement, and were continually being forgiven of their sins and cleansed from unrighteousness because their covenant God was faithful and just.

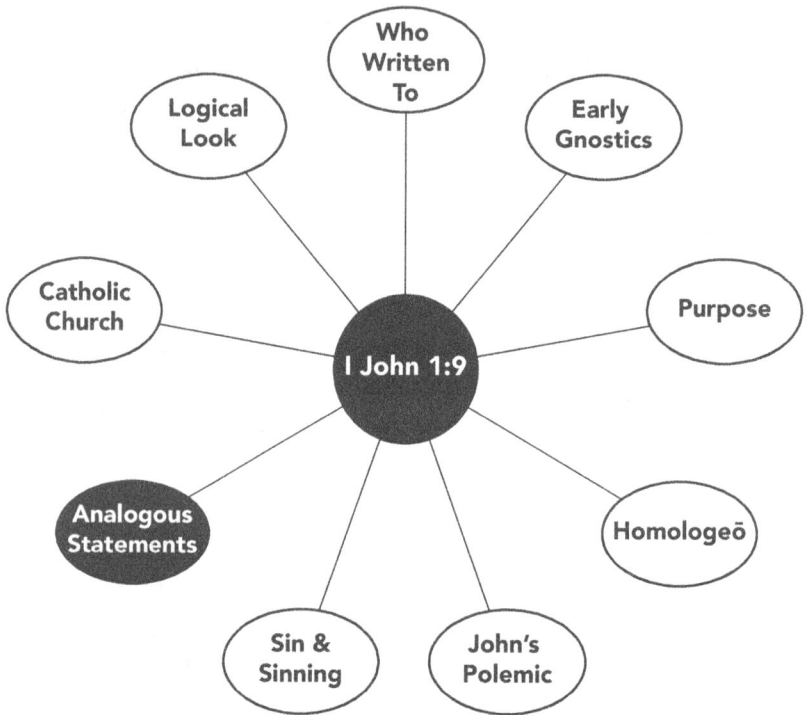

VIII

Three Analogous Statements

As we learned in the previous chapter, the apostle John dealt extensively with the subject of sin and sinning throughout his first epistle. He did so both to refute dangerous early gnostic error and to set forth vital New Testament truth on this crucial subject. There were several things John made clear about sin and sinning. First, he made it clear that sin existed. Sin was a reality, men were sinners and they sinned, and sin had to be dealt with. He informed believers that if they chose to agree with the errant early gnostics and say, "we have no sin," they would be deceiving themselves and would be void of the truth (I John 1:8). Second, he made it clear that both sinners and saints could sin and did sin. He notified his spiritual children that if they chose to agree with the early gnostics and say, "we have not sinned," they would be making God a liar and His Word would not be in them (I John 1:10). Third, he made it clear that if true believers stumbled and sinned, there was a divine remedy in place to deal with their sins. He revealed that the same blood of Jesus Christ that had cleansed them of all their sins when they first believed was effectual to cleanse them of any sin they might commit as believers (I John 1:7). He revealed that if they sinned, God was faithful and just to forgive them and cleanse them from all unrighteousness (I John 1:9). And he revealed that if they sinned, Jesus was their advocate with the Father and the propitiation for their sins (I John 2:1-2).

In this chapter, we are going to study the third matter about sin and sinning that John made clear in his first epistle; the truth that if believers stumbled and sinned, there was a divine remedy in place to deal with those sins. The way we are going to study this important truth is by examining three analogous statements from John's first epistle. The word analogous means, "matching, similar, comparable, or parallel." It describes two or more things that are related, that are kindred, or that represent the same thing. Greek philosophers considered things to be analogous if they shared the same idea, expressed the same pattern, or represented the same philosophy. Analogous statements are statements that are kindred, that share the same basic idea, and that communicate the same essential truth.

The three analogous statements we will examine in this chapter are found in I John 1:7, in I John 1:9, and in I John 2:1-2. Although these three statements do not consist of the same exact words, they do communicate the same essential truth. That essential truth is that the Father God, in His great wisdom and keen foresight, put in place for all who would believe in His Son and be saved through faith in Him a divine remedy to deal with any sins they would commit after they were saved. Examining this beautiful and essential truth as it is expressed in each of the three analogous statements will shed more light on John's familiar words in I John 1:9, further enhancing our understanding of what he really meant by those words.

The First Analogous Statement

John's statement in I John 1:7 is the first analogous statement we will consider. He wrote,

> "But if we walk in the light, as he is in the light, we have fellowship one with another, and the blood of Jesus Christ his Son cleanseth us from all sin."
>
> I John 1:7

John's statement in this verse was in direct contrast to his previous statement in I John 1:6 where he had written,

> "If we say that we have fellowship with him, and walk in darkness, we lie, and do not the truth."
>
> I John 1:6

John's contrasting statements in I John 1:6 and I John 1:7 high-lighted two distinct groups of people that his spiritual children could be aligned with depending on the choice they would make about who and what they would follow. They would either remain part of the family of true believers or they would join the early gnostics in their error. If they chose to join the errant early gnostics and walk in dark-ness while claiming to be in fellowship with God, then they would be lying and not doing the truth (I John 1:6). But if they choose to remain in the light as God was in the light, then they would have fellowship with one another and with God and the blood of Jesus Christ, God's Son, would continually cleanse them from all sin (I John 1:7).

The English word "cleanseth" in I John 1:7 is translated from the Greek word *katharizō*. *Katharizō* could mean, "to make clean, to cleanse from physical stains and dirt, to clean a utensil, to cleanse by curing a person, to free from defilement of sin, to free from guilt of sin." In I John 1:7, John used *katharizō* in the third person, present tense, active voice, and indicative mood. The fact that he used *katharizō* in the third person reveals that the cleansing of sin was being accomplished by a third person—in this case, Jesus' blood. His use of *katharizō* in the active voice meant that the object doing the action of cleansing sin was the subject of the statement; in this case, the blood of Jesus. His use of *katharizō* in the indicative mood meant that the cleansing of sin he was referring to was something that was actually occurring, not just something that was possible. And the fact that he used *katharizō* in the present tense meant that the cleansing of sin he was referring to was presently occurring.

According to Greek scholars, the present tense of a Greek verb most often denoted continuous action; in other words, an action that was always in progress or in a state of persistence. John's reference to the cleansing of all sin in I John 1:7 was not, then, a reference to the initial, complete cleansing of all past sins by the blood of Jesus which had occurred when his spiritual children had first called upon the name of the Lord and were saved. His reference to the cleansing of all sin was also not a reference to a cleansing of sin that might happen at some point in the future. The, "cleanseth (*katharizō*) us from all sin," that John was referring to in I John 1:7 was the cleansing of sin that was presently and continuously being accomplished on behalf of true believers by the blood of Jesus.

When John penned the conditional words, "But if we walk in the light," he was not suggesting that only if believers reached a certain required high standard of walking in the light would they qualify themselves to be cleansed of all sin. In fact, if that was what John had been saying, he would have been teaching a performance based cleansing of sin for believers. Those who could be cleansed of all sin were not, however, some special class of super-believers who were meeting a required high standard of walking in the light. Those who could be cleansed of all sin were, rather, those who had come into the light, had been saved, and were now walking in the light and in fellowship with God. In other words, they were true believers. What John was expressing in I John 1:7 was that New Covenant believers walking in the light, unlike early gnostic sinners walking in darkness, would continue to experience that, "the blood of Jesus Christ his Son cleanseth us from all sin." They would continue to experience being cleansed of sin because they met the condition required for them to be cleansed of sin; they were born of God and in the light.

When John wrote in I John 1:7 that, "the blood of Jesus Christ... cleanseth us from all sin," he was expressing the powerful and amazingly reassuring New Testament truth that true believers—those walking in the light—continued to experience the cleansing action of Jesus' blood if they sinned. The blood that Jesus shed on the cross was not only effectual, then, in having cleansed all the past sins of those who had called upon the name of the Lord and were saved; His blood was also continually effectual in cleansing believers of any sin they committed in the present.

The ongoing cleansing of believers' sin by Jesus' blood is one of the most necessary and wonderful provisions of the New Covenant. This powerful and beautiful truth would quiet the minds of those who were in the light and chose to remain in the light, affirming to them that if they did stumble and sin, they would not become permanently unclean or unrighteous and would not be abandoned or disowned by God, but would be cleansed by the blood of Jesus. John was wonderfully clear that because of the persistent efficacy of the blood of Jesus to cleanse sin, true believers' cleanness, righteousness, and right relationship with God would not be put in jeopardy if they stumbled and sinned.

According to the apostle John, the divine purgative dispatched from the heart of God and poured out by His Son on the cross of Calvary was not only sufficient to cleanse the sin of every sinner; it was also effectual to cleanse the sin of every believer. The effectual blood of Jesus Christ, as the epistle to the Hebrews revealed, "speaketh better things than that of Abel" (Hebrews 12:24). Whereas the blood of Abel cried out, "Vengeance for my death!" the blood of Jesus continually declares, "I was poured out to cleanse you of every past sin you committed as a sinner and to cleanse you of any sin you commit as a believer!" Because of His great love and surpassing wisdom, God planned and instituted this divine remedy to deal with the sins believers commit. The blood that Jesus shed on the cross is not only completely efficacious to cleanse all the sins of every sinner who comes to God through faith in Jesus Christ; it is also completely efficacious to cleanse every sin committed by every believer. God's children can walk in full confidence and rejoice with great joy because of this wonderful New Testament reality!

The Second Analogous Statement

The second analogous statement we will examine in this chapter is found in I John 2:1-2. There, John penned these enlightening and encouraging words of New Covenant truth,

> *"My little children, these things write I unto you, that ye sin not. And if any man sin, we have an advocate with the Father, Jesus Christ the righteous: And he is the propitiation for our sins: and not for ours only, but also for the sins of the whole world."*
>
> *I John 2:1-2*

John's words in this passage are analogous to the words he wrote in I John 1:7. In other words, they communicate the same essential truth. In his first analogous statement, John stated that those who walked in the light—true believers—would experience the continual cleansing of any sin they committed by the blood of Jesus. In his second analogous statement, John expressed that if his little children—true believers—stumbled and sinned, their sins would be forgiven because God made provision for their sins by ordaining Jesus Christ the righteous to be their advocate with the Father and the propitiation for their sins. John's statements in I John 1:7 and I John 2:1-2 expressed the same essential truth; they were analogous statements.

An Advocate With the Father

John informed believers in I John 2:1-2 that if any of them sinned, they had, "an advocate with the Father." The English word "advocate" is translated from the Greek word *paraklētos*. John used this word to characterize the ministry that Jesus Christ is presently engaged in before the Father on behalf of true believers. The *paraklētos*, according to Greek dictionaries, was, "a person who pled the case of another before a judge; who was a legal assistant, a counsel for defense, an intercessor, or an attorney." The role of the *paraklētos* was to represent his clients before a judge concerning their legal matters. The *paraklētos* never initiated his defense by admitting his client's guilt, by condemning his client before the judge, or by capitulating to a plea deal offered by the accusing party; even if he suspected that his client might be guilty. It was the duty of the *paraklētos* to do everything in his power to prove that his client was not guilty of the charges brought against him. If, however, at the end of the case, his client was found by the judge to be guilty, then it became the duty of the *paraklētos* to ensure that no unjust penalty was levied against his client.

Strong's Concordance suggests that in I John 2:1, *paraklētos* describes Jesus Christ in his exaltation at God's right hand, pleading with the Father for the pardon of believers' sins. The fact that believers have a *paraklētos* with the Father raises this obvious question: "Why do

New Covenant believers need a *paraklētos* with the Father if they have a Savior and are already forgiven and cleansed of all their past, present, and future sins?"

The reason New Covenant believers need a *paraklētos* with the Father is because even after they are saved, forgiven, and cleansed of all their past sins, have received a new righteous nature, and are in covenant with God, they will stumble and sin and their sins will have to be dealt with. The Father foreknew this. He knew that His own sons and daughters who would be born of Him, who would love Him, and who would be in fellowship with Him would still have unrenewed minds and would still be dealing with bodies that had carnal appetites and passions. He knew that none of His children could be perfect; He knew they would sin. Because He knew that His children would sin even after being forgiven of all their past sins, He ordained Jesus to represent them as "advocate with the Father." Jesus Christ the advocate is one of the great New Covenant provisions the Father God planned and put in place to deal with the matter of sins His children would commit.

When believers sin, Jesus the *paraklētos* pleads and intercedes before the Father on their behalf, presenting a strong and compelling case. He pleads the powerful merits of His own redemptive work and argues the complete efficacy of His blood to cleanse every sin. He contends that what He did in His suffering and death and through the shedding of His blood was everything necessary to cleanse the sins of every sinner, to cleanse the sins of every believer, and to satisfy the justice of God. The *paraklētos* presents to the Father all the legal realities of the New Covenant brought into force through His suffering and death. And He reminds the Father to be faithful and just—as I John 1:9 states that He is—and to forgive believers and cleanse them from all unrighteousness according to His promise.

When Jesus intercedes before the Father on behalf of believers who have sinned, He doesn't argue that no sin has been committed. He argues, rather, that based on His finished work as Savior of the world, all penalties have been paid, all punishment has been meted out, and full justice has been served. He argues that on the basis of His finished work, New Covenant believers have a legal right to be forgiven of whatever sins they have committed and to be cleansed from any stain of unrighteousness. As advocate with the Father, He guarantees that no believer will be punished for their sins, but will keep their place of being clean, of being not guilty, of being righteous, and of having permanent reconciled status with God. He ensures that no injustice will be done by the judge in assigning a penalty to a believer who has already been declared not guilty and has already been pronounced permanently righteous.

When Jesus presents a believer's case to the Father, He doesn't argue for the forgiveness of their sins on the basis of their sincere intentions or on the basis of any good works they have done. He does not argue for the forgiveness of their sins on the basis of the surpassing mercy and profound love of the Father. He also does not argue for the forgiveness of their sins on the basis of their appropriate heart sorrow or because they have properly "confessed their sins." He argues for the forgiveness of their sins, rather, on the basis of the complete efficacy of His own shed blood. He argues for the forgiveness of their sins on the basis of His finished work and on the basis of the legal realities of the New Covenant which God Himself established, which He (Jesus) procured, and which believers entered into through faith in His (Jesus') name. In each and every case, Jesus Christ, believers' advocate with the Father, prevails with the Father-judge and wins the case. The advocate always prevails because His evidence is overwhelming and His argument is irrefutable!

The important role Jesus fulfills as believers' advocate with the Father was confirmed by the apostle Paul in Romans 8:33-34 where he wrote,

> "Who shall lay any thing to the charge of God's elect? It is God that justifieth. Who is he that condemneth? It is Christ that died, yea rather, that is risen again, who is even at the right hand of God, who also maketh intercession (entygchanō) for us."

> Romans 8:33-34

According to Strong's Dictionary, the meaning of the Greek verb *entygchanō* Paul used in this passage that the English word "intercession" is translated from means, "to meet a person, especially for the purpose of conversation, consultation, or supplication; to pray or to entreat another." This is exactly what Jesus Christ does for believers as their advocate with the Father. He is at the Father's right hand, interceding for believers, supplicating and entreating the Father, making His argument so that no charge against any believer and no condemnation of God's elect will stand. If a charge is made against any believer, Jesus Christ the advocate will present an irrefutable case for forgiveness, for cleansing, and for righteous standing. He will always prevail with the Father because His testimony is based on established facts and because the Father is faithful and just.

In this passage from the Roman epistle, Paul asked and answered two important questions concerning the status of New Covenant believers on the matter of their guilt or innocence. First, he asked, "Who shall lay any thing to the charge of God's elect?" In other words, "Who can accuse God's elect of a crime, assert that they are guilty, and succeed in having that accusation prevail?" The answer to that question is that the only person qualified to bring a charge of guilt or to make a declaration of "Guilty" concerning God's elect is the judge of all the earth; God Himself. Rather than charging His elect with a crime or declaring them guilty, however, God is their justifier (Romans 3:26) and has permanently justified them, declaring them, "Not Guilty." Second, he asked, "Who is he that condemneth?" In other words, "Who can bring a judgment unto punishment against one of God's elect and have that condemnation validated and upheld?" The answer to that question is that the only person with the authority to condemn God's elect is Jesus Christ Himself. But Jesus Christ, rather than accusing the elect, is their advocate at the Father's right hand, making intercession for them and arguing for their legal righteous standing. The glorious fact of the matter is that the only two persons in all the universe who have the authority to bring charges against God's elect or to condemn them chose to forgive, to cleanse, to save, and to justify them! And one of those persons, Jesus Christ, is currently advocating for and making intercession with the other person, the Father, for the elect. What an awesome salvation from sins and a continual provision for the forgiveness of any future sins the Father has put in place for His own!

This same beautiful truth about Jesus' present day ministry as advocate with the Father is beautifully expressed in Hebrews 7:24-25. In this passage, we find the same Greek word *entygchanō* that Paul used in Romans eight again translated to the English word "intercession." Referring to the present day ministry of Jesus, the author of Hebrews wrote,

> *"But this man* (Jesus Christ), *because he continueth ever, hath an unchangeable priesthood. Wherefore he is able also to save them to the uttermost that come unto God by him, seeing he ever liveth to make intercession* (entygchanō) *for them."*
>
> *Hebrews 7:24-25*

After finishing His redemptive, justifying, cleansing, and saving work as Savior of the world, Jesus Christ was ordained by the Father to, "an unchangeable priesthood." Operating from His office as high priest, Jesus is, "able also to save them to the uttermost that come unto God by him." Jesus' present day ministry as high priest ensures that if believers sin, even in terrible ways, they will not become unclean, unrighteous, and unacceptable to God. They will not lose their right standing with Him and be exiled back into the darkness of death. How does Jesus, the great high priest, "save (believers) to the uttermost"— all the way to the end? He does so by, "ever (living) to make intercession for them."

Though believers can make no claims to God on their own merits, there is one with God who pleads their case and on whom they can rely to manage their interests before Him. Jesus Christ is that person. He is believers' advocate with the Father and their great high priest. He appears before God to this end; that He may exercise on behalf of believers the full power and complete efficacy of His own sacrifice. His intercession with the Father is a continual expression of His suffering and death and a persistent and present application of His cleansing blood for all the sins of all true believers. The fact that God does not and will not impute believers' sins to them, no matter how vile, is because He has full regard for Jesus' work as Savior of the world, full knowledge of the persistent efficacy of His blood, and complete confidence in the case He presents on behalf of believers as their advocate, intercessor, and high priest.

The Propitiation for Sins

According to the apostle John, Jesus is not only believers' advocate with the Father; He is also the propitiation for their sins. He wrote,

"And he (Jesus) is the propitiation for our sins: and not for ours only, but also for the sins of the whole world."

I John 2:2

John expressed this same beautiful truth in chapter four of his epistle when he wrote,

"In this is love, not that we loved God, but that He loved us and sent His Son to be the propitiation for our sins."

1 John 4:10

With his words in these two passages, John revealed that God so deeply loved every person who would be born into the earth that He sent His Son to deal with the devastating problem of sin. Through His suffering, the shedding of His blood, and His death and resurrection, Jesus dealt a death blow to sin and moved it out of the way, making it possible for the Father to have an intimate and eternal relationship with all who would accept His love and receive His free gift of eternal life. Because of His great love, God appointed Jesus to be the propitiation for, "the sins of the whole world." Not even the worst sinner need be excluded from the scope of God's mercy, from the effect of Jesus' sacrifice, and from the power of Jesus' blood because the efficacy of His propitiation extends to "whomsoever." When any sinner turns to God in faith, every sin they have ever committed is propitiated—moved out of the way—so that they can connect with God in a righteous, justified, forgiven, and clean relationship.

Interestingly, John wrote in I John 2:2 that, "he (Jesus) is the propitiation for our sins: and not for ours only, but also for the sins of the whole world." With these words, John revealed that Jesus is not only the propitiation for the sins of all lost sinners; He is also the propitiation for the sins of all saved believers. He stated that Jesus, "is (not was) the propitiation for our sins." The fact that Jesus is the propitiation for the sins of believers reveals that believers will sin and indicates that their sins must be dealt with; they must be propitiated. If believers did not sin or if there was no need to deal with believers' sins, there would be no need for Jesus to be the, "propitiation for our (believers') sins."

The Greek word John used in both I John 2:2 and I John 4:10 that is translated to the English word "propitation" is the word *hilasmos*. *Hilasmos* is a noun and is defined as being, "the atonement, the expiation, the propitiation; the means of appeasing." The English word "propitiation" usually refers to, "that means whereby someone's anger is either averted or satisfied, resulting in mercy being bestowed upon the one who caused the anger." In every New Testament Scripture where the word *hilasmos* is used, it is used in the context of sins (I John 2:2; 4:10; Hebrews 2:17). The scriptural conception of the effect of the propitiation is that it moves the sin that separates man from God out of the way, making way for God's mercy and forgiveness and ensuring an unimpeded relationship with Him. In His role as the *hilasmos* for believers' sins, Jesus deals with the sins believers commit that could be an obstacle in their fellowship with the Father, moving those sins out of the way.

As the *hilasmos*, Jesus propitiates for every sin of every believer who has entered into relationship with the Father through faith. The blood that He once shed and which He will shed only once qualifies Him to be that effectual propitiation for the sins of both sinners and believers. As the propitiation, Jesus not only ensures that every sin of every sinner who comes to God in faith is propitiated so that they can enter into covenant relationship with Him; He also ensures that no sin any believer commits will get in the way of their fellowship with the Father. John wanted his spiritual children to understand and to be confident that the same Jesus Christ who was the propitiation for their sins when they first believed was also the propitiation for every sin they might commit as believers. It was true that Jesus "was" the propitiation for their sins, but it was also true that Jesus "is" the propitiation for their sins. Jesus' role as the propitiation for believers' sins is one of the great provisions the Father God put in place for His children in the glorious New Covenant. It is one of the, "things which God hath prepared for them that love him" (I Corinthians 2:9).

Advocate and Propitiation

The profoundness of the New Covenant truth the apostle John set forth in I John 2:1-2 should not be underestimated. In his few, but significant words to his spiritual children in that passage, he disclosed that Jesus, God's Son, was both their advocate with the Father and the propitiation for their sins. Of course, the same reality is true for believers today. Right now, Jesus is advocating before the Father on behalf of believers on the basis of His finished work and on the basis of the efficacy of His shed blood. Right now, Jesus is the propitiation for believers' sins, dealing with those sins and moving them out of the way so they don't occlude believers' fellowship with their Father.

In this second analogous statement from I John 2:1-2, John expressed the same essential truth he had expressed in I John 1:7. That essential truth was the glorious reality that in the New Covenant, God planned and put in place everything necessary to deal with the sins believers would commit after they were saved. With this truth, John assured his spiritual children that their beautiful new life in Christ and their joyful relationship with God could not be ruined by a committed sin. If they sinned, they were not doomed again to spiritual death and to the penalties of their sins. If they sinned, they would not become unclean or alienated from the Father in an unreconciled state. This powerful truth John presented to his spiritual children in I John 2:1-2 would stir to praise and calm to peace the heart of every believer.

The Third Analogous Statement

The third analogous statement we will examine in this chapter is the main focus of our study. In I John 1:9, John wrote,

> *"If we confess our sins, he is faithful and just to forgive us our sins, and to cleanse us from all unrighteousness."*
>
> *I John 1:9*

In I John 1:9, John expressed the same essential truth he expressed in both I John 1:7 and in I John 2:1-2. Some scholars suggest, in fact, that John's statements in I John 1:7 and I John 1:9 were an example of Hebrew synonymous parallelism where one statement followed another, both communicating the same essential meaning, each lending strength and richness to the single message. The essential New Testament truth John expressed in I John 1:9, in I John 1:7, and in I John 2:1-2 was that by the foreknowledge and great wisdom of the Father and by the saving work of Jesus Christ, true believers had put in place for them and had made available to them a divine remedy for any sins they might commit. Because the once shed blood of Jesus is ever effectual to cleanse believers' sins and because Jesus is both the propitiation for believers' sins and their advocate with the Father, God will always be faithful and just to forgive believers of the sins they commit and to cleanse them from all unrighteousness.

Forgiven and Cleansed

The English word "forgive" in I John 1:9 comes from the Greek word *aphiēmi. Aphiēmi* means, "to leave something, to not discuss something, to let something go, to give up a debt." According to John, *aphiēmi* is what God does concerning the sins that believers commit. He doesn't keep those sins continually in mind, doesn't berate His children for committing those sins, doesn't discuss those sins, and doesn't hold believers accountable for the debt of those sins. Rather, God lets believers' sins go and releases their debt. He does this, not because believers are so wonderful, not because they have done enough good works, not because they sorrowfully entreat Him to forgive them, and not because they verbally admit all their sins to Him in a "confession session." God forgives believers' sins, rather, as John clearly stated, because He is faithful and just.

John declared that God was faithful and just to, "cleanse us from all unrighteousness." The English word "cleanse" in I John 1:9 is translated from the Greek verb *katharisē*. This word can mean, "to make clean, to cleanse from physical stains, to heal a leper, to free from defilement of sin and from faults, to purify from wickedness, to free from the guilt of sin, to purify and consecrate by cleansing or purifying." Interestingly, *katharisē* was used by John in both I John 1:7 and I John 1:9 to reference the cleansing of believers' sins and their purification from all unrighteousness. The only difference between the way John used *katharisē* in I John 1:7 and in I John 1:9 is that in I John 1:9, he used *katharisē* in a different tense; in the aoristic, active, subjunctive tense.

The condition of *katharisē* being in the aorist tense in I John 1:9 suggests that the nature of the cleansing John was referencing was a general and continuous action being performed rather than a specific, one time responsive action connected to a specific action on the part of another. This use of *katharisē* suggests that John was not referring to a scenario where a believer, feeling guilty for a specific sin they had committed, approached God in prayer, verbalized their specific sin, and said they were sorry for that sin and then God, in response to that action of "admitting one's sin," cleansed that believer of that specific sin. John's use of *katharisē* in the aorist tense suggests, rather, that the cleansing of sins in I John 1:9 is something that God is regularly engaged in on behalf of all true believers. In the New Covenant, God cleanses believers from their sins on the basis of the shed blood of His Son and on the basis of Jesus' finished work, not in response to a believer's sorrowful admission to Him of sins they have committed. If God only forgave believers after they specifically admitted each of their sins to Him, then it is very likely that most believers are currently unforgiven.

The fact that John used *katharizō* in the active tense in I John 1:9 indicates that the subject of the sentence was the one performing the action of cleansing. This means that in I John 1:9, God was performing the action of cleansing believers from all unrighteousness. God has the legal right, even the legal obligation, to cleanse New Covenant believers from any unrighteousness because the blood that Jesus shed was for the purpose of cleansing the sins of all people; sinners and saints alike.

The condition of *katharizō* being in the subjunctive tense in I John 1:9 means that the action of being cleansed is possible, but that it is conditional. By using *katharizō* in this way, John revealed that being cleansed by God is not something that automatically happens, but that His cleansing is conditioned upon something. This certainly agrees with the cause clause of John's conditional statement in I John 1:9 where he wrote, "If we confess our sins." The condition which must be met in order for God to cleanse a believer's sins is not, however, the action of that believer verbally admitting each and every specific sin they have committed to Him, but is the condition of a person being a true believer, as evidenced by their alignment and agreement with God concerning sin and sinning and concerning their own sins; in other words, as evidenced by the fact that they "*homologeō* our sins." If a person is a true believer, as evidenced by the fact that they "*homologeō* our sins," then God will be continually cleansing that person from any unrighteousness that results from their sinning. The condition which must be met for a person's sins to be continually forgiven and for them to be continually be cleansed is not, then, that they privately confess each and every one of their specific sins to God, but that they are a true believer; a confessor; one who "*homologeō* (their) sins."

What did John mean in I John 1:9 by his words, "cleansed from all unrighteousness?" Was he suggesting that believers' legal righteous standing with God was revoked and they became unclean and unrighteous every time they sinned and had to be recleansed and reinstated to right standing with God? Was he communicating that a believer's cleanness and righteousness was undone every time they committed a sin and they had to be recleansed and made righteous again in their spiritual nature? If this was what John was communicating, then he was revealing that believers' cleanness and right standing with God was in continual jeopardy. Thankfully, however, that is not what John meant by his words, "cleansed from all unrighteousness."

To help us understand what John meant by his words, "cleansed from all unrighteousness," we can consider the well known parable Jesus told about the prodigal son (Luke 15:11-32). In this parable, the prodigal son left his father's house and spent time in riotous living, wasting his inheritance. He finally ended up in a pig pen, eating pig food. Even in this terrible condition, however, the prodigal son had not become a "non son." His genetic material had not mutated and he was not legally estranged from his father, even though he was living a long distance away from him. And even though he groveled with the swine, lived in the mud and the muck, and became dirty, he was not "stained" beyond cleansing.

In the same way, believers do not become "non-sons" or "unrighteous" or "unsaved" or "permanently stained with sin again" when they commit a sin or even when they live for a season in a lifestyle of sinning. But just as the prodigal son created distance between himself and his father and got dirty on the outside, so when believers sin, they create distance in their intimacy with the Father and get "dirty." And just as the prodigal son needed to be washed and cleaned up and have a fresh robe put on him after his time in the mud and the muck, and just as he had to be reunited to intimate fellowship with his father, so too, when believers transgress God's will and sin against Him, they need be cleansed of their "unrighteousness"—cleansed of the stain of their unrighteous actions. They need to have the dirtiness of sinning removed from their righteous robes and be reunited to the intimacy of the Father's embrace.

James may have been referring to this when he exhorted believers with these words,

"Draw nigh to God, and he will draw nigh to you. Cleanse (kath-

arizō) *your hands, ye sinners; and purify your hearts, ye double minded."*

James 4:8

The word "cleanse" James used in this passage is the same Greek word *katharizō* John used in both I John 1:7 and I John 1:9. In his very practical, everyday Christianity style, James exhorted believers who were not living as they should to draw nigh to God and to, "Cleanse your hands...and purify your hearts." James' words seem to suggest that some believers needed to be cleansed because they had "dirtied their hands" with sinful actions and "spotted their hearts" with ungodly thinking or deeds. He was not saying that these individuals had become unsaved and needed to be saved again, but was clearly expressing that they were not living as they should and needed to clean up.

We could also consider the experience Jesus and His disciples shared after they celebrated the feast of the Passover and just prior to Jesus being apprehended in Gethsemane. After they shared the Passover meal, Jesus girded himself with a servant's towel, took some water, and began to wash His disciples' feet. Peter, feeling awkward because Jesus was serving him in this fashion, asked Him, "Lord, are you really going to wash my feet?" Jesus answered, "If I don't wash you, you have no part with me." Peter, in his typical exuberant fashion, responded, "Lord, not my feet only, but also my hands and my head!" Jesus responded to Peter with these words,

> *"He that is washed needeth not save to wash his feet, but is clean every whit..."*

John 13:10

With these words, Jesus revealed that those who were already washed and who were "clean every whit" did not need a full washing, but did sometimes need to "wash (their) feet." Those who weren't willing to have their "feet" washed, according to Jesus, had no part with Him. But those who were with Him did not need to be completely washed because they were already clean through their relationship with Him. In a prophetic way, which Peter would later understand (John 13:7), Jesus revealed that those who were truly part of Him were already clean and did not need a total cleansing, but might need an occasional washing of their "feet" because their "feet," often in contact with the "dirt in the world," could become "dirty."

The symbolism in Jesus' prophetic act is profound. True believers don't need to be completely "rewashed" if they sin and get dirty because they have already been thoroughly cleansed by the blood of Jesus Christ. But they may need to have "their feet" washed because they have contacted the "dirty world." What Jesus did in washing His disciples' feet was a prophetic foreshadowing of how things would transact for believers in the wonderful New Covenant if they sinned and "got dirty."

Speaking by the Holy Spirit and through the apostle John to the spiritual leader and the church at Sardis, Jesus said,

> *"Thou hast a few names even in Sardis which have not defiled their garments; and they shall walk with me in white: for they are worthy."*
> *Revelation 3:4*

Jesus said concerning the church in Sardis that there were a few believers who had not soiled their garments. His words suggest that there were a significant number of believers in Sardis who had soiled their garments. He did not say, however, that those who had soiled their garments had become unsaved or were permanently unclean and would be rejected by God. Thanks to the wisdom of God, believers who are in relationship with God in the more excellent New Covenant do not lose their sonship, do not lose their righteousness or right standing, and do not lose their salvation if they sin. It does seem, however, as happened with some in Sardis, that when believers sin, they have, "defiled their garments," and need to be cleansed of the stains of their unrighteous deeds.

It is important to understand that the word "righteousness" is not only used in the New Testament Scriptures to refer to believers' legal and permanent right standing with God and to their new spiritual nature, but is also used to describe believers' right living in their daily walk with God. A believer can be being unrighteous in their deeds even though they are righteous in their spirit and righteous in their legal standing with God. Believers should understand that when they sin, they do not become unrighteous in their spiritual nature and do not lose their right standing with God, but they have been unrighteous in their actions.

The unrighteousness that believers sometimes need to be cleansed of, which John addressed in I John 1:9, is not an unrighteousness in their spiritual nature or an unrighteousness in their legal standing with God. The unrighteousness believers sometimes need to be cleansed of is an unrighteousness in their actions which can cause a "temporary staining" of their "righteous robes" and a "dirtying of their feet." Because the sins believers commit can stain them and because sinning can "make their feet and hands dirty" and muddy them up a bit, they need to be cleansed "from all unrighteousness." That cleansing, according John's words in I John 1:9, is being continually accomplished for believers—those who *homologeō* their sins—by their faithful and just God.

It is crucial for believers' spiritual well being to understand and to embrace the significant New Testament truth that they do not become legally unrighteous or permanently unclean if they sin. One's faith and confidence concerning their cleanness and their righteousness and their reconciled relationship with God must not be based upon their own daily performance, but must be rooted in and grounded upon the New Covenant promises they have received and based upon the Father's fidelity to His own Word and promises.

Faithful and Just

In I John 1:9, John stated,

"...he (God) *is faithful and just to forgive us our sins, and to cleanse us from all unrighteousness."*

I John 1:9

The English word "faithful" in I John 1:9 comes from the Greek word *pistos*. *Pistos* was a word used to describe persons who showed themselves trustworthy and dependable in the transaction of business, in the execution of commands, or in the discharge of official duties. A person who was *pistos* was, "one who could be relied on to do what was right." The fact that God is "faithful" to forgive believers' sins and to cleanse them from all unrighteousness means that He is trustworthy and dependable in transacting that spiritual business. He will honor the blood that Jesus shed for the forgiveness and cleansing of sins. He will abide by the terms of the New Covenant which He planned and established and that Jesus put into force through His suffering, the shedding of His blood, His death, and His resurrection. Because God is *pistos*, it is absolutely certain He will forgive the sins New Covenant believers commit. Because God is *pistos*, it is absolutely certain He will cleanse them from all unrighteousness. God's faithfulness is the firm ground upon which believers can rest their faith in this important aspect of spiritual life.

According to John, God is also "just" to forgive believers' sins and to cleanse them from all unrighteousness. The English word "just" comes from the Greek word *dikaios* which refers to, "rendering to each his due and, in a judicial sense, passing righteous judgment on others, whether that righteous judgment is expressed in words or is shown by the manner of dealing with them." The Greek word *dikaios* is interpreted "righteous" forty one times in the New Testament. To do something in a just or righteous way meant, "to do what is the right thing to do," or, "to do something in the right way." The fact that God is just to forgive believers' sins means that He does what is legally right. He passes righteous judgment on believers when they have sinned and deals with their sins in a right and righteous way.

Because God is just, He does what is legally required by the terms of justice. Although it is a legal reality that sins must be paid for, it is also a legal reality that sins have been paid for. The sins of all people in all places and at all times were paid for by Jesus' suffering and death and by the shedding of His blood. When God forgives believers' sins and cleanses them, He is not acting in a merciful or kind or long-suffering way. He is, rather, "justly rendering what is due" and "passing righteous judgment" according to the legal and immutable terms of the New Covenant in Jesus' blood.

It is very important to take note of the fact that in I John 1:9, John did not characterize God as merciful and compassionate to forgive believers' sins. He didn't use heart language to characterize the Father God who forgives the sins of His children, but used legal, covenant language. Certainly, God is loving and kind; He expressed His great love and profound kindness by planning a great salvation for all mankind and by sending His own Son to die for sinners (John 3:16). But when God forgives believers' sins and cleanses them from all unrighteousness, He is being faithful to the promises that His great love caused Him to make and being just to follow the terms of the eternal covenant that His great kindness caused Him to plan. If God refused to forgive believers' sins or punished believers for their sins, He would be breaking His own word, violating the New Covenant, and ignoring the paid in full sacrifice of His own Son. He would be being unfaithful and unjust.

Conclusion

Each of the three analogous statements we examined in this chapter—I John 1:7, I John 1:9, and I John 2:1-2—communicate one incredible and significant New Covenant truth. That truth is that the Father God, in His great wisdom and keen foresight, put in place for all who would one day become His children through faith in Jesus Christ a divine remedy to deal with any sins they might commit after they had become part of His family. John expressed in each of the three analogous statements that if true believers—those who walk in the light (I John 1:7); those who *homologeō* their sins (I John 1:9); John's spiritual children (I John 2:1-2)—missed the mark and sinned, their sins would be forgiven and cleansed. John's spiritual children could be completely confident that the righteousness and the right standing with God they had received through faith in Jesus their Savior was being safeguarded by the ever effective blood of Jesus, by their faithful and just God, and by Jesus, their advocate with the Father and the propitiation for their sins. According to John, believers could know with certainty that because they were "walking in the light people" the blood of Jesus Christ would continually cleanse them of any sin they might commit (I John 1:7). They could be confident as God's children that the same Jesus Christ who was the propitiation for every sin they committed when they were sinners was also the propitiation for sins they would commit as believers and was their advocate with the Father if they sinned (I John 2:1-2). And they could know with calm assurance that because they were those who *"homologeō* our sins"—because they were true believers—God would be faithful and just to forgive them of any sins they committed and would cleanse them from all unrighteousness (I John 1:9).

Looking at I John 1:9 through the lens of the three analogous statements confirms for us that the true remedy for the sins believers commit is not a required action of admitting each and every sin to God, but is the provision that the all wise Father God already put in place to deal with those sins. Jesus' blood is effectual to cleanse (I John 1:7). God is faithful and just to forgive believers' sins and to cleanse them from all unrighteousness (I John 1:9). And Jesus the righteous is advocating with the Father and serving as the propitiation for believers' sins (I John 2:1-2). Examining this beautiful and powerful New Testament truth in the unique ways it is expressed in each of the three analogous statements has provided us with further insight into John's words in I John 1:9 and enhanced our understanding of what he really meant by those words.

In the three analogous statements we studied in this chapter, John was basically communicating this message:

> "You who are true believers—you who walk in the light and in fellowship with God; you who *homologeō* with God on the subject of sin and concerning your own sins; you who are my spiritual children—can be completely confident that the same blood of Jesus that washed away your sins and cleansed you

from all unrighteousness when you first believed is equally effective to cleanse you of any sin you commit as believers. You can be confident that your faithful and just Father God will forgive your sins and cleanse you according to the terms of the New Covenant you are part of through faith in Jesus Christ. And you can be confident that Jesus Himself is your advocate with the Father and the propitiation for any sins you commit."

Why is this View of I John 1:9 Important ?

In this chapter, we looked at I John 1:9 from the point of view that John's statement in I John 1:9 was one of three analogous statements that expressed the same essential truth concerning the remedy the Father God put in place for the forgiveness and cleansing of sins that His children, New Covenant believers, might commit. The insights we gleaned in this chapter confirm what we have been learning throughout our study and shine more light on John's words in I John 1:9. When we realize that each of the three analogous statements we studied reveal the beautiful remedy God put in place to facilitate the forgiveness and cleansing of believers' sins, it further illuminates our understanding of his words in I John 1:9.

Looking at I John 1:9 through the lens of the three analogous statements helps us to see with greater clarity that in I John 1:9 the apostle John was not communicating to believers that in order to be forgiven of sins they had committed, they had to admit each and every one of those sins to God in a special time of confession, but was revealing the same essential truth he revealed in I John 1:7 and in I John 2:1-2. That truth was that true believers—characterized in I John 1:9 as those who *homologeō* their sins—are continually being forgiven and cleansed of sins they commit because God, in His profound wisdom and keen foresight, provided ahead of time the remedy for the forgiveness of sins they would commit. John's words in I John 1:9 reveal that

God forgives the sins that believers commit, not in response to their sorrowful admission of each and every one of those sins to Him in a special time of confession, but because He is faithful and just.

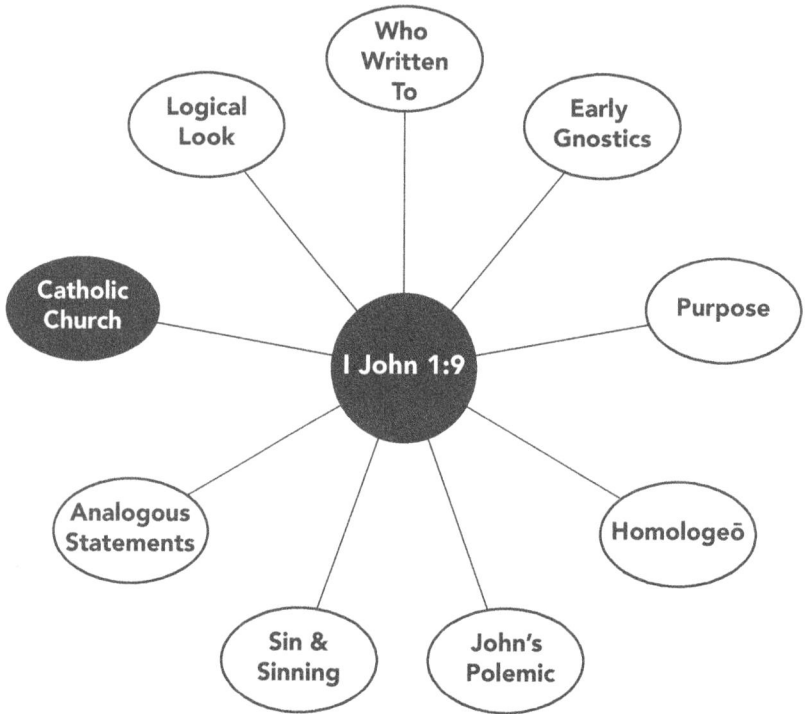

IX

The Catholic Church's Sacrament Of Confession

Although most protestant Christians are not very familiar with the doctrines and sacraments of the Catholic church, the Catholic church has had a significant role in shaping Christian doctrine and practice throughout the world. This is nowhere more evident than in the matter of how Christians interpret John's words in I John 1:9. Because of the significant influence the Catholic church has had on how believers understand I John 1:9, we will briefly consider the doctrine and practice of the Catholic church called the Sacrament of Confession.

In the Catholic church, there are seven sacraments held dear and practiced. One of those sacraments is the Sacrament of Confession. The Sacrament of Confession is the practice members of the Catholic church follow of verbally acknowledging sins they have committed to ordained Catholic priests so that they can be forgiven and absolved of those sins. The Catholic church believes that the Sacrament of Confession, also called the Sacrament of Penance, was instituted by Jesus Himself when He first appeared to the apostles after His resurrection. Breathing on them, He said, "Receive the Holy Spirit. For those whose sins you forgive, they are forgiven; for those whose sins you retain, they are retained" (John 20:22-23). The Catholic church believes that Jesus, knowing that He would not always be physically present with the church on earth, transferred the authority to forgive sins to other men—specifically to the Catholic priesthood—so that the church would always be able to offer the forgiveness of sins to future generations.

Although the Catholic church believes that the pardon for all sins comes ultimately from Christ's finished work on Calvary, they also believe that Jesus ordained two primary means for peoples' sins to be forgiven. The first means He ordained for the forgiveness of sins was baptism. Baptism, which should follow a person's original confession of faith in Jesus, was given to take away the sin nature they inherited from Adam and to facilitate the forgiveness of all the sins they had committed before they believed in Jesus Christ. A second means for the forgiveness of sins ordained by Jesus was for the purpose of dealing with the sins that Christians would commit after they were saved. That means, according to the Catholic church, is the Sacrament of Confession.

The Catholic church believes that the purpose of the Sacrament of Confession is to facilitate the forgiveness of sins that Christians commit and to reconcile them back to God. They believe that when Christians sin, they deprive themselves of God's grace and make it likely that they will sin even more. The only way for Christians to escape this downward cycle is to be genuinely sorry for their sins and to acknowledge their sins, asking for God's forgiveness through the instrument of a Catholic priest. It is through the Sacrament of Confession, Catholics believe, that Christians' sins are forgiven and that God's grace is restored, cleansing Christians and empowering them to once again resist sin. Members of the Catholic church are encouraged to confess their of sins often, but are required to participate in the Sacrament of Confession at least once a year.

According to Catholic doctrine, three things are required of a Christian for them to participate in the Sacrament of Confession in a worthy manner. First, they must be truly sorry for their sins. Second, they must confess their sins fully; in kind and in number. Third, they must be willing to do penance and make amends for their sins. Once a confession of sins is made, the priest must decide whether to forgive or to retain the sins that were confessed. If a priest judges the Christian who is confessing their sins to be truly sorry, he must absolve their sins because Christ's passion merited forgiveness for every repentant sinner.

Some wonder whether the Catholic church believes that Christians can speak directly to God about their sins and be forgiven without making a confession to a priest. On the most basic level, the answer of the Catholic church to that question is, "Yes." They believe, however, that although God can forgive a Christian without that Christian making their confession of sins to a priest, it requires that the Christian comes to God with a perfect motive. If they confess their sins with an imperfect motive, it reveals that they have not fully turned from their sins and turned back to God. Rather than excluding Christians who cannot rise to the occasion of having a perfect motive, the Catholic church believes that Jesus gave the Sacrament of Confession to the church. Through this Sacrament—by confessing one's sins to a priest—Jesus can forgive and lift up every Christian, even when their heart sorrow for sin is weak and imperfect.

The Catholic church believes that Catholic Christians who confess their sins to a priest are better off than non-Catholics who speak directly to God about their sins. They believe this for several reasons. First, they believe they are better off because the Catholic Christian is seeking forgiveness in the way Christ intended. Second, they believe they are better off because by admitting their sins to a priest, the Catholic Christian learns a lesson in humility; a lesson which would be forfeited if they spoke directly to God in private prayer. Third, they believe they are better off because Catholic Christians receive sacramental graces that non-Catholic Christians do not receive. Fourth, they believe they are better off because the Catholic Christian is assured by the priest that his sins are forgiven and does not have to rely on a subjective feeling. Lastly, they believe they are better off because the Catholic Christian can obtain sound advice from a priest about how to avoid sinning in the future.

Recently, Pope Francis, the current Pope of the Catholic church, granted spiritual authority to certain individuals called "super confessors" and sent them all throughout the world to take believers' confessions. He did this so that Catholic Christians everywhere could be absolved of their sins. This practice is not, however, prescribed or described anywhere in the New Testament. And it certainly was not this kind of confession of sins that the apostle John was referring to in I John 1:9.

Why Is This View of I John 1:9 Important?

Looking at I John 1:9 from the point of view of the teaching of the Catholic church brings to our attention another reason why the common interpretation of I John 1:9 has been so widely and for so long accepted by the church. Although many Christians are unaware of the doctrine of the Catholic church called "The Sacrament of Confession," almost all Christians have been influenced by that doctrine. They may have been influenced by the mental image of Catholic Christians going to the confessional booth at the Catholic church and making their confession to a priest. They may have been influenced by the Catholic church's concept of "confessing our sins" because that doctrine is so deeply rooted in the Catholic church. No matter how it has occurred, most Christians have been influenced by the doctrine of the Catholic church concerning "the confession of sins" and, consequently, have had their understanding of I John 1:9 influenced.

Although the great majority of protestant Christians don't follow the Catholic church's Sacrament of Confession, the mental image of someone going to confession and the Catholic doctrine and practice of the confession of sins has significantly influenced how churches and believers throughout the world understand John's words, "If we confess our sins." With confession theology woven deeply into the fabric of a major church denomination and with confession imagery projected onto the minds of countless believers, it is easy to see how the words, "If we confess our sins," in I John 1:9 came to be understood to mean, "if a Christian sorrowfully articulates to God each and every sin they have committed." Unfortunately, the church at large, influenced to some degree by the Catholic church, has misinterpreted I John 1:9 and, based on that misinterpretation, put forth errant teaching which has produced rituals and practices that the apostle John never intended to teach by his words in I John 1:9.

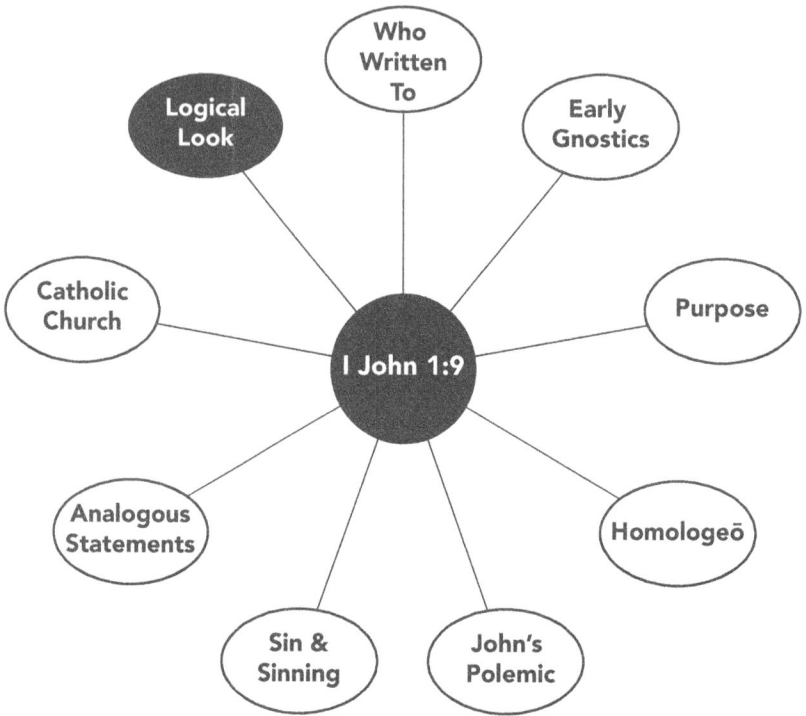

X

A Logical Look At I John 1:9

When searching for the best interpretation and most accurate meaning of any Scripture, it is important to consider the logical implications of possible interpretations of that Scripture to determine if those interpretations agree with other fundamental truths of Scripture and are harmonious with God's ways and His nature, or if they are contrary to other fundamental truths of Scripture and do not fit well with God's ways and His nature. Employing a logical and thoughtful approach when seeking to determine the best interpretation of a Scripture is not an ungodly or merely academic exercise. Rather, being logical and thoughtful in our approach to Scripture is a good and godly endeavor. God Himself, after all, is supremely intelligent and logical. Just a cursory glance at creation, a limited familiarity with His written Word, or an elementary knowledge of His great plan of salvation reveals that He is not only loving and powerful, but is very intelligent and logical. According to Scripture, "In the beginning was the *logos*...and the *logos* was God." The *logos*, the Word of God, the logic of God, was manifested in the flesh. He is the second person of the Godhead and His name is Jesus Christ. To be logical in our consideration and interpretation of Scripture is not to be contrary to God and His ways, but is to be like Him.

The English word "logic" is derived from the Greek word *logos*. The method of *logos* was taught in ancient Greece and Rome as a systematized approach to the practice of deduction. Deduction is the practice of thinking carefully about all the knowable facts of a matter for the purpose of arriving at a correct conclusion about that matter. The method of logic, then, is the method of examining important evidence concerning a matter and thinking carefully about that evidence in order to arrive at a right conclusion about that matter. The goal of logic is to come to a right conclusion about something by the means of reasonable and deductive thinking.

A logical approach to the interpretation of God's Word is one of the approaches we should employ as we seek to understand what God intended to reveal to us in the Scriptures. Especially in the case where a Scripture is difficult to understand or where coming to a right conclusion about its meaning is paramount to believers and to the church, every means possible should be employed to understand what God was communicating in that Scripture; including the method of thinking logically about various possible interpretations of that Scripture.

Some believers suppose that employing logical reasoning to the interpretation of Scripture is not a legitimate approach. Although it is certainly true that even the most strenuous academic efforts to understand Scripture can fail if God hides His truth or does not aid by His Holy Spirit, it is also true that thinking logically about God's Word blends beautifully with a prayerful, humble, and Holy Spirit guided approach. To think logically about Scripture and to thoughtfully consider various possible interpretations of particular Scriptures is not a wrong or an ungodly endeavor, but is a good and godly endeavor. And asking questions about the common interpretations of particular Scriptures is not a bad thing; it is a good thing. It causes us to study more, to think more, and to pray more as we endeavor to understand God's Word. When we think logically and carefully as well as prayerfully and humbly about a Scripture, we have a very good chance of arriving at the right interpretation of that Scripture. Concerning any Scripture we are studying, we should eventually be able to say, "I understand what God was revealing in this Scripture; it makes sense to me."

The important point of view from which we will examine I John 1:9 in this chapter is the logical point of view. We will do this by thoughtfully considering various implications of the common interpretation of I John 1:9. If those implications suggest that the common interpretation of I John 1:9 is contrary to other Scripture or is not compatible with other important New Covenant truth, then we will have to seriously consider whether the common interpretation of I John 1:9 is a valid interpretation.

In this chapter, we will be asking and answering this question: "If the common interpretation of I John 1:9 is correct, what logical conclusions does that interpretation lead us to?" Let's move forward now and consider several implications and conclusions that are demanded by the common interpretation of I John 1:9, employing logical thinking to shine more helpful light on John's important words.

Sinners' Sins and Believers' Sins

One of the more troubling implications of the common interpretation of I John 1:9 is it suggests that it may be more difficult for believers to be forgiven of sins they commit than it is for sinners to be forgiven of all their past sins. If it is true, as the common interpretation of I John 1:9 suggests, that believers must admit to God each and every sin they commit before He will forgive those sins, then God's own sons and daughters, partakers of the new and better covenant through faith in Jesus Christ, must meet far more stringent requirements in order to receive the forgiveness of their sins than sinners must meet. If we accept the common interpretation of I John 1:9 and also accept the simple gospel as it is presented throughout Scripture, then we must conclude that every lost sinner, even the darkest of the dark and the most vile of the vile, can be forgiven and cleansed of every terrible sin they committed by simple faith in Jesus Christ while God's own sons and daughters who He ransomed from death, who He purchased with the blood of His own Son, and who He loves with an eternal love, can only be forgiven and cleansed of sins they commit if and after they admit every one of those sins to Him. If the familiar and commonly accepted interpretation of I John 1:9 is the correct interpretation, then we must conclude that unlike the full scale, immediate, faith-based forgiveness of sinners' sins, the forgiveness of believers' sins is a "sin by sin, day by day, confession-based forgiveness of sins." This conclusion, based on our logical consideration of the commonly accepted interpretation of I John 1:9, is deeply troubling and certainly raises questions about that interpretation.

This logical consideration of the common interpretation of I John 1:9 raises serious questions. We have to ask, "Could it be possible that we, the children of God's love and the inheritors of a better covenant based on better promises, are in a worse position with God concerning the forgiveness of sins than sinners are?" We have to ask, "Could it be that our heavenly Father forgives sinners the moment they believe the gospel and rejoices with all His angels in heaven, but withholds forgiveness from His own children until they dutifully admit each and every sin to Him in a time of confession?" We have to ask, "Could it be possible that by the simple faith act of embracing God's free gift of salvation, without offering any recitation of past sins, a sinner who has lied, cheated, stolen, murdered, abused, and ruined the lives of others can be immediately forgiven and cleansed of all their past sins and immediately enter into true fellowship with the Father, but God's own children must remain in an unforgiven state and in a place of broken fellowship with their Father until they confess every one of their sins to Him?" We have to ask, "Is it possible that the Father God, because of His great love and on the basis of the suffering, the shedding of blood, and the death of His only begotten Son, is willing and even happy to immediately blot out the, 'handwriting of ordinances that was against,' every sinner (Colossians 2:14), but will not forgive the sins of His own children unless and until after they participate in a required act of confession?"

The only way to respond to this gross inconsistency between the way God immediately and joyfully forgives even the worst of sinners, but, according to the common interpretation of I John 1:9, withholds forgiveness from His own children until they admit each of their sins to Him in a time of confession is to question whether the common interpretation of I John 1:9 is the correct interpretation. This disturbing implication of the common interpretation of I John 1:9 gives us no other choice.

A Works Based Covenant?

There is another troubling implication of the common interpretation of I John 1:9; an implication suggested by the obvious corollary to the common interpretation of I John 1:9. If, in I John 1:9, John was informing believers that, "If you admit your sins to God, then He will forgive your sins and cleanse you," he was also informing them that, "If you do not admit your sins to God, then He will not forgive your sins and cleanse you." This unavoidable corollary highlights one of the most serious problems with the common interpretation of I John 1:9; that problem being that every believer who has not admitted to God all the sins they have committed is currently in an unforgiven and unclean state. But could it be true that every Christian who has not admitted to God each and every sin they have committed is not forgiven and is unclean? That is what the common interpretation of I John 1:9 clearly suggests.

If the commonly accepted interpretation of I John 1:9 is the correct interpretation, then we must accept that we who once trusted our lives to God in complete faith and believed on Jesus Christ to be forgiven of all our past sins are now part of a covenant where we cannot be forgiven of sins we commit unless and until after we admit each and every one of those sins to God. We must accept that we who were saved, forgiven, and cleansed of every past sin by simply believing in our hearts that God raised Jesus from the dead and acknowledging with our mouths that Jesus Christ was Lord (Romans 10:17) are now part of a confession-based forgiveness of sins system. If the commonly accepted interpretation of I John 1:9 is the correct interpretation, we must accept that we who were once completely forgiven and cleansed now have a substantial "works-burden" requirement laid upon us in order to remain forgiven, clean, and in fellowship with our Father. If the common interpretation of I John 1:9 is the correct interpretation, then we are in a fragile relationship with God, always living on the edge of being unforgiven, unclean, and out of fellowship with Him. I have no doubt that the common interpretation of I John 1:9 has been a significant hindrance to many believers because the confession-based forgiveness system suggested by that interpretation would cause many to worry endlessly about whether or not they had properly confessed all their sins to God and to wonder, therefore, whether they were currently unforgiven and unclean.

If I John 1:9 means that the forgiveness and cleansing of sins is dependent upon believers properly admitting all their sins to God, then I John 1:9 does not harmonize well with other crucial New Testament teaching and does not fit well with the beautiful realities of the better covenant that believers are part of through faith in Jesus Christ. If the commonly accepted interpretation of I John 1:9 is the correct interpretation of I John 1:9, we cannot but say to ourselves, "This far better New Covenant we are part of through faith in Jesus Christ includes some very unexpected, hard to bear, fear-inspiring requirements." This disconcerting, logical implication of the common interpretation of I John 1:9 makes it difficult to accept that the common interpretation of I John 1:9 is the correct interpretation.

What if We Don't Confess Our Sins to God?

There is another very important matter for us to consider in a logical way as we endeavor to discover the correct interpretation of Johns' words in I John 1:9. If his words in I John 1:9 mean that believers must admit each and every sin they commit to God in order to be forgiven and cleansed of those sins, then believers must be aware of every sin they commit and must take the time to admit every one of those sins to God. Thinking logically about this, we must ask ourselves this question, "What happens if a believer is honestly unaware of some of the sins they have committed?" And we must ask, "What happens if they fail to confess to God even one of the sins they have committed?" The only logical conclusion to these questions based on the common interpretation of I John 1:9 is that any believer who is unaware of a sin they have committed or fails to admit to God a sin they have committed will not be forgiven and cleansed of that sin; they will be in an unforgiven and unclean state. The version of Christian life suggested by the common interpretation of I John 1:9—a life where believers must carefully note and dutifully admit each and every sin they commit to God in order to be forgiven of those sins—is a very precarious "life of faith."

Something we must acknowledge along these lines is that many believers sin on a daily basis. Even if some of their sins are minor, they are still sins. For example, a believer might be jealous of someone else's spiritual gifts or covet another person's home. They might entertain some secret, lustful thoughts, even though they never act on those thoughts. They might do a good thing, but do it with a selfish motive, wanting to be seen and praised by others. The Holy Spirit might have urged a believer to pray for a brother or sister in the Lord, but they did not pray and so were disobedient. They might pass along words of gossip that are hurtful to others. They might be proud of their knowledge or of their calling. Even though these kinds of sins may not seem very serious, they are still sins and, according to the common interpretation of I John 1:9, must be confessed to God or they will not be forgiven.

If it is true that by his words in I John 1:9, the apostle John intended to communicate to believers that the sins they committed could only be forgiven and cleansed if they were enumerated and admitted to God, then many believers are currently in serious spiritual trouble. Why are many believers currently in serious spiritual trouble? Because it is nearly impossible for any believer to be one hundred percent aware of or perfectly do the work of admitting to God each and every sin they have committed. And, according to the commonly accepted interpretation of I John 1:9, if a believer has not confessed every one of their sins to God, then they are not forgiven and cleansed of those sins. If the common interpretation of I John 1:9 is the correct interpretation of John's words, we must conclude that all unconfessed sins are unforgiven sins. The negative consequence of failing to comply with the requirement to confess one's sins suggested by the common interpretation of I John 1:9 can only lead us to the logical conclusion that a majority of Christians are currently in an unforgiven and unclean state. This conclusion is extremely troubling, but it is the only logical conclusion to the commonly accepted interpretation of I John 1:9.

What About New Believers?

Another matter we must consider pertaining to the common interpretation of I John 1:9 concerns new believers and young disciples. Currently, the important work of evangelism is going on all through-out the world. Sinners are being saved every day. The precious fruit of the earth is being reaped and new disciples are continually being added to the church. This effectual work of the church in evangelism is a wonderful thing for the heavenly Father, makes all of heaven rejoice, and is life from death for those who become God's sons and daughters through faith in Jesus Christ.

But what happens to new converts and young believers who don't know that according to the common interpretation of I John 1:9, they must confess every sin they commit in order to remain forgiven and clean? Is their ignorance of this "truth" a legitimate excuse for not confessing their sins? Or have all these new converts and young believers fallen back into an unclean and unforgiven state just hours or days after being gloriously saved and forgiven and cleansed from all their past sins? If the common interpretation of I John 1:9 is the correct interpretation, then many of God's new sons and daughters, recently delivered from sin and death and made clean by the blood of Jesus, are unclean and unforgiven once again.

Can we accept as true that our loving and wise Father God designed and inaugurated a better New Covenant if new believers and young disciples who have not yet been taught the "truth" of I John 1:9 fall back into an unforgiven and unclean state the very first time they sin? What kind of a new and better covenant would that be? Perhaps, rather than wondering why our all wise Father God didn't do a better job of designing the New Covenant, we should wonder whether the common interpretation of I John 1:9 is the correct interpre-tation. Along with other matters we have already considered in this chapter, this matter concerning the spiritual state of new believers and young disciples who sin after they are saved, but are unaware of the "truth" that they must confess their sins to God in order to be forgiven of those sins certainly calls into question the veracity of the common and widely accepted interpretation of I John 1:9.

Is Fellowship With God Broken When We Sin?

There is another serious matter we must consider concerning the common interpretation of I John 1:9. That matter concerns whether or not believers' fellowship with the Father is broken when they sin and remains broken until they properly confess their sins. I spoke recently with one minister who told me he firmly believed that any time a Christian sinned, their fellowship with God was broken and remained broken until they confessed their sins according to the common interpretation of I John 1:9. Only after they had confessed their sins, he said, would their fellowship with God be restored.

Can what this minister said be true? Is the fellowship between God and His children and between the Lord Jesus and His people so fragile that one unconfessed sin leads to a breach in that fellowship? Do we, as God's children, cut our friends off or refuse to talk to a family member just because of one unkind word or one minor offense? Scripture teaches that love covers a multitude of sins (I Peter 4:8). Could it be that God is love, but He cuts us off from fellowship if we commit one sin and only restores us to fellowship after we admit that sin? The heavenly Father did not teach us to cut off fellowship with a brother or sister who committed one offense against us. Could it be that He is less forgiving of offenses and sins than He expects us to be?

It is certainly true that God is holy and that sin is an offense against Him. But even after Adam and Eve sinned, God came seeking them in the garden, found them, and spoke to them. All throughout the Old Testament, God spoke with and fellowshipped intimately with unsaved and unclean Old Covenant saints. Could it be true, then, that the Father and the Lord Jesus close the door of fellowship on believers when they sin and keep that door closed until such time as that believer fulfills a mandated confession of sins? Interestingly, Jesus told one of the churches in Revelation that He was standing at their door and knocking, making it clear that He desired for believers to open the door of fellowship to Him (Revelation 3:20). Jesus was not only not closing the door of fellowship on those believers; He was trying to persuade them to open the door of fellowship to Him. He certainly did not tell them, "Only after you confess every one of your sins to God will I open the door and fellowship with you again." In fact, He said that if they would just hear His voice and open, He would come in and fellowship with them.

Before the foundation of the world, God made a plan to redeem the lost and bring them into His family as sons and daughters. In the fullness of time, He sent forth His Son, Jesus Christ, who suffered, shed His blood, died, and was raised from the dead to accomplish that plan. God swore the promises of His covenant with an oath and offered those who would receive His gift of eternal life words of commitment like, "I will never leave thee, nor forsake thee" (Hebrews 13:15). Jesus told His disciples, "lo, I am with you always, even unto the end of the world" (Matthew 28:20). God is totally committed to His own people. He who began a good work in lost sinners will continue to perform that work until Jesus comes again (Philippians 1:6). Scripture is clear that the Father God and the Lord Jesus and the Holy Spirit are totally committed to their covenant people; to their own children.

Perhaps our fellowship with the Father isn't as fragile and as prone to "breakups" as some have suggested. Perhaps our relationship with the Father isn't like the relationship of two teenagers who become a couple and then break up and then become a couple again and then break up again; in and out of their relationship every few days. Perhaps some ministers have inappropriately used the common interpretation of I John 1:9 to leverage God's people to stay in line spiritually or to fill the altars at church services, preaching to them that their fellowship with God was broken when they sinned and that they must come to the altar and confess their sins in order to restore that fellowship.

Could it be true that if a believer was unaware of even one sin they had committed or if they failed to admit to God even one sin they had committed, He would turn His back on them, shut His door, not forgive them, not cleanse them, and cut off fellowship with them? Some believe, based on the common interpretation of I John 1:9, that this is exactly how things work in the New Testament. But can this possibly be true? If the New Covenant, based on the finished work of Jesus Christ and entered into by faith, is indeed a better covenant based upon better promises, then the familiar and commonly accepted interpretation of I John 1:9 cannot be the correct interpretation.

If it was true, as the common interpretation of I John 1:9 suggests and as many believe, that a believer's fellowship with God is broken when they sin and remains broken until they confess their sins to Him and are forgiven, then every believer who has any unconfessed sin in their life is currently not in fellowship with Him. Their fellowship with God is broken and can only be restored through the act of the confession of sins. If this is true and if this is how things work in the New Covenant, then believers' fellowship with God is like a revolving door turning all day long, in and then out, in and then out, their fellowship with God in continual jeopardy.

If the common interpretation of I John 1:9 is the correct interpretation of I John 1:9, then we must conclude that a great majority of Christians are currently not in fellowship with God due to unconfessed sin in their lives. And if the common interpretation of I John 1:9 is the right interpretation of I John 1:9, then a believer's relationship with God cannot possibly be a beautiful and joyful and confidence filled relationship. More likely, believers who embrace the common interpretation of I John 1:9 will find themselves in a state of continual anxiety, worried that when they sin, God will shut the door on them and break fellowship with them until they confess their sins to Him. Under the scenario of the common interpretation of I John 1:9, some Christians may actually spend more time outside of fellowship with God than in beautiful fellowship with Him. A life of joyful and faith filled fellowship with God would be very difficult, maybe impossible, if the common interpretation of I John 1:9 was the correct interpretation.

Why Don't Believers Confess Their Sins?

Another matter to consider logically concerning I John 1:9 can be introduced by this question: "If most Christians truly believe the common interpretation of I John 1:9—that believers must confess their sins to God in order to be forgiven of those sins—then why don't most believers regularly confess their sins to God?" Over the span of time that I have been conducting this study and writing this book, I have asked many fellow believers what they think I John 1:9 means and then asked them if they regularly confess their sins to God. Almost no one I spoke to over this time span of four years said that they regularly admitted their sins to God in a time of confession even though they all said they believed the common interpretation of I John 1:9.

Why wouldn't believers who embraced the common interpretation of I John 1:9 act in harmony with their own beliefs and be diligent to confess their sins? Could it be that they were not actually convinced in their hearts that the common interpretation of I John 1:9 was an accurate interpretation? After all, if they truly believed that the common interpretation of I John 1:9 was correct, wouldn't they be deeply concerned about whether or not their sins were forgiven and wouldn't they be diligent, therefore, in admitting their sins to God? Could it be that the many believers I talked to didn't confess their sins to God on a daily or weekly or even monthly basis because their own hearts were not convicted by the Holy Spirit that the common interpretation of I John 1:9 was actually the correct interpretation?

Some of the believers and ministers I talked to over the past few years told me that they "kind of" believed the common interpretation of I John 1:9, but did not believe that if they failed to admit their sins to God, they would become unclean and unforgiven. Could it be that one reason some Christians "kind of" believe the common interpretation of I John 1:9, but are not strongly convinced that they have to regularly confess their sins to God is because they have never been offered an alternative interpretation of I John 1:9 that their heart could truly "lock onto" and concerning which they could say a strong, "Yes, that is the correct and true meaning of John's words in I John 1:9 and it bears witness with my heart?"

Think about your own Christian life and your own relationship with God. Do you confess your sins to God every day or every week? Or, while generally holding to the common interpretation of I John 1:9, do you neglect to make a regular practice of confessing your sins to God? Have you ever sensed in your heart that your heavenly Father was warning you that because you failed to confess your sins to Him, you were currently unforgiven and unclean? Has the Holy Spirit, your indwelling helper, ever urged you to properly confess your sins lest you remain unforgiven and unclean? Has the Lord ever told you, "My child, you are not currently forgiven and you are not currently clean because you have not properly confessed your sins"? If you have an authentic relationship with God, love Him, know His Word, are generally obedient to Him and enjoy good fellowship with Him, but are not a regular confessor of your sins, why hasn't your Father dealt with you about this matter? Why hasn't the Holy Spirit been speaking to you along these lines?

Could it be that the reason the Father and the Son and the Holy Spirit have not been dealing strongly with believers all over the world about their failure to confess each and every one of their sins to God is because the common interpretation of I John 1:9 is not, in fact, the correct interpretation I John 1:9? And could it be that most believers have only held loosely to the common interpretation of I John 1:9 because they were never offered a better interpretation that their hearts could connect with; an interpretation that resonated with their spirit and with the Holy Spirit who indwells them? This is another important matter to ponder as we consider whether or not the common interpretation of I John 1:9 is the correct interpretation.

Where Are the Other Scriptures?

Another matter we must consider logically concerning the common interpretation of I John 1:9 can be introduced by this important question: "If John's words in I John 1:9 really mean that in order

for believers to be forgiven and cleansed of sins they have committed, they must first confess each one of those sins to God, why isn't
this very important truth represented anywhere else in the epistles?"
Thinking logically about this matter, it would certainly seem that if
the common interpretation of I John 1:9 was the correct interpretation
of I John 1:9, then this absolutely critical truth would be clearly represented other places in the epistles. That is not, however, the case. In
fact, nowhere in the epistles can we find teaching that collaborates the
interpretation of I John 1:9 that most Christians embrace; the interpretation that believers must confess the sins they commit to God in order
to be forgiven of those sins and cleansed.

If the common interpretation of I John 1:9 is the correct interpretation, why didn't the apostle Paul write to believers about the important practice of confessing their sins to God? This would have been be
a very significant matter in regards to daily Christian life and should
have been addressed. Why didn't the apostle Peter teach believers
about the important practice of the confession of sins in his two epistles or exhort believers to be diligent in that practice? Why didn't the
apostle James, who wrote the most practical, daily Christian living
epistle, at least mention to believers the necessity of confessing their
sins to God so they could be forgiven and cleansed? If the common
interpretation of I John 1:9 is, indeed, the correct interpretation of I
John 1:9, and if it is necessary for believers to admit their sins to God
in order to be forgiven and cleansed of their sins, then why didn't at
least one leading New Testament author teach this essential truth in
their writings, or at least refer to it? The fact that no other author of a
New Testament epistle even mentioned the confession of sins leads
us to this obvious question: "Is it possible that the reason the apostles
Paul, Peter, and James as well as Jude and the author of the Hebrew
epistle didn't write to believers about the necessity of confessing their
sins to God so that they could be forgiven and cleansed is because
the confession of sins to God is not a New Testament doctrine or a
required Christian practice?"

We know that the authors of other New Testament epistles wrote

to believers and churches about sin and sinning and about sinful practices. For example, the apostle Paul communicated to the Corinthian
believers that they should repent of their sins, especially their fornication, and turn to godly and righteous living (II Corinthians 12:20-
21; 13:2). He also communicated extensively with them about the
young man living in an incestuous relationship with his father's wife.
Interestingly, both in his specific direction to the Corinthian believers
about the young man who was sinning and in his general directions to
them about sinning, he didn't say anything about confessing their sins
so that they could be forgiven and cleansed of their sins.

In his letter to the Roman believers, Paul asked this question
concerning sinning,

> "What shall we say then? Shall we continue in sin, that grace may
> abound?"
>
> *Romans 6:1*

Notice that in this important question to the Roman believers
about continuing to sin after they had been saved and delivered from
sin, Paul did not ask, "Shall we continue in sin only to have to repeatedly confess to God the sins we commit so that we can be forgiven?"
His words in Romans 6:1 suggest, rather, that when believers sin, God's
grace continues to abound without them performing any special act or
without them praying any special prayer. Paul's words suggest that
if believers sinned, even if they continued in sin for a season, God's
grace would continue to flow to them without any confession of sins
on their part. Paul was not, of course, encouraging believers to sin.
In fact, his retort to the possibility of believers continuing in sin was
a strong, "God forbid" (Romans 6:2). Nevertheless, Paul's words in
Romans 6:1 about believers sinning are worth thinking about in the
context of our study; especially taking note of the fact that he didn't
mention anything to them about confessing their sins to God so they
could be forgiven and cleansed.

Based on what we know from his many epistles, Paul never taught
that believers must engage in the practice of admitting their sins to

God in order to be forgiven and cleansed of sins they had committed; and he certainly never exhorted believers to confess their sins. The same thing is true of the apostle Peter. He did not teach anywhere in his epistles that believers must confess their sins to God in order to be forgiven. The same is true concerning the apostle James and concerning Jude. Given these facts, we must accept that if the common interpretation of John's words in I John 1:9 is, in fact, the correct interpretation of his words, that interpretation is not collaborated or supported anywhere else in the epistles. Perhaps it is true then, as I have been suggesting throughout this study, that John's statement in I John 1:9 was not a teaching that believers must admit to God the sins they had committed in order to be forgiven and cleansed of those sins, but was an important conditional statement he penned in his polemic against early gnostic error concerning sin and sinning where he characterized true believers as those who agreed with God concerning sin and sinning and openly acknowledged their agreement.

Over Eight Hundred Instructions

Along this same line of thinking, it is interesting to consider the fact that the New Testament epistles contain over 800 present imperative tense instructions exhorting New Covenant believers about things they should do. These hundreds of present imperative tense instructions direct those who are receiving the instructions—believers—that they should continually and habitually perform the action that is directed. These instructions suggest a long-term commitment to the action stated; in other words, they describe and direct a consistent manner of living.

For example, believers in Thessalonica were instructed to, "stand fast, and hold the traditions which ye have been taught, whether by word, or our epistle" (II Thessalonians 2:15). The Roman Christians were instructed to, "Let not sin therefore reign in your mortal body, that ye should obey it in the lusts thereof" (Romans 6:12). The Ephesian believers were told to, "Put on the whole armour of God, that ye may be able to stand against the wiles of the devil" (Ephesians 6:11).

Timothy was charged to, "Study to shew thyself approved unto God, a workman that needeth not to be ashamed, rightly dividing the word of truth" (II Timothy 2:15). Believers were exhorted by Peter to, "desire the sincere milk of the Word that ye may grow thereby" (I Peter 2:2). These are just a very few examples of the more than 800 present imperative tense instructions written to believers in the New Testament. What is fascinating and noteworthy in light of our study is that among these hundreds of present imperative tense instructions recorded in the epistles and directed toward believers, not one of them exhorts believers to admit their sins to God in order to be forgiven.

If we took time to read the hundreds of present imperative tense instructions found in the epistles, we would gain a very expanded scope of understanding about how believers are expected to conduct their daily lives in Christ. Among those many instructions, we would find instructions about how to think, about how to speak, about fighting, about praying, about loving, about worshipping, about standing, about running, about giving, about resisting, about holding fast, about bearing burdens, and about many other things. Very importantly for us to realize in the context of this study is the fact that in the extensive list of present imperative tense instructions presented to believers in the epistles, there is not one instruction to, "admit your sins to God so that you can be forgiven and cleansed of those sins." The fact that there is not even one present imperative tense instruction in the epistles that exhorts believers to admit their sins to God in order to be forgiven and cleansed suggests that it is highly unlikely that the confession of sins to God is a necessary action for believers to engage in before they can be forgiven of sins they commit.

Among the hundreds of instructions directed to believers about how they should live and what they should regularly do there is no instruction that they must admit their sins to God in order to be forgiven and cleansed. This fact strongly suggests that the longly held belief that believers must admit their sins to God in order to be forgiven of their sins is not a sound belief. The fact that there is not one present imperative tense instruction directed to believers that they should confess their sins to God lends strong support to the argument I have been presenting throughout this study; the argument that John's words I John 1:9, were not, in fact, a teaching that believers must admit to God each and every sin they commit in order to be forgiven and cleansed of those sins.

The further we proceed in our study and the more we consider John's words in I John 1:9, the more it appears that his words were not, in fact, a teaching revealing that believers must admit their sins to God in order to be forgiven, but were one of several important conditional statements he penned in his polemic against the early gnostic error that was flourishing in the region.

Conclusion

In this chapter, we considered the commonly accepted interpretation of I John 1:9 in a logical manner, thinking carefully about various implications of that interpretation. As we considered those various implications, it seemed more and more likely that the common interpretation of I John 1:9 was not the most accurate interpretation of John's words in that verse. In fact, our logical consideration of the commonly accepted interpretation of I John 1:9 revealed that it does not harmonize well with New Testament doctrine in general and is not compatible with the glorious, beautiful, faith based, freeing New Covenant in Jesus' blood. After all, the Father God sent His Son to set men free from sin and death and from law and works, not to bind them up in a works based forgiveness of sins system that would be nearly as burdensome as the Old Covenant sacrificial system.

When we consider John's words in I John 1:9 from a logical point of view, it seems that we can only reach this conclusion: The apostle John never intended his words in I John 1:9 to mean that only if and only after believers admit each and every sin they commit to God and ask Him to forgive those sins will God forgive and cleanse them of those sins. The logical implications of the common interpretation of I John 1:9 strongly suggest, rather, that a different interpretation of

John's words should be sought; an interpretation that is more harmonious with New Covenant truth.

Why Is This View of I John 1:9 Important?

It is very important when seeking to discover the true meaning of any Scripture to think carefully about the logical implications of various possible interpretations of that Scripture. Doing so helps us discover if those possible interpretations are harmonious with other important Scripture truths or if they are incompatible with other important Scripture truths. For New Covenant Christians, it is most important to determine if an interpretation of a New Testament Scripture is harmonious with other important truths of the New Covenant and can be collaborated by other New Testament Scriptures or if that interpretation is not harmonious with other important truths of the New Covenant and cannot be collaborated by other New Testament Scriptures.

In this chapter, we looked at I John 1:9 from a logical point of view, thinking carefully about various implications of the commonly accepted interpretation of John's words to determine if that interpretation was harmonious with other Scripture and compatible with other New Covenant truth or if it was not harmonious with other Scripture and not compatible with other New Covenant truth. Looking at I John 1:9 from this logical point of view has been very valuable in helping us examine the common interpretation of I John 1:9. After examining the common interpretation of I John 1:9 from a logical point of view, enough concerns have been raised to cause us to seriously question that interpretation and wonder if there might be a better and more accurate interpretation.

XI

What Does I John 1:9 Really Mean?

A s we have progressed from chapter to chapter in our study, we have learned many important things about the apostle John's first epistle and discovered numerous enlightening facts about his words in I John 1:9. We learned about the activity of the errant early gnostics in the region where John was living and ministering. We discovered who John wrote his first epistle to and why he wrote it. We determined what the Greek word *homologeō* would have meant to believers of John's day. We examined John's powerful polemic, learned about his attention to the subject of sin and sinning in his first epistle, studied three analogous statements, and considered the common interpretation of I John 1:9 from a logical point of view. As we studied and discovered many important and enlightening facts, the commonly accepted interpretation of John's words in I John 1:9 seemed less and less likely to be the correct interpretation.

Looking at I John 1:9 from various important points of view in previous chapters has given us an important base of knowledge, has contributed essential context to John's words, and has provided us with the degree of light necessary to reach a correct interpretation of I John 1:9. In this chapter, I will set forth with as much clarity as possible what I believe the apostle John intended to communicate to his spiritual children by his words in I John 1:9, giving the best sense of what his words in I John 1:9 really mean. The important question I will endeavor to answer in this chapter is: "What did the apostle John originally intend to communicate to his spiritual children by his words in I John 1:9?"

I John 1:9 Was a Counter Statement

In chapter six, we learned that the apostle John's words in I John 1:5 through I John 2:11 constituted a polemic against early gnostic error on the subject of sin and sinning. We saw that throughout his polemic, he employed a back and forth, alternating statements style, using six "say statements" and a similar number of counter statements in order to create a stark contrast between early gnostic error and their ungodly lifestyle in the dark and true Christian doctrine and believers' godly walk in the light. John's words in I John 1:9 comprised one of the very important counter statements he penned in his polemic to help him create that stark contrast between the beliefs and sayings and lifestyle of the errant early gnostics and the beliefs and sayings and lifestyle of true believers. The counter statement he penned in I John 1:9, a statement which characterized true believers—what they believed and said and what was, therefore, true of them—was strategically positioned between and answered to the two "say statements" he penned in I John 1:8 and I John 1:10—statements which characterized the early gnostics and their error and what was true of them.

It is essential to an accurate interpretation and a correct understanding of John's words in I John 1:9 to realize that his words were not a teaching about what believers must do in order to be forgiven of sins they commit. His words, rather, comprised one of the very important counter statements he penned in his polemic against early gnostic error on the subject of sin and sinning. Let's briefly review his three statements in I John 1:8-10 to confirm that his words in I John 1:9 were, indeed, a counter statement to his statements in I John 1:8 and I John 1:10.

In I John 1:8, John wrote,

"If we say that we have no sin, we deceive ourselves, and the truth is not in us."

I John 1:8

John's conditional "If we say" statement in John 1:8 characterized the errant early gnostics—what they believed and said about sin and the fact that they were self-deceived and void of the truth. His words also served as a warning to true believers to not follow them. Because the early gnostics believed that the spirit of man came from God and was pure, they believed that they had no sin nature. That is why they said, "we have no sin." Their thinking on this matter was completely contrary to God's truth, however, which is why John said that they were self deceived and that, "the truth is not in (them)." John wanted his spiritual children to be aware that if they joined the early gnostics in their error and said, "we have no sin," they would also be deceived and void of God's truth.

In I John 1:10, John wrote,

"If we say that we have not sinned, we make him a liar, and his word is not in us."

I John 1:10

John's conditional "If we say" statement in I John 1:10 character-ized the errant early gnostic belief that there was no such thing as sin or sinning and their belief that since their pure spirit and their evil body did not effectually connect, they could live carnal, fleshly lives in their bodies and it would not affect their spirit, their spiritual life, or their relationship with God. The early gnostics believed that just as the purity of a golden ring could not be affected by setting it in pig dung, so the pure spirit of man could not be affected by any carnal deed done in the body. Because of this belief, they said, "we have not sinned." Their thinking on this matter was completely contrary to God's truth, however, and that is why John said that they made God a liar and, "his word is not in (them)." Like his words in I John 1:8, John's words in I John 1:10 served as a warning to his spiritual children to not follow the errant early gnostics. He wanted them to understand that if they joined them in their error and said, "we have not sinned," they would also be in disagreement with God, would be making Him a liar, and His Word would obviously not be in them.

In I John 1:9, John penned a counter statement that characterized true believers—what they believed and said, how they lived, and what was true of them—and served as an encouragement to his spiritual children to continue their firm agreement with and open acknowledgment of God's truth on the matter of sin and sinning. His counter statement in I John 1:9 contrasted the "say statements" of early gnostic error he penned in I John 1:8 and 1 John 1:10. In I John 1:9, he wrote,

> *"If we confess our sins, he is faithful and just to forgive us our sins, and to cleanse us from all unrighteousness."*
>
> *I John 1:9*

In complete contrast to the early gnostics John characterized in I John 1:8 and I John 1:10 who denied that they had a sin nature and denied that they sinned, true believers, "confess *(homologeō)* our sins." In other words, true believers acknowledged that sin existed, acknowledged that men were sinners, and acknowledged that they had sinned if they had thought, spoken, or acted in ways that God had characterized as sin. True believers did not disagree with what God had said about sin. They did not deny that men had a sin nature, did not deny that men sinned, and did not deny that they had sinned if, indeed, they had sinned. True believers, unlike the early gnostics who did not have God's truth or His Word in them, aligned themselves with God, had His truth living in them, agreed with what His Word said about sin and sinning, and agreed with Him that they had sinned if they had done anything contrary to His truth and His commandments. That is the action John was communicating by his words, "If we confess our sins."

John penned his important counter statement in I John 1:9 to reveal the stark contrast between the beliefs, the saying, and the life-style of early gnostics concerning sin and sinning and what was, therefore, true of them, and the beliefs, the saying, and the lifestyle of true believers concerning sin and sinning and what was, therefore, true of them. His statement in I John 1:9 also alerted believers to the fact that they had a choice to make. If they joined the early gnostics in their error, they would also be deceived and void of the truth and would be taking a position contrary to God and His Word. If, on the other hand, they continue to hold their posture of alignment with God and His truth and continued to speak in agreement with Him about sin and about their own sins, they would continue to be forgiven of any sins they committed and would be cleansed from all unrighteousness by their faithful and just God.

In a concise fashion, the three statements John penned in I John 1:8-10 highlighted the stark contrast between the early gnostics and true believers on the matter of sin and sinning. His statement in I John 1:9 revealed that the belief and speaking of true believers who agreed with God about sin and sinning and about their own sins was in direct contrast to the belief and speaking of the early gnostics who disagreed with God and said, "we have no sin," and, "we have not sinned." John's statement in I John 1:9 was one of the very important contrasting statements he penned in his polemic to make clear to his spiritual children what would be true of them if they remained aligned with and continued to speak in agreement with God and His truth concerning sin and sinning.

John's words in I John 1:9 were a counter-statement of Christian truth to the two "If we say" statements representing early gnostic error that he penned in I John 1:8 and I John 1:10. His words in I John 1:9 must be read and interpreted in that light—with the understanding that I John 1:9 was not a stand alone statement, but was part and parcel of the extended argument he was making against dangerous early gnostic error. When we view I John 1:9 this way, giving serious consideration to its critical context, we realize that John's words in I John 1:9 were not a teaching about what Christians must do in order to be forgiven and cleansed of sins they had committed, but were an important part of his argument against early gnostic error on the subject of sin and sinning. When we view I John 1:9 with this crucial fact in mind, John's words are properly illuminated.

I John 1:9 Was a Characterizing Statement

Throughout his first epistle, John characterized the errant early gnostics and true believers as two completely different groups of individuals. One way he did this was by using unique descriptive words for each group. For example, he described the errant early gnostics as "deniers," "antichrists," "liars," "seducers," "false prophets," and "children of the devil." In contrast, he described true believers as those who were "born of God," as those who "walked in the light," as "the children of God," as "brethren," as "righteous," and as "my little children."

Another way John characterized the errant early gnostics and true believers as two completely different groups of individuals—a way that is very important for us to understand when seeking to discover the best interpretation of I John 1:9—was by describing errant early gnostics as those who did not *homologeō* with God and describing true believers as those who did *homologeō* with God. For example, in chapter two of his epistle, John wrote,

> *"Who is a liar but he that denieth* (arneomai) *that Jesus is the Christ? He is antichrist, that denieth* (arneomai) *the Father and the Son. Whosoever denieth* (arneomai) *the Son, the same hath not the Father: he that acknowledgeth* (homologeō) *the Son hath the Father also."*
>
> *I John 2:22-23*

John characterized the errant early gnostics as liars who denied that Jesus was the Christ, denied the Father and the Son, and denied the Son. These deniers did not *homologeō* with God's testimony about His Son and, according to John, they, "hath not the Father." In stark contrast to the early gnostics deniers were true believers who, "*homologeō* (acknowledgeth) the Son." These confessors-true believers agreed with God's testimony about His Son and, according to John, they, "hath the Father also." In other words, they were born of God and in true fellowship with Jesus Christ and with the Father. In this passage, John used the matter of whether or not a person *homologeō* to create a stark contrast between two groups of individuals. Those who did not *homologeō* were "liars-deniers-sinners" who were not in relationship with the Father or the Son. Those who did *homologeō* were "confessors-agreers-believers" who were in relationship with the Father and the Son.

In the fourth chapter of his first epistle, John again used the matter of whether or not a person *homologeō* with God to distinguish between errant early gnostic sinners and true believers. He wrote,

> *"Beloved, believe not every spirit, but try the spirits whether they are of God: because many false prophets are gone out into the world. Hereby know ye the Spirit of God: Every spirit that confesseth (homologeō) that Jesus Christ is come in the flesh is of God: And every spirit that confesseth (homologeō) not that Jesus Christ is come in the flesh is not of God: and this is that spirit of antichrist, whereof ye have heard that it should come; and even now already is it in the world."*
>
> I John 4:1-3

The early gnostics did not *homologeō* (confess) that Jesus Christ had come in the flesh. John labeled them as "false prophets," said that they were speaking by, "that spirit of antichrist," and described them as, "not of God." In other words, they were not true believers. True believers, on the other hand, did *homologeō* (confess) that Jesus Christ had come in the flesh. According to John, they were speaking by the influence of the Spirit of God and were, "of God." Again, John created a stark contrast between errant early gnostic deniers and true believer agreers, characterizing them as two distinct groups of individuals by his use of the word *homologeō*. He characterized the errant early gnostics as those who did not *homologeō* (confess) and characterized true believers as those who did *homologeō* (confess).

Near the end of his first epistle, John employed the word *homologeō* to characterize true believers as those who agreed with God's testimony that Jesus was the Son of God and the Savior of the world. He wrote,

> *"And we have seen and do testify (martyreō) that the Father sent the Son to be the Saviour of the world. Whosoever shall confess (homologeō) that Jesus is the Son of God, God dwelleth in him, and he in God."*
>
> I John 4:14-15

Concerning those who *homologeō* (confessed) that Jesus was the

Son of God, John stated that, "God dwelleth in (them), and (they) in God." In other words, they were true believers. Again, he used the matter of whether or not a person *homologeō* to distinguish between two groups of people. True believers *homologeō* with God and with His truth that Jesus of Nazareth was the Son of God. Errant early gnostics did not *homologeō* with God and with His truth that Jesus of Nazareth was the Son of God.

John not only used the matter of whether or not a person *homologeō* with God concerning who Jesus of Nazareth was to distinguish between true believers and errant early gnostics. He also used the matter of whether or not a person *homologeō* with God about sin and sinning and about their own sins to distinguish between true believers and errant early gnostics. In I John 1:8-10, he penned these three statements,

> *"If we say that we have no sin* (errant early gnostics), *we deceive ourselves, and the truth is not in us. If we confess* (homologeō) *our sins* (true believers), *he* (God) *is faithful and just to forgive us our sins, and to cleanse us from all unrighteousness. If we say that we have not sinned* (errant early gnostics), *we make him* (God) *a liar, and his word is not in us."*
>
> I John 1:8-10

I am going to paraphrase John's three statements in I John 1:8-10 to make it even more clear how he used the matter of whether or not a person *homologeō* with God and His truth concerning sin and sinning to distinguish between true believers and errant early gnostic sinners. This is essentially what John said:

> "If a person says that they do not have a sin nature, suggesting that they are pure and blameless and don't need a Savior to save them from sin, then they are self-deceived and God's truth is not in them. They are a denier of what God said. If, on the other hand, a person is aligned with God and His truth and agrees with Him about sin and about their own sins, speaking with one voice with Him—if they are a confessor—

then they are a true believer, born of God and in an authentic relationship with Him. Because they are a true believer, they will continue to experience the forgiveness of their sins and a cleansing from all unrighteousness because God is faithful to His Word and just to follow the terms of the covenant He made with them through Jesus Christ. But if a person says they have not sinned when they have done things that God has characterized as sin, then they are disagreeing with God and basically calling Him a liar, denying that His Word is true. In that case, it is obvious that God's Word is not in them. They are a denier of what God has said."

We could also paraphrase John's words in I John 1:8-10 this way:

"If we say that we have no sin, then we are deceived and the truth is not in us—we are not true believers, but are lost sinners. But if we don't deny sin and don't deny that we have sinned when we have, in fact, sinned, but agree with God about sin and sinning and agree with Him that we have sinned when we have sinned, then we reveal ourselves to be true believers. Because we are true believers, our faithful and just God continually forgives our sins and cleanses us. If we sin, but say that we have not sinned, then we are calling God a liar and His Word is not in us—we are not true believers, but are lost sinners."

This, then, is the essence of what John was communicating with his spiritual children in his three conditional, characterizing statements in I John 1:8-10:

"If you say, 'I have no sin,' you are self deceived and the truth is not in you. If, on the other hand, you agree with God and with His truth, acknowledging sin to be sin and acknowledging that you have sinned when you have thought, said, or done things that God has characterized as sin, then you can carry on with confidence knowing that because you are a true believer, your faithful and just God will forgive your sins and cleanse you. But if you sin and then say, 'No, I have not sinned,' you are basically calling God a liar and refusing to acknowledge that the things He has characterized as sins are, in fact, sins. If you are sinning, but say that you are not sinning, then His truth is not in you and His Word has no place in your heart."

John's statements in I John 1:8 and I John 1:10 characterized those who did not *homologeō* with God about sin and about their own sins as persons who were self-deceived and in whom God's truth and His Word had no place. Those individuals were the errant early gnostics. John's statement in I John 1:9 characterized those who did *homologeō* with God about their sins—who agreed with God's truth and His Word about sin and sinning and agreed with Him concerning their own sins—as those who would continue to experience the forgiveness of their sins and would be continually cleansed from any stain of unrighteousness because God was faithful and just. Those individuals were true New Covenant believers.

John's statement in I John 1:9 was one of several significant characterizing statements he penned in his polemic against early gnostic error on the subject of sin and sinning as he endeavored to help his spiritual children recognize who and what was of God and His truth and who and what was not of God and His truth. His characterizing statement in I John 1:9 expressed the "aligned with God" spiritual posture and the "speaking in agreement with God" action of true believers concerning sin and sinning, setting them in stark contrast to the "not aligned with God" posture and the "speaking in disagreement with God" action of the errant early gnostics.

Understanding that I John 1:9 was a statement which characterized true believers as agreers with God and with what He had said is absolutely essential to a right interpretation of I John 1:9. To understand what John intended to communicate in I John 1:9, we must realize that his words were not a teaching about what believers must do to be forgiven if they sinned, but was a statement that characterized those who agreed with God about sin and about their own sins as true believers whose sins were continually being forgiven and cleansed. I want to repeat this crucial fact: John's words in I John 1:9 were not an instruction about what believers must do to be forgiven and cleansed if they had sinned, but were a statement about what true believers believed, what they said and did, and what was, therefore, true of them. True believers, unlike errant early gnostics, were not deniers of sin and sinning, but were confessors of sin and sinning. In other words, they agreed with God about sin and about their own sins. In I John 1:9, then, John was not telling believers, "This is what you must do when you have sinned in order to be forgiven and cleansed of your sins," but was saying, "If you are a person who speaks in agreement with God about sin and about your own sins, then you are clearly a true believer. Because you are a true believer, your sins are continually being forgiven and you are continually being cleansed by your faithful and just God."

What John really meant by his words in I John 1:9 can be further clarified by the answer to this question: "Are you a confessor or a denier?" If a person said that they had no sin and said that they had not sinned, they were a denier. If they were a denier, then they were deceived, they were against the truth, and the Word of God was not in them. If they were a denier, they were not saved, were not in fellowship with God, and were not a true believer. If, on the other hand, a person aligned with and agreed with God about sin and about their own sins, then they were a confessor. If they were a confessor, then they were in the light, they were in relationship with the Father and the Son, and they were a child of God. If they were a confessor, they were saved and a true believer. And if they were a confessor, their sins would continually be forgiven and they would be continually cleansed because their covenant God was faithful and just. The question that might be suggested by John's words in I John 1:9 was not, then, "Did you, child of God, confess to God each and every one of the sins you committed so that you can be forgiven?" The question suggested was, rather, "Are you, reader of my epistle, a confessor of sins or a denier of sins? Are you a person who is aligned with God and His Word, who agrees with God and His Word, and who speaks in agreement with God and His Word on the subject of sin and sinning or are you contrary to God and His Word and a denier of what He has said about sin and sinning?"

As I wrote earlier, the apostle John's words in I John 1:9 characterized the "we align with God" posture and the "we agree with God" profession of true believers concerning sin and sinning. Unlike errant early gnostic unbelievers who said, "we have no sin," and, "we have not sinned," true believers, "*homologeō* our sins." They agreed with God, conceded that He was right concerning whatever He had said on the subject of sin and sinning, and openly acknowledged their agreement. As well, if they had thought, said, or done anything that God had characterized as sin, they agreed with Him and acknowledged that they had sinned. When John wrote his words, "If we confess (*homologeō*) our sins, he is faithful and just to forgive us our sins, and to cleanse us from all unrighteousness," he was communicating this message:

"If, unlike the individuals I characterized in I John 1:8 and I John 1:10, we are individuals who agree with God about sin and agree with God concerning our own sins, openly acknowledging that He is right about everything He has said concerning sin and sinning, it reveals that we are, indeed, true believers in relationship with God through faith in Jesus Christ. Because we are true believers, our covenant God will continue to forgive our sins and cleanse us from all unrighteousness."

I John 1:9 Was a Conditional Statement

Throughout his first epistle, the apostle John created a stark contrast between early gnostic error and New Covenant truth. He did this not only to expose the early gnostics and their dangerous error, but also to alert his spiritual children to the fact that they had choices to make concerning the errant teachings they were hearing and the ungodly influences they were experiencing. They could choose to abandon the truth they had embraced from the beginning and embrace error, speaking in disagreement with God and turning to an ungodly lifestyle in the dark, or they could choose to remain stead-fast in the truth they had embraced from the beginning, continue to agree with God and His Word on all matters, including the matter of sin and sinning, and continue their fellowship with Him in the light.

To make sure his spiritual children were aware of the serious dangers of early gnostic error and to prevent them from being seduced into that error and into a sinful lifestyle, John penned five consecutive "If we" conditional statements revealing to believers who they would be or would become depending on the choices they might make. He wrote,

> *"If we say that we have fellowship with him, and walk in darkness, we lie, and do not the truth: But if we walk in the light, as he is in the light, we have fellowship one with another, and the blood of Jesus Christ his Son cleanseth us from all sin. If we say that we have no sin, we deceive ourselves, and the truth is not in us. If we confess our sins, he is faithful and just to forgive us our sins, and to cleanse us from all unrighteousness. If we say that we have not sinned, we make him a liar, and his word is not in us."*
>
> *I John 1:6-10*

In these five verses, the words "we" and "us" referred to true believers, including the apostle John. John used the words "we" and "us" because his spiritual children were facing the danger of early gnostic error and were at risk of embracing that error and departing from the truth. His words in each of the five conditional "If we" state-ments in I John 1:6-10 revealed that his spiritual children were at risk of making a decision to depart from God's truth and to follow after error. He was doing everything in his power to prevent that from happening.

In each of his five conditional "If we" statements in I John 1:6-10, John was dealing with significant spiritual matters and revealing to his spiritual children that they had significant choices to make. In each statement, he presented what would be true of them if they chose to do what he had written in the cause clause of that statement. In his three negative "If we" statements—I John 1:6, 8, and 10—he informed believers that if they chose to do what he had written in the cause clause of those statements, they would be lying, they would be deceiving themselves, they would not be doing the truth, God's Word would not be in them, and they would be making God a liar. In his two positive "If we" statements—I John 1:7 and 9—he informed believers that if they chose to do what he had written in the cause clause of those statements, they would have true fellowship with one another, the blood of Jesus would continually cleanse them of their sin, and God, who was faithful and just, would forgive their sins and cleanse them from all unrighteousness. John's three negative "If we" statements in I John 1:6, 8, and 10 informed believers who they would be and what their life would look like if they chose to walk in darkness, to say they had no sin, and to say they had not sinned. His two positive "If we" statements in I John 1:7 and I John 1:9 informed believers who they would be and what their life would look like if they chose to continue their walk in the light and in fellowship with God and chose to continue to *homologeō* their sins.

John's "If we" statement in I John 1:9, like his other four "If we" statements, was a conditional statement, revealing what would be true of his spiritual children if they did what he wrote in the cause clause of that statement. John began his conditional statement in I John 1:9 with the word "If" because he was setting up a hypothetical situation for his spiritual children to consider. Rather than embracing early gnostic error, saying what they said and living how they lived (I John 1:6, I John 1:8, and I John 1:10), they should choose to, "*homologeō* our sins." They should agree with God by saying what He said about sin and by acknowledging that they had sinned if, indeed, they had sinned. John did not want his spiritual children to be deceived and say, "we have no sin," and, "we have not sinned" (I John 1:8 and 10). Rather, he wanted them to remain sound in God's truth and, "*homologeō* our sins" (I John 1:9). In other words, he wanted them to continue agreeing with God's Word on the subject of sin and sinning and, if they had missed the mark of God's will and sinned themselves, agree with God and acknowledge that they had sinned. Choosing to remain in this spiritual posture and choosing to continue the action of agreeing with God would reveal that they were, indeed, true believers. And because they were true believers, they would be forgiven of their sins and cleansed by their faithful and just God.

In his five conditional "If we" statements in I John 1:6-10, John was dealing with major doctrinal and lifestyle issues concerning sin and sinning. I John 1:9 was one of the five significant conditional "If we" statements he penned to alert his spiritual children to the reality that given the ungodly influence of the early gnostics in the region where they lived, they had serious choices to make. What were they going to do? Would they choose to abandon the truth they had embraced and join the early gnostics in their error and their ungodly lifestyle in the dark, saying what they said and living how they lived? Or would they choose to remain in agreement with God and with His Word, stay steadfast in the truth they had embraced from the beginning, walk with God in the light, and continue to *homologeō* their sins? The choice John wanted his spiritual children to make was expressed by his words in I John 1:7 and I John 1:9. He wanted them to continue their true fellowship with God in the light and continue to *homologeō* their sins. John hoped, and no doubt prayed, that his spiritual children would not be seduced by the dangerous error concerning sin and sinning they were being exposed to, but would continue steadfast in their walk in the light and continue to "*homologeō* our sins."

This insight into John's conditional "If we" statements in I John 1:6-10 aids us greatly as we endeavor to reach the most accurate interpretation and best understanding of what he was communicating to believers by his words in I John 1:9. The essence of the important choice he presented to his spiritual children in I John 1:9 could be expressed by this question:

"Will you choose to remain in alignment and in agreement with the truth of God you already embraced on the matter of sin and sinning and continue to be forgiven of your sins and cleansed from all unrighteousness, or will you choose to disagree with God's truth and His Word, embrace the error of the early gnostics, saying, 'we have no sin,' and, 'we have not sinned,' and be deceived, be void of God's truth and His Word, make God a liar, and return to a walk in darkness?"

I John 1:9 Was Not About Talking to God

Due to many years of thinking a certain way about John's words in I John 1:9, most believers, when reading or considering I John 1:9, unconsciously insert the words "to God" after the words, "If we confess our sins," and think, "If I admit my sins to God, He will forgive them." Most believers suppose that when John wrote, "If we confess our sins," he meant, "If we admit our sins to God," or, "If we ask God to forgive our sins." It is very important to note, however, that the apostle John did not write, "If we confess our sins to God." He wrote, "If we confess our sins." The unconscious inserting of the words, "to God," after the words, "If we confess our sins," has served to perpetuate the misunderstanding of John's words in I John 1:9, making it seem that he was informing believers that they had to say something to God about their sins before He would forgive their sins and cleanse them. The very important truth of the matter, however, is that John did not write anything in I John 1:9 about believers speaking to God.

Earlier in our study, we learned that the Greek word *homologeō* the apostle John used in I John 1:9 was also used several places in the gospels, was used by John in his gospel, was used in the book of Acts, and was used in several New Testament epistles other than John's first two epistles. Nowhere in any of those places did *homologeō* characterize the action of a person admitting to God the sins they had committed or characterize the action of a person asking God to forgive their sins. In fact, there is only one place in all the New Testament where *homologeō* might have characterized speaking to God; and that was in Hebrews 13:15. As we have learned, the word *homologeō* was used almost exclusively in the New Testament to describe the action of a person openly speaking before others their heart agreement with what God had said. For example, when John the Baptist confessed (*homolo-*

geō) that he was not the Christ, but was the voice of one crying in the wilderness, he was not speaking to God, but was speaking openly to others, expressing his personal convictions which were in agreement with what God had said about him in Scripture through the prophet Isaiah. As well, when Paul confessed (*homologeō*) at his trial, he was not speaking to God, but was speaking openly before men; speaking his convictions which were based upon and in agreement with what God had said in Scripture. And when Jesus said, "If you confess (*homologeō*) me before men," He was not describing a person speaking privately to God, but was describing a person's open declaration before others of their heart conviction which was in agreement with God's testimony about who Jesus was.

We also learned earlier in our study that the apostle John used the Greek word *homologeō* several places in his first two epistles other than in I John 1:9. Nowhere in those other places did he use *homologeō* to characterize a person admitting to God the sins they had committed or asking God to forgive them of their sins. Rather, in all the places he used *homologeō*, he used it to describe a person openly expressing their agreement with God and with what He had said. He used *homologeō* to describe a person's internal posture of alignment with God and their external action of speaking in agreement with what He had said; agreeing with His truth and His testimony and speaking with one voice with Him. For example, when John wrote, "Whosoever shall *homologeō* (confess) that Jesus is the Son of God, God dwelleth in him, and he in God," he was not describing the action of a person speaking privately to God about their sins, but was describing the action of a person openly acknowledging before others their heart conviction that Jesus was the Son of God, which conviction was in agreement with God's testimony. When he wrote, "he that *homologeō* (acknowledgeth) the Son hath the Father also," he was not describing a person privately asking God to forgive their sins, but was describing a person speaking openly and publicly before others about their heart agreement with God's testimony that Jesus of Nazareth was His Son.

In nearly every place in the New Testament and in every place in John's two epistles, individuals who *homologeō* (confessed) were not speaking to God, but were openly declaring their heart agreement with God before others; speaking with one voice with Him. To *homologeō* did not mean, then, "to speak privately to another person" but meant, "to openly speak one's heart agreement with another; that another usually being God."

We must give serious consideration to this very important fact concerning *homologeō* when interpreting John's words in I John 1:9. The reality of the matter is that if by his words, "If we *homologeō* our sins," John meant, "if we admit our sins to God," that would be the only place in the whole New Testament where the word *homologeō* was used to characterize a person privately admitting their sins to God. Even more importantly, that would be the only time the apostle John used the word *homologeō* to characterize a person privately admitting their sins to God, or speaking to God at all.

The way *homologeō* was used throughout the New Testament and the way *homologeō* was used by the apostle John in his first two epistles lends a great amount of support to my assertion that the familiar and commonly accepted interpretation of I John 1:9 is not the correct interpretation. Based on the dictionary definitions of *homologeō* and based on how *homologeō* was used throughout the New Testament, especially by the apostle John, it is highly unlikely that John intended his words, "If we confess (*homologeō*) our sins," to be understood to mean, "If we admit our sins to God," or, "If we ask God to forgive our sins." Rather, the way *homologeō* was used throughout the New Testament, especially by the apostle John in his first two epistles, strongly suggests that John's words, "If we confess our sins," referred to the action of true believers agreeing from their hearts with God about sin and sinning and openly speaking their agreement.

The fact that John did not include the words "to God" with the words, "If we confess our sins," and the substantial evidence we have discovered concerning how the word *homologeō* was employed throughout the New Testament and by the apostle John in his first two epistles strongly suggests that John's words, "If we confess our sins," did not refer to the action of believers privately admitting their sins to God so that they could be forgiven of those sins, but referred to the action of true believers agreeing with God and openly speaking their agreement with whatever He had said on the subject of sin and sinning; including agreeing with Him that they had sinned if they had thought, said, or done anything that He had characterized as sin.

The action of *"homologeō* our sins" in I John 1:9 was not, then, the action of believers privately admitting their sins to God in order to secure His forgiveness, but was the action of believers openly speaking their agreement with God on the subject of sin and sinning and openly speaking their agreement with God concerning any sins they had committed. The person who confessed (*homologeō*) their sins in I John 1:19 was not a believer who privately admitted their sins to God so that He would forgive their sins and cleanse them, but was a believer who openly acknowledged their internal alignment and agreement with God concerning sin and sinning and concerning their own sins.

Paraphrases of I John 1:9

Based on everything we have learned up to this point in our study, I am going to offer several paraphrases of John's words in I John 1:9. These paraphrases represent what I believe the apostle John intended for his spiritual children to understand by his words and will serve to reinforce and add more light to our growing understanding of I John 1:9.

Paraphrase of I John 1:9:

"But if we choose to align with God—with His truth and His Word—openly agreeing with what He has said about sin and about our sins, then we are true believers, standing steadfast in His truth and speaking in unison with Him. Because we are true believers in covenant with God—as clearly evidenced by the fact that we *homologeō* our sins—our covenant God will continue to be faithful and just in His actions toward us, forgiving our sins and cleansing us from all unrighteousness."

Paraphrase of I John 1:9:

"If—unlike those who disagree with God, saying that they
have no sin and saying that they have not sinned and who
are deceived and void of the truth—we agree with God's
truth that sin exists and that sinning occurs and agree and
acknowledge that we have sinned ourselves when we have,
in fact, sinned, we clearly identify ourselves as true believers. Because we are true believers, our covenant God will
be faithful and just toward us, forgiving us of any sins we
commit and cleansing us from all unrighteousness."

Paraphrase of I John 1:9:

"If, however, we are those who have come into internal alignment and speaking agreement with God and His truth about
sin and about our own sins and continue in that alignment
and agreement, then we represent ourselves to be true believers. Because we are true believers, we will continue to experience the benefits of the better New Covenant in Jesus' blood;
we will be forgiven of our sins and cleansed from all unrighteousness by our faithful and just God.

Paraphrase of I John 1:9:

"If, however, you choose to agree with God's Word concerning
sin and sinning and agree with Him when you have sinned,
and if you don't wander into error and deny God's Word on
the subject of sin and sinning, that confirms that you are,
indeed, a true believer. Because you are a true believer, you
can know with certainty that God will forgive you of any
sins you commit and cleanse you from any stain of unrighteousness. This wonderful New Covenant benefit belongs to
you through faith in Jesus Christ."

Paraphrase of I John 1:9:

"If, rather than disagreeing with God and His Word about sin and about your own sins, you *homologeō* your sins—if you submit to God's truth, align with Him, openly agree with Him about sin and sinning, and openly agree with Him that you have sinned when you have sinned—then you distinguish yourself as a true believer. As a true believer, you can be confident that your Father God will be faithful to His Word of promise and the oath that He swore and will be just in His actions toward you. He will continue to forgive your sins and cleanse you from any stain of unrighteousness according to His promises in the New Covenant."

Paraphrase of I John 1:9:

"But if, unlike the deniers and deceivers I characterized in I John 1:8 and I John 1:10, you "*homologeō* your sins"—you accept God's Word as truth, submit to His truth, and speak with one voice with Him concerning sin and your own sins—then as a true believer, you can be confident that God will be faithful to His promise and just in keeping covenant, forgiving you of any sins you commit and cleansing you from all unrighteousness."

Paraphrase of I John 1:9:

"If, on the other hand, we choose to remain 'aligners' and 'agreers' with God and continue to be 'confessors'—openly speaking our agreement with Him concerning sin and concerning our own sins—then we can be certain that God will be continually faithful to His promises and just in His actions toward us, forgiving us and cleansing us of any sins we commit."

Paraphrase of I John 1:9:

"But if, unlike the disagreers-deniers-unbelievers I characterized in I John 1:8 and I John 1:10, you are an agreer-con-fessor-believer, then you can be sure that your sins will be forgiven by your faithful and just Father. He will forgive your sins, not because you admit every one of them to Him in a private time of confession, but because you are an agreer-con-fessor-believer in covenant with Him through faith in His Son, Jesus Christ, and because He is faithful and just."

What Does I John 1:9 Really Mean?

Based on all the significant information we have gathered and all the meaningful insights we have gained in our study, I am confi-dent that John's words in I John 1:9 were neither an invitation to early gnostic sinners to be forgiven, to be cleansed of their sins, and to be saved or a teaching revealing to believers that in order to be forgiven and cleansed of sins they had committed, they were required to admit each and every one of those sins to God in a time of confession. John's words in I John 1:9 were, rather, an important conditional statement characterizing those who agreed with God about sin and sinning and about their own sins as true New Covenant believers whose sins were continually being forgiven and who were continually being cleansed from all unrighteousness. In stark contrast to early gnostic sinners who disagreed with God about sin and sinning, saying things like, "we have no sin," and, "we have not sinned," and who were character-ized by John as those who were deceived, who were void of truth, who were walking in darkness, and who were liars, true believers agreed with God about sin and sinning and agreed with God about their own sins—they "*homologeō* (their) sins"—and were characterized by John as those whose sins were being forgiven and who were continually being cleansed from all unrighteousness by their faithful and just God.

Contrary to the familiar and common interpretation of I John 1:9, the apostle John did not write his words in I John 1:9 to inform believ-ers about a New Testament practice they must engage in called "the confession of sins" where they would admit each of their sins to God so that He could forgive their sins and cleanse them. His words were not a revelation that a believer's admission of sins to God was a prerequisite for the forgiveness of their sins. John wrote his words in I John 1:9, rather, to inform his spiritual children who had already *homologeō* with God's message that Jesus of Nazareth was the Son of God, was the Christ, and was the Savior of the world that due to dangerous, errant teachings about sin and sinning being fostered in the region where they lived, they had a very important decision to make. Would they abandon the truth of God they had previously embraced and join the errant early gnostics saying things like, "we have no sin," and, "we have not sinned," or would they hold steady to God's truth, remain aligned with Him, and continue to speak in agreement with what He had said? Would they choose to disagree with what God had said about sin and sinning or would they, "*homologeō* our sins?"

John penned his words in I John 1:9 as part of his effort to expose early gnostic error concerning sin and sinning, to alert his spiritual children to that error, to refute that error, and to persuade believers he loved to remain steadfast in the faith and firm in the truth they had embraced. He wanted his spiritual children to remain aligned with God's Word and to continue speaking in agreement with His truth concerning sin and concerning their own sins. If they abandoned the truth and abandoned God's Word and joined the early gnostic sinners, then no matter what positive claims they made about themselves, they would be sinning, they would be in the dark, they would be deceived, and they would be void of God's Word and His truth. It is abundantly clear, based upon the many direct and disquieting statements John penned in his first epistle, including his important statement in I John 1:9, that he was endeavoring to arrest the attention of his spiritual children and persuade them to continue walking down the right path.

John wrote his words in I John 1:9 because he wanted his spiritual children to agree with God and with His Word and acknowledge that sin existed. He wanted them to agree with God and with His Word about what things were sins and openly express that agreement. And if they had sinned, he wanted them to agree with God and with His

Word and acknowledge that they had sinned. In other words, John wanted his spiritual children to *"homologeō* (their) sins." Rather than being carried away by the error of the early gnostics who disagreed with God, refused His truth, deceived themselves, lived as they wished, and said, "we have no sin," and, "we have not sinned," his spiritual children should, *"homologeō* our sins." They should concede that God was right about sin and sinning, should not refuse to accept as truth what He had said about sin and sinning, and should speak with one voice with Him, acknowledging that sin existed and acknowledging that they had sinned when they had sinned.

The action of confessing (*homologeō*) our sins that John expressed by his words in I John 1:9 was not, contrary to the common interpretation of I John 1:9, the action of a believer making required admissions to God of sins they had committed so that He would forgive their sins and cleanse them. The action of confessing (*homologeō*) our sins that John expressed by his words in I John 1:9 was not, contrary to the commonly accepted interpretation of I John 1:9, the action of believers making private requests to God in times of prayer, asking Him to forgive their sins. Rather, the action of confessing (*homologeō*) our sins that John expressed by his words in I John 1:9 was the action of believers taking and maintaining a spiritual stance of alignment with God and openly expressing their agreement with Him on the subject of sin and sinning and concerning their own sins. The voice believers spoke with when they *homologeō* our sins was not the voice of "sorrowfully admitting one's sins to God in private prayer" or the voice of "pleading with God for the forgiveness of one's sins," but was the voice of "openly agreeing with what God had said on the subject of sin and sinning and openly agreeing with God about one's own sins."

John's words, "If we confess our sins," in I John 1:9 did not describe a required spiritual activity believers must engage in so that God would forgive their sins. His words, rather, described the spiritual posture and the speaking in agreement action of true believers concerning whatever God had said on the subject of sin and sinning. If God said that sin exists, that the sin nature of men must be dealt with, and that men's sins must be forgiven and cleansed, true believers agreed with Him and "said the same thing." If God said concerning a specific thought, word, or deed, "That is a sin," true believers submitted to His truth, conceded that He was right, and said, "I agree with God; that thought, word, or deed is a sin." And if true believers thought, said, or did something that God had characterized as a sin, they acknowledged that He was right and said, "What I did was sin. I submit to God's Word and agree with Him. I have sinned."

What John was really expressing by his words in I John 1:9 was that unlike the errant early gnostics who openly disagreed with God on the subject of sin, claiming that they had no sin and that they did not sin, true believers did not deny that there was sin or deny that they had sinned when God's Word made it abundantly clear that all men were sinners and that they, themselves, had sinned. True believers were in allegiance with God and openly professed their agreement with whatever He had said about sin. If they had done something that God said was sin, they agreed with Him and acknowledged that they had sinned. They said, "I sinned. And I know that I sinned because God said in His Word that what I did is sin."

When true believers confess their sins in the way John intended his words to be understood, they are not engaging in a required spiritual practice of verbally admitting their sins to God so that He can forgive and cleanse them. They are not kneeling in contrition, admitting their guilt to God and requesting that He be merciful to them and forgive them. They are not prostrating themselves before God, sorrowfully expressing their guilt and enumerating their failings to Him in a required act of religious contrition so that they can secure absolution from Him. Rather, when true believers confess their sins in the way John intended his words to be understood, they are standing in alignment with God and speaking in agreement with God on the subject of sin and sinning and concerning their own sins. They are holding a posture of solidarity with God's Word and with God's truth on the subject of sin and sinning and openly professing that solidarity. They are "speaking with one voice with God" and are "in unison with Him" concerning the subject of sin and sinning and concerning their own sins.

Conclusion

For we who are true believers to confess our sins in the way the apostle John intended his words in I John 1:9 to be understood consists of nothing more and nothing less than for us to be aligned with God and with His Word on the subject of sin and sinning, to agree openly with His truth about what things are sins, and to agree with Him and acknowledge that we have sinned if we have thought, said, or done something that He characterized as sin. For we who are true believers to confess our sins is not for us to regularly and repeatedly engage in the practice of admitting our sins to God so that we can be forgiven, but is for us to hold a permanent posture of alignment with God and to openly speak our agreement with Him about sin and sinning.

For us to *homologeō* our sins is not to admit each and every sin we have committed to God in a time of confession hoping that He will forgive those sins. To *homologeō* our sins is not to admit our guilt to God in a private time of prayer and beseech Him to forgive our sins. To *homologeō* our sins, rather, is to agree with God on the subject of sin and to agree with Him that we have sinned if, in fact, we have done things that He has characterized as sin. To *homologeō* our sins is to openly acknowledge our agreement with God and with His Word, speaking with one voice with Him concerning sin and our own sins.

When we confess our sins in the way John meant his words to be understood, we are agreeing with God and His Word, openly saying the same things He has said about sin. If God said, "Being covetous is a sin," we say, "It is a sin to be covetous." And if we have been covetous, we acknowledge, "I have sinned because God said that being covetous is a sin." If God said, "Gossiping is sin," we say, "It is a sin to gossip." And if we have gossiped, we say, "I have sinned because God's Word says that gossiping is a sin." If God said, "Stealing is a sin," we say, "Stealing is a sin." And if we have stolen something, we acknowledge, "I have sinned because God said that stealing is a sin." As true believers, we do not disagree with God about what sin is and we don't refuse to acknowledge that we have sinned when His Word makes it clear that we have sinned. Rather, we agree with God and openly acknowledge our agreement. That is what John meant by his words in I John 1:9. And that is what it really means to "confess our sins."

Fortunately for true believers and for the whole church, the familiar and commonly accepted interpretation of I John 1:9 is not the correct interpretation. There is, in fact, no God-ordained or God-required New Covenant spiritual practice called "the confession of sins" that believers must engage in before they can be forgiven of sins they have committed. John's words in I John 1:9 are not a teaching that believers must admit every one of their sins to God before He will forgive their sins and cleanse them. His words in I John 1:9, rather, characterize the action of true believers openly agreeing with what God has said about sin and sinning and openly agreeing with God when they have sinned.

XII

What Should I Do If I Have Sinned?

Throughout this study, we have learned important truths about I John 1:9 and about John's first epistle. In the previous chapter, I summarized our study up to this point and offered an interpretation of I John 1:9 that is sound and accurate, that is supported by its general and immediate contexts, and that harmonizes with the teachings of the New Testament and with all Scripture. The interpretation I offered is consistent with the way the Greek word *homologeō* was used throughout the New Testament and is in agreement with the way John used *homologeō* in his first two epistles. The interpretation I offered fits very well with the purpose of John's first epistle, fits beautifully with the other conditional statements he penned in his polemic against early gnostic error on the subject of sin and sinning, and makes perfect sense in its general and immediate contexts. The interpretation I offered is also harmonious with the teachings of the New Testament epistles and their emphasis on the complete success of Jesus' finished work in undoing the necessity of any of man's works to receive and to maintain righteousness and right standing with God. The interpretation of I John 1:9 I offered will set believers free from unnecessary ritual and needless fear and can serve as an important building block in believers' foundation of full confidence in God and in the complete and eternal salvation He provided through His Son, Jesus Christ.

If you have previously embraced either the most common interpretation of I John 1:9—that believers must admit to God each and every sin they commit in order to be forgiven and cleansed of those sins—or the less common interpretation—that I John 1:9 and the first chapter of John's first epistle was written to early gnostic sinners as an evangelistic message—hopefully this study has enriched your understanding and enlightened your mind as to what I John 1:9 really means. As we are concluding our study, you might be asking yourself, "What should I do with the insights I have gained from this study? How can I incorporate what I have learned into my daily Christian life and into my relationship with God? And if I don't have to admit to God each and every sin I commit in order to be forgiven of those sins, what should I do if I have sinned or am sinning?" In this final chapter, I will address these questions and show you how to implement what you have learned into your daily Christian life; especially focusing on how you should relate to God if you have sinned or if you are living a lifestyle of sin.

No Confession Sessions Are Necessary

My main objective in writing this book was to set forth an argument based on Scriptural and historical information to make it clear that neither the most common and familiar interpretation of I John 1:9—that believers must admit to God each and every sin they have committed in order to be forgiven and cleansed of those sins—or the less common interpretation of I John 1:9—that John's words in I John 1:9 were an invitation to gnostic sinners to be saved—are correct interpretations. Rather, as I argued throughout this study, John's words in I John 1:9 were one of several important conditional statements he penned in his first epistle revealing that given the significant influence of the early gnostics in the region, believers had a choice to make about what they would believe and say about sin and sinning and how they would live. The choice they should make, rather than agreeing with the early gnostics and disagreeing with God, saying, "we have no sin," and, "we have not sinned," was to, "*homologeō* our sins." Rather than following the early gnostics in their error, true believers should remain aligned with God and with His Word, remain submitted to His truth, and continue to speak in agreement with Him on all matters concerning sin and sinning; including their own sins.

In the wonderful New Covenant, the forgiveness of believers' sins is not set in motion only if and only after they complete a required act called "The confession of sins to God." In other words, God does not refuse to forgive believers of their sins until after they have admitted their sins to Him in a time of confession. Rather, in the New Covenant, God forgives believers' sins because of the finished work of His Son Jesus Christ, because of the blood that He shed on the cross, and because of His current role as advocate with the Father and the propitiation for believers' sins. God forgives the sins of His sons and daughters, not as a merciful response to their admission of sins, but because He is faithful to His own promises and just to follow the terms of the New Covenant that He planned and which His Son Jesus brought into force through the shedding of His blood and His death. God is not, then, merciful and kind to forgive believers' sins after they obediently admit their sins to Him in a time of confession. Rather, God is faithful and just to forgive believers' sins because the New Covenant He designed and that His Son Jesus brought into force through the shedding of His blood and His death put everything in place that is necessary for the forgiveness and cleansing of sins that believers commit.

We learned in chapter five that the Greek word *homologeō* was never used in the New Testament to represent the action of a person privately admitting their sins to God in order to be forgiven or of asking God to forgive their sins. In Scripture, the action of making requests to God for anything were always described by verbs like "ask," "beseech," "supplicate," "request," or "implore." What does this important information tell us about what John meant by his words, "If we *homologeō* our sins?" It tells us that his words, "If we *homologeō* our sins," do not represent the action of believers privately admitting their sins to God so that they can be forgiven or the action of asking God to forgive their sins.

Along these lines, we can consider John's words to his spiritual children in I John 2:1-2; paying close attention not only to what he did say in those verses, but also taking careful note of what he did not say. He wrote,

"My little children, these things write I unto you, that ye sin not.

> *And if any man sin, we have an advocate with the Father, Jesus*
> *Christ the righteous: And he is the propitiation for our sins: and not*
> *for ours only, but also for the sins of the whole world."*
>
> *I John 2:1-2*

Notice that in these important words to his spiritual children, John did not write, "And if any man sin, he must confess his sin to God so that God can forgive his sin and cleanse him." In the most direct and clear words from his first epistle concerning believers sinning, the apostle John said nothing about what believers must do if they sinned. He said nothing to his spiritual children about the necessity of confessing their sins to God so that they could be forgiven. Rather, he followed his words, "And if any man sin," by referring to the remedy God had already put in place for them if they sinned. Rather than informing believers that if they sinned, they must admit their sins to God, he informed them that if they sinned, they had an advocate with the Father and a propitiation for their sins. John's words in I John 2:1-2 are very important words to consider, not only because of the important things he revealed concerning what God prepared and put in place for believers if they sinned, but also because he said nothing to his spiritual children about what they must do if they sinned. He most certainly did not tell them, "If you have sinned, you must confess your sins to God."

It is absolutely essential to understand and embrace the important truth that as New Covenant believers, we are not forgiven of sins we commit only if and only after we fulfill a required action of admitting our sins to God or a required action of asking God to forgive us. The forgiveness of our sins is not dependent upon us confessing our sins. There is, in fact, no confession of sins practice taught in the New Covenant that is required to initiate God's action of forgiving our sins. The forgiveness of the sins we commit is not dependent upon our admission of those sins to God, but is part and parcel of the New Covenant provision that the all wise Father God put in place for us. We are forgiven of sins we commit because long ago God put the divine remedy in place for the forgiveness of sins we would commit. God forgives our sins, not because we admit our sins to Him or because we humbly ask Him for forgiveness, but because of the past work of His Son, Jesus Christ in His death and resurrection and in the shedding of His blood and because of His present work as advocate with the Father and the propitiation for our sins. God forgives our sins, not because we obediently confess our sins to Him, but because He is faithful and just.

As a New Covenant believer, you are not required to list the sins you have committed and enumerate those sins to God in a sorrowful manner during a "time of confession" in order to qualify yourself to be forgiven and cleansed of those sins. You do not need to "put on sackcloth and ashes" in an act of contrition, tearfully asking God to forgive you, pulling on His emotions and trying to persuade Him to be merciful. You do not have to follow the teaching of the Catholic church and "go to confession" to tell your sins to a priest in order to be absolved of those sins. You don't need to be afraid that if you didn't confess a specific sin to God or didn't ask Him to forgive you of a specific sin, you have unconfessed sin in your life that will cause bad things to happen to you, that will remove God's protection over your life, that will cause God to ignore your prayers, or that will put your eternal destiny at risk. The truth of the matter is that there is no teaching in the New Testament, including in I John 1:9, that instructs you to engage in an accounting of your sins to God in a practice called "The confession of sins" so that He will you forgive you and cleanse you of sins you have committed.

This truth I am stating—that New Covenant believers are not required to admit each and every sin they have committed to God or required to ask God to forgive them of specific sins before He will forgive those sins—is the significant New Covenant truth I am presenting in this study. This important truth does not mean, however, that sin does not matter. This important truth does not mean that God winks at sin and does not care if you sin. And this important truth does not mean that you shouldn't say something to God about your sin or shouldn't make any serious decisions about changing your life if you are sinning. Sin and sinning do matter to God; and sin and sinning should matter to you.

Since the forgiveness of sins we commit is not predicated upon, initiated by, or dependent upon our admission of those sins to God or by asking Him to forgive those sins, what should we do if we have sinned? How should we interact with our Father and with our Lord Jesus? What should we say to them? And what should we do if we have been living a consistently sinful lifestyle? Throughout the remainder of this chapter, I will provide answers to these questions and address other important matters concerning sin and sinning.

You Should Experience Conviction if You Sin

Contrary to what some seem to think, believers are not delivered from having a conscience when they are saved. It could be, and perhaps it should be, that a believer's consciousness of sins they commit is actually heightened after they are saved. After all, their heart is no longer a heart of stone, but of flesh. They have a new inner nature that is righteous and the Holy Spirit of God is living in them. And if they are receiving God's Word and renewing their minds to His truth, they will become more conscious of His will and know when they are violating it. Those who are truly born of God, who share His nature, who have the Holy Spirit living in them, who love God, and who are learning His ways will desire to, "do those things that are pleasing in his sight" (Colossians 1:10). And they will know in their hearts and in their conscience when they are not doing those things.

Some ministers teach that when a believer feels guilty for sinning or has any sense of shame or remorse if they have sinned, they are too sin conscious. These ministers, often leaning on two passages from the epistle to the Hebrews, suggest that for a believer to have any sense of guilt, any remorse, or any shame when they have sinned is not a good thing. One of these passages says,

> "How much more shall the blood of Christ, who through the eternal Spirit offered himself without spot to God, purge your conscience from dead works to serve the living God?"
>
> Hebrews 9:14

In this passage, the author of Hebrews revealed one of the wonderful and powerful effects of Jesus' blood upon a person who is saved. He said that the blood of Christ purges a person's conscience from dead works. Notice, however, that the writer did not say that the blood of Christ delivers believers from having a conscience. He also did not say that the blood of Christ purged the believer's conscience from any feelings of guilt if they sinned. He said, rather, that the blood of Christ purged the believer's conscience, "from dead works to serve the living God." In other words, after a person is born of God, is cleansed of their sins by Jesus' blood, and has received a new nature, they are no longer fixated on participating in works of darkness or focused on fulfilling their own selfish desires, but are attuned to the things of God, desiring to serve Him.

Some ministers also lean a little too heavily on this passage from Hebrews,

> *"For the law having a shadow of good things to come, and not the very image of the things, can never with those sacrifices which they offered year by year continually make the comers thereunto perfect. For then would they not have ceased to be offered? because that the worshipers once purged should have had no more conscience of sins."*
>
> *Hebrews 10:1-2*

This passage confirms that Old Covenant sacrifices were unable to cleanse a person from sin, stating that if those sacrifices had been enough, "the worshipers once purged should have had no more conscience of sins." This passage also points to the complete effectiveness of the one time sacrifice of Jesus Christ. The application of His blood to the lives of those who come to God through faith results in them no longer being overwhelmed by a guilty conscience for past sins that have been completely cleansed. They understand that they have been washed in Jesus' blood, that their sins have been forgiven, that their hearts have been made new, and that they have right standing with God.

True believers experience a great sense of relief in their conscience knowing that they are delivered from the debt of sin they could not pay, are cleansed from the deep stain of sin that could not be washed away by animal sacrifices or by any good works, and are no longer unclean before God. The strong and persistent guilty conscience that once accompanied being unsaved, unreconciled, and unclean has been removed. This is the purging of the conscience that the writer of Hebrews was referring to. Having one's conscience purged from dead works and from the persistent sense of guilt does not mean, however, that believers should have no conscience at all or mean that they should never have a sense of guilt or remorse if they sin.

Certainly, New Testament believers should not live in fear like some of God's Old Covenant saints who realized that the sacrifices offered for the cleansing of their sins brought only a temporary covering of those sins. When they committed more sins, more sacrifices were necessary. In the far better New Covenant, saints have been cleansed of all their past sins and provision is in place for the forgiveness and cleansing of any sins they commit after they are saved. When believers are taught correctly concerning these glorious truths, they will be confident and heart-light because they know that they have been cleansed from all their past sins, know that they will be cleansed of any sins they commit in the future, know that they are completely free from the penalty of sin, and know that they have permanent right standing with God. That is what it really means to, "(have) no more conscience of sins."

When a person is saved, all their past sins are forgiven, all their debts are paid, they are completely cleansed from the stain of sin, and they have legal right standing with God. This revelation of the forgiveness of sins and of the divine cleansing that occurred by the blood of Jesus Christ sets believers' minds free from the heavy burden of being guilty before God. Those who have been cleansed of their sins need not live with an overwhelming guilty consciousness or sin consciousness, but should be conscious of their cleanness and of all the wonderful realities of their new life in Christ. They should be conscious that they are forgiven of all their past sins, that they are righteous in their new nature, that they are reconciled to the Father, that they are sons and daughters of God, and that they are children of the light.

While it is absolutely true that believers have been cleansed of all their past sins, made righteous, and set free from the penalty of their sins, it is not true that believers have been set free from having a conscience. If believers sin, their conscience should know that they have sinned. They should not interpret every guilty feeling as a sin consciousness trying to rule them or Satan trying to condemn them. When believers sin, they should know in their conscience that they have done wrong and they should experience a sense of remorse and regret. Why should believers have these feelings? Because they are born of their Father God and have His nature. Their heart of stone has been removed and their new heart is sensitive to God. And the Holy Spirit of God now lives in them. When true believers sin, the indwelling Holy Spirit, their new righteous nature, and their conscience will notify them that they have sinned. And because they realize that they have sinned, they will feel remorse and may feel ashamed.

Sometimes I hear ministers say, "Believers should not be sin conscious." Without a doubt, there is some truth in their words. Believers should not have such a pervasive consciousness of already forgiven sins that they worry and fear, wondering if their old sins and maybe even some of their more recent sins have not been forgiven and that they are unclean and unrighteous before God. If believers are constantly burdened with persistent guilty thinking concerning past sins, they are, in fact, too sin conscious and not conscious enough of what God has done for them in Christ. Some ministers, however, have gone too far, suggesting that if believers have any feelings of guilt, any sense of shame, or any remorse for wrong doing, they are too sin conscious. Some ministers even recommend that believers refuse any guilty feelings because they have "been set free from a sin consciousness." Others say that any feelings of guilt or shame that believers experience when they have sinned is just, "Satan, the accuser, trying to condemn you."

Some believers, not wanting to be sin conscious because they have heard wrong teaching along these lines or because they don't like the feelings of guilt, may actually ignore signals from their own hearts or from the Holy Spirit notifying them that they have sinned. If believers continually ignore the voice of their conscience, they can sear their conscience and become insensitive to it (I Timothy 4:2). If believers ignore the witness of the Holy Spirit, they might grieve Him (Ephesians 4:30). Believers should be careful, then, about going too far with attempts to have no consciousness of sin if they have sinned. They should not try so hard to quench guilty feelings or a sense of remorse that they become unaware of when they are sinning.

It is important to understand that if your conscience is guilty because you have sinned, that is not a bad thing. In fact, that is actually a good thing. The voice of your conscience is not something you should ignore because you are worried that you might be too sin conscious. There is, after all, a significant difference between "being too sin conscious" and "having a conscience." While you should not be overwhelmed with guilty feelings because of sins you committed before you were saved or because of more recent sins you may have committed, you should have a conscience and you should pay attention to it. A careful and balanced posture must be reached in this important area of spiritual life lest you ignore messages coming from your own heart, from the Father God, from the Lord Jesus, and from the Holy Spirit informing you that you missed the mark and sinned.

Your Heart May Condemn You

In his first epistle, the apostle John wrote these enlightening words about how believers' own hearts would notify them if things were out of order in their lives,

> "For if our heart condemn us, God is greater than our heart, and knoweth all things. Beloved, if our heart condemn us not, then have we confidence toward God. And whatsoever we ask, we receive of him, because we keep his commandments, and do those things that are pleasing in his sight.
>
> I John 3:20-22

The English word "condemn" in these verses is translated from the Greek word *kataginōskō*. *Kataginōskō* most commonly means, "to find fault, to blame, to show that something is wrong." It comes from the prefix *kata* which means, "according to, or from," and the word *ginōskō* which means, "to learn, to know, to gain knowledge of, to perceive, or to feel." The word *kataginōskō* suggests a communication of knowledge or information from another source. This meaning of *kataginōskō* and how it is used in the context of John's words in I John 3:20-22 suggests that when a believer's heart condemns them, information is being transmitted from their heart—from their conscience, from their inner man—to their thinking mind. This message from the heart informing the mind that something wrong has been thought, something wrong has been said, or something wrong has been done causes a sense of guilt or a feeling of remorse.

The beautiful truth John revealed in I John 3:20-22 was that a believer's own heart would notify them when they had thought wrong, spoken wrong, or done wrong. Their inner man—their new heart and righteous spirit—would alert their thinking mind that something was not right in their walk with God. It would inform them that they were out of alignment, were not living as they should, and were sinning. John indicated that this message from a believer's heart to their thinking mind—this *kataginōskō*—could negatively impact their confidence toward God; especially in the area of asking and receiving from Him.

According to John, it could also be the case that a believer's heart did not condemn them. If a believer's heart did not condemn them, it meant that their inner man—their born again spirit; their renewed conscience—had no negative message to send to their thinking mind to inform them that they were out of alignment with God, living unrighteously, walking in darkness, or sinning. When a believer was thinking right, behaving righteously, walking in the light, and living in agreement with God's Word, there would be no alerting message from their heart to notify them that they were out of alignment with the Father and there would be no sense of guilt about how they were living. According to John, the believer whose heart did not condemn them had, "confidence toward God." In other words, they had confidence to approach God, to ask for things in prayer, and to receive the things they asked for because they knew in their heart that they were living in a way that pleased Him.

John's enlightening words in I John 3:20-22 reveal that true believers can know from their own conscience if they are thinking, speaking, or living in ways that are not in agreement with God's will. They can know from the witness of their own hearts if they are not pleasing their heavenly Father. John's words also reveal that true believers can know from their hearts, from their inner man, from their own conscience, when they are walking righteously, living in agreement with the will of God, and pleasing their heavenly Father.

Interestingly, Paul used the word *kataginōskō* in his letter to the Galatians in reference to a situation where he publicly corrected Peter. He wrote,

> *"But when Peter was come to Antioch, I withstood him to the face, because he was to be blamed* (kataginōskō).*"*
>
> *Galatians 2:11*

During a visit to Antioch, the apostle Peter had happily fellowshipped with Gentile believers, even eating meals with them. But when Jewish believers connected to James came from Jerusalem to Antioch, Peter became worried about what they would think of him associating with Gentile believers and so he stopped fellowshipping with them. Others, including Barnabas, followed Peter's example. Paul publicly rebuked Peter for his hypocrisy and later informed the Galatians when he wrote, "I withstood him (Peter) to the face, because he was to be blamed (*kataginōskō*)."

What was it that Paul did when he "blamed" (*kataginōskō*) Peter? He communicated a message to Peter showing him that his thinking was wrong and how he had acted was wrong. When Paul "blamed" Peter, he didn't tell him that he was a terrible person, say that there was no hope for him, or suggest that he would be punished for his hypocrisy. He simply notified Peter that what he had done was wrong.

This *kataginōskō* from Paul to Peter—this revealing and corrective message from another source—afforded Peter an opportunity make a correction in his thinking and change the way he behaved toward Gentile believers.

The condemning (*kataginōskō*) that a believer's heart might do is not intended to produce feelings of overwhelming guilt and shame, but to reveal wrong thinking, wrong speaking, or wrong acting so that believers can make important corrections in their lives. The purpose of the *kataginōskō* is to notify a believer that something is out of order in their life so that changes can be made.

There is a beautiful statement in I John 3:20-22 that I want to point your attention to. John wrote,

> *"For if our heart condemn* (kataginōskō) *us, God is greater than our heart, and knoweth all things."*
>
> *I John 3:20*

The apostle John expressed a glorious truth in this verse. He said that even if our hearts condemn us, God is greater than our hearts and knows all things. What does that mean? It means that God is not going to refuse our requests, ignore our cries, or turn His back on us until everything is in perfect order in our lives. Our Father God is not like that. He is very sympathetic. He knows that we are human and understands that we have weaknesses. He knows we will not always do things perfectly. He knows that we will fail. He knows that we will sin. And our Father God is greater than our hearts, even when our hearts condemns us. He will not to deal with us according to our failures or according to our sins, but according to His own nature and according to the New Covenant He made with us through Jesus Christ.

Always remember that even if your heart condemns you—if your heart is informing you that you have sinned and that things are out of order in your life—you should not fall into a funk or into a depression, supposing that everything is ruined in your relationship with God and that He is going to refuse your prayers, punish you, or reject you. Your heart might be informing you that you are out of alignment with

Him and what your heart is telling you may be absolutely true. But God is greater than your heart. He knows everything. He is faithful and true. And He is your Father!

If you are lacking confidence because you know that you have missed the mark and sinned, remember that God is greater than your heart and realize that He understands everything. Just trust His love, rest steadfast in faith in the better New Covenant, make necessary corrections in your life, and remember that your confidence should always be in your faithful Father God and in His Word, not in your own performance.

You Should Homologeō With God

One of the important things we learned in our study is that throughout his first two epistles, the apostle John employed the Greek word *homologeō* to help him reveal the stark contrast between early gnostic error and their ungodly lifestyle in the dark and Christian truth and the godly lifestyle of true believers in the light. According to John, the early gnostics did not *homologeō* with God. They disagreed with Him, did not align with His truth, denied what He had said, and did not embrace His Word. They did not *homologeō* with the record God gave of His Son; that eternal life was to be found in Him (I John 5:11). They did not *homologeō* with God that Jesus of Nazareth was His Son and Savior of the world (I John 4:14). They did not *homologeō* with the witness of the Holy Spirit that Jesus was the Christ and did not *homologeō* with God's testimony that Jesus was God manifested in the flesh (I John 2:22, 4:3). They also did not *homologeō* with God on the subject of sin or concerning their own sins. In fact, on the matter of sin and sinning, they disagreed with God completely, saying, "we have no sin," and, "we have not sinned" (I John 1:8, 10).

True believers, in stark contrast to the early gnostics, did *homologeō* with God. They embraced His Word and agreed with His truth; speaking with one voice with Him. They did not refuse His testimony about His Son, but conceded that He was right (I John 2:23; 5:10). They believed God's record that He had sent His own Son to earth to suffer and die and to be raised again from the dead as Savior of the world; defeating death, destroying the works of the devil, and overcoming the travesty of sin (I John 4:14-15). They *homologeō* with the witness of the Holy Spirit that Jesus was the Christ (I John 2:22, 4:3) and *homologeō* with God that Jesus of Nazareth was, indeed, God manifested in the flesh. True believers also *homologeō* their sins (I John 1:9). They did not deny God's truth that men were sinners or disagree with God's testimony that He had sent His Son to earth to save men from their sins. They did not claim, "we have no sin," disagreeing with God's Word that all men were sinners in need of a Savior, or say, "we have not sinned," when, according to God's Word, they had sinned. True believers agreed with God about sin and sinning and about their own sins; true believers "*homologeō* our sins."

Christianity is often called, "The great profession." It has come to be known by those beautiful words because one of the most significant characteristics of true believers is that they align themselves from the heart with God—with His truth and with His Word—and they boldly, openly, and joyfully profess their agreement with Him. One of the meanings of *homologeō* is, "to declare something openly because one is deeply convicted of facts that have been presented." True believers do this very thing. They live with a strong heart conviction that whatever God has said in His Word is the truth and they speak out openly; even if their open profession results in rejection, mocking, persecution, or death.

One very important thing we can glean from our study is an awareness that a very significant aspect of authentic Christianity is to *homologeō* with God. True believers agree with God and with His testimony as set forth in His written Word and they openly express their agreement. True believers do not deny that God is right and do not disagree with what He has said. True believers concede that what God has said is true and openly say the same things. True believers submit themselves to God's truth, even if they don't like all of it, just as a defeated army submits to the terms of surrender the victorious army offers. True believers speak with one voice with God, joyfully

declaring their fidelity to Him and expressing their allegiance to what
He has spoken. True believers align with God from their hearts, utter-
ing a bold "Amen" to everything He has said. True believers *homologeō*!

The apostle John expressed his ardent desire that his spiritual
children remain steadfast in their agreement with God when he wrote
these words,

> *"Let that therefore abide in you, which ye have heard from the begin-*
> *ning. If that which ye have heard from the beginning shall remain in*
> *you, ye also shall continue in the Son, and in the Father."*
>
> I John 2:24

John exhorted believers to make sure that the truth they had
heard from the beginning continued to abide in them. He informed
them that if what they had heard from the beginning, "shall remain in
you," they would, "continue in the Son, and in the Father." The English
word "remain" in I John 2:24 comes from the Greek *menō* which means,
"to not depart." John did not want his spiritual children to depart from
the foundational truths they had heard and embraced from the beginning and run after unsound doctrines that would subvert their beliefs
and lead them into ungodly living. He wanted believers to continue in
the truth, to continue to *homologeō*, and to, "continue in the Son, and in
the Father."

This essential aspect of Christianity—the internal posture of
alignment with God and the vocal action of *homologeō*—was not something that the apostle John originated, but it was something he emphasized in his first and second epistles. A willingness to agree with God
has always been an essential aspect of a right relationship with Him.
Quoting Old Testament Scripture in His defense against Satan's temptations, Jesus stated that man should not live by bread alone, but by,
"every word which proceedeth out of the mouth of God" (Luke 4:4).
The English words, "every word," come from the Greek *pas rhema*
which means, "each and every single word." True believers receive,
embrace, submit to, align with, speak in agreement with, and live in
agreement with each and every single word God has spoken. True
believers *homologeō*!

One of the most distinguishing marks of true Christianity and one of the things that will always be challenged by both men and demons, no matter the geography or calendar date, is the absolutely essential aspect of *homologeō* with God. In every generation and in every place, one of the great challenges believers will face is the challenge to *homologeō* with God concerning everything He has said; to *homologeō* with everything written in His Word. This is a challenge you will face as well. Will you *homologeō* with God? Or will you refuse to agree with what He has said and not concede that He is right? Will you align with God and with His Word—with all the truth He has spoken—or will you be so "enlightened" and so "up to date" and so "relevant" that you fall out of alignment with Him and no longer agree with what He has said?

One of the significant take aways from this study is to understand that as true believers, we must posture ourselves in alignment with God on all things and remain in alignment with God on all things; including the important subject of sin and sinning. We must not be afraid to openly acknowledge our agreement with Him. We must not hesitate to speak with one voice with Him and to boldly say the same things He has said. We must not waffle about and be double minded, trying to straddle the fence, picking and choosing what things we prefer to agree with Him about. We must make up our minds to always align with Him, to always align with His Word, and to say with David,

"I esteem all thy precepts concerning all things to be right; and I hate every false way."

Psalm 119:128

As true believers, we must *homologeō* with God. Why? Because that is what true believers do!

You Should Homologeō Your Sins

As we have learned throughout our study, John's words, "If we confess (*homologeō*) our sins," referred to believers agreeing with God and speaking their agreement with Him on the subject of sin and sinning in general and agreeing with God and acknowledging that they had sinned if they had thought, said, or done anything He had characterized as sin. The apostle John wrote his words in I John 1:9 to characterize for his spiritual children what true believers looked like and what true believers said and did. He did not want his spiritual children to be deceived and to follow the early gnostics who said, "we have no sin," and, "we have not sinned." He wanted them, rather, to, "*homologeō* our sins." He wanted them to remain in agreement with whatever God had said on the subject of sin and sinning and to agree with God that they had sinned if, according to His Word, they had sinned. He wanted them to be agreers with what God had said, not to be deniers of what God had said.

One thing that is being robustly challenged in this generation is the veracity and the applicability of what God has said in His written Word on the subject of sin and sinning. Many who say that they are in fellowship with God and claim to be walking in the light do not *homologeō* with God on the subject of sin. Many, in fact, are doing exactly what the early gnostics did. While making claims like, "We are in fellowship with God; we are enlightened; we have not sinned," they are living in disagreement with what God has clearly said in His Word and breaking His commandments. Some errantly think they are more enlightened and more up to date and more relevant than others and suppose that they know God in a more profound way than "starchy, fundamental, old-fashioned, Bible thumping, religious believers."

If you are a true believer in relationship with God through faith in Jesus Christ, you must "*homologeō* your sins." In other words, you must submit and align yourself with God, with His Word, and with His truth on the subject of sin and sinning. If God says that sin exists and that men are sinners and need a Savior, you must *homologeō* and say, "Yes, sin exists and men are sinners and need a Savior." If God's Word characterizes a particular deed as a sin, you must not disagree with Him and say, "Well, I just don't think that particular deed is a sin." You must *homologeō*, rather, and say, "If God said that is a sin, then it is a sin." As well, if you think, say, or do something that God has characterized as a sin, you must not say, "I have not sinned," but must *homol-ogeō* your sins. You must submit to God and agree with His Word and say, "God said in His Word that what I did is a sin. I agree with Him. What I did is a sin. I have sinned."

To *homologeō* your sins in the way John intended his words in I John 1:9 to be understood is to do the same thing you did when you first *homologeō* that Jesus of Nazareth was Lord and Savior. You heard the gospel—God's message about who Jesus was and what He had done—and responded from your heart in agreement with His message, saying the same thing. You confessed with your mouth, "I believe that God loves me and that He sent His Son, Jesus, to die for my sins." This is the essence of *homologeō* and is precisely what you do when you *homologeō* your sins. You hear the message of truth God has set forth in His Word about sin and sinning and you respond from your heart in agreement with Him; you say the same thing. If you have lied, you agree with God and say, "I have sinned because God said in His Word that lying is a sin." If you have gossiped about others, you don't say, "Well, a little chit chat about someone doesn't really hurt." You agree with God, rather, and say, "I know that I have sinned because Scripture reveals that gossip is a sin." If you are coveting your neighbor's new car, you don't say, "Well, just because I envy him for his success and want his car, that doesn't mean I have done anything wrong." You realize, rather, that according to God's Word, you are coveting; you are sinning. And you say, "I have been coveting. That is wrong; that is sin." If you have sinned, you don't deny it, try to excuse it, or say with the early gnostics, "(I) have not sinned." Rather, you *homologeō* your sins.

If you are currently living a lifestyle of sinning, but are saying to others or to yourself, "I have not sinned," or, "I don't agree with Scripture that what I am doing is a sin," then you are not *homologeō* your sins. You are refusing, denying, and not conceding that God is right and not agreeing that His Word is the truth. If, for example, you lie persistently, but say, "It's no big deal; people lie all the time; I'm basically a good person," you are not *homologeō* your sins. If you use harsh or demeaning words toward others, but say, "Well, they got what they deserved; all I did was tell them the truth about how horrible they are," you are not *homologeō* your sins. If you are living a lifestyle that God has clearly revealed in His Word to be sin—being drunk, committing adultery, being a glutton, always in strife with others, living a homosexual life, gossiping, jealous, prideful, or full of covetousness—and you won't submit to what the Scriptures say and agree with God that these things are sins and that you are sinning, then you are not *homologeō* your sins.

True believers *"homologeō* our sins." That doesn't mean, as we have learned, that true believers must admit each and every one of their sins to God in a special "confession session" in order to persuade Him to extend His mercy and forgive them. It means, rather, that true believers agree with God and agree with His Word about what sin is and agree with God and agree with His Word that they have sinned if, in fact, they have thought, said, or done something that His Word reveals to be a sin. It means that believers posture their hearts in alignment with God's truth concerning sin and sinning and openly acknowledge that they have sinned if they have thought, said, or done something that He characterized as sin.

Do not refuse to *homologeō* your sins. In other words, agree with God's Word about sin and sinning and do not deny that you sinned if you sinned, but acknowledge that you sinned. Be synchronized with God and "sing in unison with Him" on the matter of sin and sinning and concerning your own sins. Don't be a sin denier or a sin disagreer or a sin excuser or a sin explainer. Rather, be a sin confessor and *homologeō* your sins because that is what true believers do!

You Should Apologize to God if You Sin

Understanding that in I John 1:9, John was not teaching that believers must admit each and every sin they commit to God in order to be forgiven and cleansed of those sins, how should we relate to God if we have sinned? Should we be sorrowful for our sins? Should we apologize to God if we have sinned ? Should we repent of our sins? If John's words in I John 1:9 do not mean that we must verbally admit our sins to God in order to be forgiven and cleansed of those sins, then what should we do if we sin? Should we go on living as if nothing happened? Should we speak to God about our sins and make things right in our fellowship? How should we relate to our heavenly Father and to our Lord Jesus if we have sinned and offended them?

Along these lines, it is important for us to remember that although our relationship with God is founded upon a very secure legal contract, our relationship with Him is not just about that legal contract. Jesus didn't come to earth, suffer, shed His blood, die, and rise again from the dead just to procure for us a legal and binding contract with God. He also didn't shed His blood on the cross just to deliver us from hell and open the way for us to live in a better place called heaven after we die. Jesus also suffered, shed His blood on the cross, died, and rose again from the dead to remove the insurmountable impediment of sin that stood between us and God so that we could enter into beautiful fellowship with the Father and with His Son, Jesus Christ. Our great salvation which was secured by the work of Jesus Christ is not just about a legal contract or just about avoiding hell and going to heaven. It is also about entering into and remaining in joyful personal and intimate fellowship with the Father God and with His Son Jesus Christ. John expressed this beautiful reality when he wrote,

> *"That which we have seen and heard declare we unto you, that ye also may have fellowship with us: and truly our fellowship is with the Father, and with his Son Jesus Christ."*
>
> I John 1:3

As true believers, we should love our heavenly Father and our Lord Jesus and care deeply about the quality of our fellowship with them. And we should realize that any sin we commit, whether it is committed privately or against another person, is a violation of our fellowship with them. When, through Nathan's words, David became profoundly aware of his sin of committing adultery with Bathsheba and of killing her husband Uriah, he said to Nathan, "I have sinned against the Lord" (II Samuel 12:13). The book of Psalms records these heartfelt, sorrowful words he spoke to the Lord when he realized what he had done,

"Against thee, thee only, have I sinned, and done this evil in thy sight."

Psalm 51:4

When we sin, even if our sin is against another human being, we do damage to our personal fellowship with God. Although we do not become legally estranged from Him, distance is often created in our fellowship because we have been offensive to Him. Whenever an offense is committed in any relationship, remorse should be felt by the person who committed the offense and a heartfelt apology should be offered to the person who was offended. Making a heartfelt apology by saying, "I am truly sorry," is the first step to putting a strained relationship back in good order; not in the legal sense, but in the intimate, fellowship sense.

If, for example, a husband spoke harshly to his wife, he should be sorry for what he had done and should sincerely apologize to her saying, "I am truly sorry that I spoke harshly to you." This action would not, of course, result in him getting remarried. He was legally married before he offended his wife and he would likely remain legally married even if he didn't apologize. When the husband sincerely apologizes for his offense, he is endeavoring to make things right with his wife so that there will be no emotional distance between them or lack of intimacy in their relationship. He is acting to restore the peace and the pleasure and the connection in their relationship. By admitting his failing and apologizing, he is making the right move and doing the right thing, seeking to restore the right dynamic in their fellowship.

In the same way, if you have offended God by violating His will and sinning against Him, you should feel remorse, you should apologize to Him, and you should take steps to make things right with Him—not in the legal sense, but in the personal fellowship sense. Your heavenly Father is a person. Your Lord Jesus is a person. The Holy Spirit is a person. They have feelings; they can be saddened, grieved, and offended. So if you have done something offensive or sinful in your relationship with God, you should feel sorrowful. You should acknowledge your offense to Him, take responsibility for your sin, apologize, and make things right. That is part of maintaining rich and healthy fellowship with Him.

If you are the kind of son or daughter who can offend your heavenly Father without any sense of remorse or without any concern about your fellowship with Him, you are too cold hearted and are not living in rich and loving fellowship with Him. If you are a believer who can sin without caring that you have offended your Lord in heaven and never apologize to Him for any transgression of His will, you may be like the early gnostics who said they knew God, but, in fact, did not know Him, were not born of Him, were not righteous, and were not in the light. After all, what good son or good daughter refuses to apologize to their earthly father or mother if they have done them wrong? How much more does your heavenly Father and your Lord Jesus and the Holy Spirit deserve the courtesy of a sincere apology from you if you have offended them by sinning against them?

Believers who can offend God with no sense of wrong doing, with no guilty feelings, and with no sorrow for their sins are not in good spiritual health. Believers who have no concern for what their heavenly Father, their Lord Jesus, or the Holy Spirit feel, and are so cold and callused that they have no regret, no shame, and no sorrow when they sin have either seared their conscience or are not actually true believers. True believers who are living in healthy fellowship with God will have a sense of remorse and feelings of guilt if they have sinned. They will feel sad and have a sense of shame when they know they have displeased their Father. And true believers will express their sorrow to God with a sincere, "I am very sorry, Lord." If you are a believer who is persisting in sin and feel nothing at all, there is definitely something wrong in your spiritual life.

True believers care deeply about their relationship with God. If they have displeased Him with their thoughts, words, or deeds, and have damaged their fellowship with Him, their heart will be sorrowful and they will apologize for what they have done. They will apologize because they are born of God, because they love Him deeply, and because they truly care about their fellowship with Him, not because they are afraid that they won't be forgiven if they don't say anything. When true believers sin, they talk to their Father about it; they apologize to Him and express that they are sorry for their failure; sorry for saying and doing things that were hurtful to Him, hurtful to others, and hurtful to themselves.

As a true believer, you should apologize to God when you sin. This action of apologizing is not, however, an "apologizing unto forgiveness." In other words, you don't apologize to God in order to pull on His heartstrings, hoping that He will see your tears, feel compassion for you, consider being merciful to you, and forgive you. As we have learned throughout our study, God doesn't forgive our sins because we confess our sins to Him. He also doesn't forgive our sins because we apologize to Him. God forgives our sins because He is faithful and just. God forgives us when we sin whether we apologize to Him or not. Apologizing to God does not initiate the forgiveness process or persuade God to forgive you. But apologizing to God does keep things right in your fellowship with Him, with the Lord Jesus, and with the Holy Spirit. If you have sinned, apologize to your Father, to your Lord Jesus, and to the Holy Spirit. Say that you are sorry and make things right with them.

Along with keeping things right in your fellowship with the Father, one of the benefits of apologizing for your sins is that it helps to unburden your conscience from the feelings of remorse and guilt you are experiencing because you know that you have sinned. In the English language, we sometimes characterize speaking honestly and from the heart as "getting things off our chest." It is often the case that until we speak honestly to a person we have offended, we feel the emotional pressure that accompanies a conflicted relationship burdened with unresolved issues. Your heart will often be burdened if you have sinned, but have not yet made things right with God. Apologizing sincerely to your heavenly Father and the Lord Jesus and the Holy Spirit when you have sinned will help to unburden your soul. It will clear your heart of the heaviness of guilt and give you the sense that all is well between you and your Father and between you and your Lord Jesus and between you and the Holy Spirit.

You Should Repent if You Have Been Sinning

In view of everything we have learned about I John 1:9 and about what the apostle John really meant by his words, "If we confess our sins," one of the important questions we must ask is, "If a believer is engaged in a persistent lifestyle of sinning, what should they do?" One of the most important answers to that question is, "They should repent." Before a believer can truly repent, however, they must understand what it means to repent.

The English verb "repent" found throughout the New Testament comes from the Greek verb *metanoeō*. The verb *metanoeō* means, "to change one's mind for the better, to think differently after, to feel a moral compunction, to reconsider." In contrast to the Greek word *pronoeo* which means, "to perceive something beforehand," *metanoeō* signifies, "to change one's mind or one's purpose after perceiving something." Most often in the New Testament, the verb *metanoeō* signified a person's change of thinking and their decisive change of living away from a life of sin and sinning toward a righteous and God-pleasing life. This change of thinking and lifestyle—this act of repenting—was embarked upon after a person realized the error in their thinking and the sinfulness of their life.

The English noun "repentance" found throughout the New Testament is translated from the Greek noun *metanoia*. The noun *metanoia* means, "to perceive afterwards." It comes from the word *meta*, which means, "after, implying a change," and the word *noeo*, "to perceive," which derives from *nous* which means, "the mind, the seat of moral reflection." In the New Testament, the noun *metanoia* most often characterized that change in a person's thinking and the consequent change in their living that occurred after they reflected upon their life and realized that the way they were thinking, speaking, and acting were not in accord with God's will and were, therefore, sinful.

According to Strong's Dictionary of New Testament Words, the Greek noun *metanoia* (repentance) represents, "the change of mind that results when one has begun to abhor their misdeeds." Strong's

Dictionary also says that *metanoia*, "embraces the recognition of sin and sorrow for those sins and the change of mind and actions that follow." Thayer's Greek Lexicon says that the Greek verb *metanoeō* can mean, "to feel sorry for what one has done; to feel sorry for offending another; to be conscious of sins and be sorrowful, desiring God's pardon." It can also mean, "to heartily amend one's conduct in a way that shows a true heart and mind change and an abhorrence for sin."

It is very important to understand how the words "repent" and "repentance" are typically used in New Testament; especially their significant connection to the issue of sin and sinning. A right understanding of the meaning and use of these words is especially important at this current hour because some ministers are suggesting that "to repent" simply means, "to change one's mind," or, "to renew one's mind with truth." Some say that repentance simply means, "to change your mind and believe the gospel." Others describe repentance as, "accepting God's forgiveness, His love, and His grace," or as, "learning the truth about who God really is."

Although "changing one's mind" is certainly an important aspect of repentance, the majority of the time the words repent and repentance are used in the New Testament, they refer to that change of living away from a lifestyle of sinning and toward a righteous life that pleases God which began with an awareness of sin and was followed with a strong decision of mind to turn from that sin. The preponderance of the use of the words repent and repentance in the New Testament Scriptures to describe the decision and the following action of turning away from sin and turning toward a righteous life suggests that to characterize repent and repentance as simply, "changing one's mind," or, "renewing one's mind in truth," or, "learning the truth about who God is," is a significant theological mistake.

It is important, of course, that believers renew their minds in God's truth. The apostle Paul prayed almost endlessly about this matter. But to equate repent and repentance with renewing one's mind in truth is a significant error because it divorces these words from their primary use in the New Testament Scriptures—to represent that action a person takes when they turn away from a life of sin and sinning and turn toward God and toward righteous living following their strong decision of mind to change after awaking to the fact that they have been living a sinful life in violation of God's Word.

The words "repent" and "repentance" used throughout the New Testament most often described a person's heartfelt, determined, and willful turning away from sin and sinning and turning toward God and righteous living following the sobering realization that things were not right in their life and that things were not right between them and God. This decisive change of mind and change of lifestyle from sinning to godliness represented by the words "repent" and "repentance" was used both of sinners turning to God in response to the gospel message (found mostly in the gospels and the book of Acts) and of believers making decisive changes from a lifestyle of sinning to a lifestyle of godliness.

The gospels are full of examples where the words "repent," "repented," and "repentance" were used by ministers like John the Baptist and Jesus to describe the action that sinners should take of recognizing their sinful nature and their sinful living, of making a decision of heart and mind to abandon their old sinful ways, and of turning, by faith, to God. In Mark 1:4, for example, the word "repentance" was used in the context of the remission of sins. Mark wrote,

"John did baptize in the wilderness, and preach the baptism of repentance for the remission of sins."

Mark 1:4

Later in Mark's gospel, we find these words which reveal that Jesus called sinners to repentance,

"When Jesus heard it, he saith unto them, They that are whole have no need of the physician, but they that are sick: I came not to call the righteous, but sinners to repentance."

Mark 2:7

In the context of His three famous parables where He revealed the Father's heart for sinners, Jesus spoke these words,

*"Likewise, I say unto you, there is joy in the presence of the angels of
God over one sinner that repenteth."*

Luke 15:10

As in the two examples I previously quoted, we recognize in Jesus'
words from Luke 15:10 the relationship between the word "repent"
and the turning away from sin and turning toward God and righteousness that it describes.

We also find the word "repent" in the book of Acts describing
sinners turning from a life of sin to a righteous life and a relationship
with God through faith in Jesus Christ. For example, on the day of
Pentecost, Peter preached,

*"Repent, and be baptized every one of you in the name of Jesus Christ
for the remission of sins..."*

Acts 2:38

In his famous sermon in the city of Athens, Paul spoke these
words,

*"And the times of this ignorance God winked at; but now comman-
deth all men every where to repent..."*

Acts 17:30

In both of these passages, the word "repent" was used in the
context of sin and described that decisive turning from sin and a life
of ignorance toward a relationship with God and a life of righteousness that followed one's realization that they were a sinner and needed
a Savior.

In Peter's second epistle, we find words which reveal God's desire
that unsaved men and women repent and turn to Him to avoid perish-
ing; which is the eternal future for any person who is not cleansed of
their sins through faith in Jesus Christ. Peter wrote,

*"The Lord is not slack concerning his promise, as some men count
slackness; but is longsuffering to us-ward, not willing that any
should perish, but that all should come to repentance."*

2 Peter 3:9

In the book of Revelation, we find these stunning words about sinners who refused to repent and turn from their sinning,

"Neither repented they of their murders, nor of their sorceries, nor of their fornication, nor of their thefts."

Revelation 9:21

In all of these passages, the words "repent" and "repentance" described the action of turning away from a lifestyle of sinning and turning toward God.

Several places in Scripture, we find the words "repent" and "repentance" used in connection with believers who, in their thinking and living, were not in alignment with God and were charged, therefore, to change. In the book of Acts, we find a situation where a man named Simon wanted to purchase the power of God to be able to lay hands on people so that they would be filled with the Holy Spirit. Peter sharply chided Simon for his evil desire, telling him,

"Thy money perish with thee, because thou hast thought that the gift of God may be purchased with money. Thou hast neither part nor lot in this matter: for thy heart is not right in the sight of God. Repent therefore of this thy wickedness..."

Acts 8:20-22

Peter informed Simon that, "thy heart is not right in the sight of God," and charged him to, "Repent therefore of this thy wickedness." The connection in this passage between a wrong heart with ungodly desires and the word "repent" is obvious.

In the Scriptures we just looked at, the words "repent" and "repentance" were not used of, "making a mental adjustment in one's thinking on any variety of matters." They did not mean, as some suggest, "to renew one's mind in the knowledge of God," or, "to come to a true understanding of God and His love." The words "repent" and "repented" represented, rather, that purposeful, heart motivated change in thinking about sin and sinning which was followed by a strong decision of mind to turn from sin to righteousness and which concluded with a change of living from an ungodly lifestyle of sin in the dark to a godly life of righteousness in the light.

Jesus Exhorted Believers to Repent

Jesus made several references to believers repenting and also admonished some believers to repent in His words to seven local churches recorded in the book of Revelation. He said this to the spiritual leader and the church in Pergamos,

> *"But I have a few things against thee, because thou hast there them that hold the doctrine of Balaam...So hast thou also them that hold the doctrine of the Nicolaitans, which thing I hate. Repent; or else I will come unto thee quickly, and will fight against them with the sword of my mouth."*
>
> *Revelation 2:14-16*

According to Jesus, some believers in Pergamos were holding to false doctrines, including the doctrine of the Nicolaitans, who were likely a subset of the early gnostics and were licentious in their lifestyle. Other believers in Pergamos were holding to the doctrine of Balaam, which apparently included sexual sins. Embracing these unclean doctrines had resulted in some believers living unclean lives. Jesus challenged those believers with the single word, "Repent." He wanted them to hear His Word of correction, realize the error of their thinking and of their ways, be sorry for their sins, make a firm decision of mind to change their lives, and then turn away from sinning toward godliness and a lifestyle in the light.

One of Jesus' strongest charges to repent in the book of Revelation was delivered to the church in Thyatira and concerned the false prophetess Jezebel. He said,

> *"Notwithstanding I have a few things against thee, because thou sufferest that woman Jezebel, which calleth herself a prophetess, to teach and to seduce my servants to commit fornication, and to eat things sacrificed unto idols. And I gave her space to repent of her fornication; and she repented not. Behold, I will cast her into*

a bed, and them that commit adultery with her into great tribula-
tion, except they repent of their deeds. And I will kill her children
with death; and all the churches shall know that I am he which
searcheth the reins and hearts: and I will give unto every one of
you according to your works. But unto you I say, and unto the rest
in Thyatira, as many as have not this doctrine, and which have not
known the depths of Satan, as they speak; I will put upon you none
other burden."

Revelation 2:20-24

Jesus revealed to the spiritual leader and the church at Thyatira that He had already given the false prophetess Jezebel a period of time to, "repent of her fornication." But Jezebel did not repent; she did not acknowledge her sin, change her thinking, and amend her ways. Some of Jesus' servants, seduced by Jezebel, were also committing fornication and eating things offered to idols. Some had gone so far into darkness that Jesus referred to them as those who knew, "the depths of Satan." He charged these believers to repent of their deeds and said that if they did not, they would face harsh consequences. It is clear from Jesus' words that the repenting He was calling for was not simply a change of mind on some Scripture topic or being enlightened to the love of God. He was calling, rather, for a radical change of heart, for a complete change in thinking, and for a change "of their deeds"—for a permanent departure from a lifestyle of sinning to a lifestyle of godliness in the light.

To the church at Laodicea, Jesus spoke these words,

"I know thy works, that thou art neither cold nor hot: I would thou
wert cold or hot. So then because thou art lukewarm, and neither
cold nor hot, I will spue thee out of my mouth. Because thou sayest,
I am rich, and increased with goods, and have need of nothing; and
knowest not that thou art wretched, and miserable, and poor, and
blind, and naked: I counsel thee to buy of me gold tried in the fire,
that thou mayest be rich; and white raiment, that thou mayest be
clothed, and that the shame of thy nakedness do not appear; and
anoint thine eyes with eyesalve, that thou mayest see. As many as I

love, I rebuke and chasten: be zealous therefore, and repent."
Revelation 3:15-19

Jesus addressed believers in Laodicea with the words, "Because thou sayest," and then mentioned things they were saying about themselves. Interestingly, all the things they were saying about themselves were positive and wonderful things. In his first epistle, the apostle John warned believers about the danger of saying wonderful things about themselves that were not actually true; things like, "we have no sin," and, "we have fellowship with God," and, "we have not sinned." It is very possible that some of the believers in Laodicea had been swayed by the errant early gnostics and joined them in saying wonderful things about themselves that were not true. Some in Laodicea said of themselves, "I am rich, and increased with goods, and have need of nothing." Jesus said something quite different about them, however. He said that they were, "wretched, and miserable, and poor, and blind, and naked." Because Jesus loved these believers, He rebuked and chastened them and charged them, "be zealous therefore, and repent." He wanted them to make a fervent response to His message, change their errant thinking, make a turn away from sinning and a lukewarm life of faith, and get on a path of right thinking and righteous living in the light.

From Jesus' words to the church in Laodicea, we understand that He will rebuke and chasten those He loves whose lives are out of order and who are living in sin and darkness. The word "rebuke," translated from the Greek *elegchō*, meant, "to reprehend severely; to chide, admonish, reprove; to show one his fault; to demand an explanation." The word "chasten," translated from the Greek *paideuō*, meant, "to chastise or castigate with words; to correct; to mold one's character by reproof; to scourge; sometimes used of a father punishing a son." Jesus wanted the believers He loved in Laodicea to respond to His rebuke and His chastening by repenting. They should heed His words, wake up to their error, get passionate in their hearts about changing, make up their minds to obey His words and to abandon their sin, and then make all the necessary changes, moving toward a godly life in the light.

Repentance in Corinth

An excellent example of New Testament repentance can be found in the apostle Paul's two letters to the Corinthian church. In those two letters, he dealt both with a young man who was living in an incestuous relationship with his father's wife and with the whole church. In his first letter to them, he addressed this situation, writing,

> *"It is reported commonly that there is fornication among you, and such fornication as is not so much as named among the Gentiles, that one should have his father's wife. And ye are puffed up, and have not rather mourned, that he that hath done this deed might be taken away from among you...To deliver such an one unto Satan for the destruction of the flesh, that the spirit may be saved in the day of the Lord Jesus. Your glorying is not good. Know ye not that a little leaven leaveneth the whole lump? Purge out therefore the old leaven, that ye may be a new lump, as ye are unleavened...Therefore put away from among yourselves that wicked person."*
> *I Corinthians 5:1-2, 5-7, 13*

In this passage, Paul not only pointed out the grave issue of sin concerning the young man living in incest with his father's wife; he also sternly chided the whole church at Corinth for being spiritually "puffed up" and for not having "mourned" about the sin that was in their midst. He informed them that the young man living in sin would be delivered to Satan for the destruction of his flesh so that his spirit would be saved in the day of the Lord Jesus (I Corinthians 5:3-5, 13). He then reproved the church again, informing them that their, "glorying (was) not good," and exhorted them to, "purge out therefore the old leaven" (I Corinthians 5:6-8, 13). The church at Corinth, in response to Paul's strong words, put the young man out of the church and began to sorrow because of their spiritual pride and because of the sin they had allowed to fester in their midst.

In his second epistle to the Corinthians, Paul addressed this situation again. He was no longer upset, however, but was rejoicing because the stern admonition of his first epistle had been heard and heeded.

The believers in Corinth had put the young man out of the church and had sorrowed themselves (II Corinthians 7:7-12). After being put out of the church, the young man recognized his sin, experienced a change in his heart, and made a change in his life. As well, the whole church at Corinth made changes in their thinking and their actions. Realizing that good fruit had resulted from his stern admonition, Paul wrote,

> *"For though I made you sorry with a letter* (his first epistle), *I do not repent, though I did repent: for I perceive that the same epistle hath made you sorry, though it were but for a season."*
>
> *II Corinthians 7:8*

The way Paul dealt with the situation of the young man living in incest with his father's wife woke up the whole church at Corinth and caused them to become sorrowful. Although Paul had originally felt some sorrow himself knowing that he had caused the believers in Corinth to sorrow, by the time he wrote his second epistle, he no longer felt that way because he knew that his stern words had led to great change. He wrote,

> *"Now I rejoice, not that ye were made sorry, but that ye sorrowed to repentance: for ye were made sorry after a godly manner..."*
>
> *II Corinthians 7:9*

Paul rejoiced, he said, not because the church in Corinth had experienced sorrow, but because the sorrow they experienced led them to repentance. He wrote, "ye sorrowed to repentance: for ye were made sorry after a godly manner." The sorrow the church in Corinth experienced was not a debilitating sorrow that led them nowhere. The sorrow they experienced was, rather, "after a godly manner." In other words, it was a sorrow connected to their relationship with God and a sorrow that moved them to repentance. The Corinthian believers changed their ways after they changed their minds after their hearts were made sorry after they became aware, through Paul's stout words, that things were not right in their church. In other words, they repented.

The VOICE translation renders Paul's words in II Corinthians 7:9 this way,

> *"Now I am glad—not because it (my first letter) caused you grief but because you were moved to make a permanent change that can happen only with the realization that your actions have gone against God—I'm glad to know you suffered no long-term loss because of what we did."*
>
> II Corinthians 7:9 VOICE

This rendering of Paul's words accurately depicts the action of repentance that took place in Corinth. It says that the Corinthian believers, "were moved to make a permanent change that can happen only with the realization that your actions have gone against God."

The Amplified Bible renders Paul's words this way,

> *"...yet I am glad now, not because you were hurt and made sorry, but because your sorrow led to repentance (and you turned back to God); for you felt a grief such as God meant you to feel..."*
>
> II Corinthians 7:9 Amplified Bible

The Amplified Bible's translation of Paul's words connects the "sorrow" that the Corinthian believers experienced to their, "(turning) back to God," and lends support to the meaning of repentance I have been emphasizing.

These two translations of Paul's words to the Corinthian church help us to understand that Scriptural repentance is much more than, "a change in one's thinking," or, "the renewing of one's mind on a variety of Scriptural subjects." Scriptural repentance, rather, is most often that change of lifestyle from sinning to godliness that begins with a realization that one's life is not in agreement with God's will. This initial realization is followed by a godly sorrow for the sin in one's life, leads to a decision of mind to turn from sinning toward righteous living, and concludes with a lifestyle change from sinning to righteous living.

Paul continued his address to the Corinthian believers in his second epistle with these words,

> *"For godly sorrow worketh repentance to salvation not to be repented of: but the sorrow of the world worketh death."*
>
> II Corinthians 7:10

The English words "godly sorrow" are translated from the Greek words *theos kata lypē*. The word *theos* means, "God, or things to do with God." The word "sorrow" comes from the Greek *lypē* and means, "an internal heaviness, a grieving of heart, internal affliction, mourning." The words *theos kata lypē* can mean, "a sorrow that comes from God," or, "sorrow of a godly type." The English word "worketh" in this verse comes from the Greek *katergazomai* which means, "performs, causes, brings about, results in." Paul's message in this passage was that a true and godly heart sorrow for sin led to the action of repenting. And the action of repenting—a turn from sinning to a righteousness life—was a decision that would never need "to be repented of."

The GNT translation renders Paul's words this way,

> "For the sadness that is used by God brings a change of heart that leads to salvation—and there is no regret in that! But sadness that is merely human causes death."
>
> II Corinthians 7:10 GNT

According to the apostle Paul, the heartfelt sorrow the Corinthian believers experienced was a result of God working in them. Their godly sorrow led them to a place of repentance—to a heart-motivated change of mind and change of lifestyle. This change of mind and lifestyle which led to salvation—to freedom, deliverance, life, joy, and peace—would never be regretted.

Near the conclusion of his second epistle to the Corinthians, Paul addressed in a more general manner the need of some believers to repent from sin. He wrote,

> "And lest, when I come again, my God will humble me among you, and that I shall bewail many which have sinned already, and have not repented of the uncleanness and fornication and lasciviousness which they have committed."
>
> II Corinthians 12:21

In this passage, Paul referred to believers in Corinth who had, "not repented of the uncleanness and fornication and lasciviousness which they have committed." By these words, Paul did not mean that some believers in Corinth had not yet received a revelation about God's love or had not yet had their minds renewed to His truth. In fact, his words seem to indicate that these believers were well aware of God's truth concerning uncleanness and fornication, but had not yet acted on what they knew. His statement that they had not yet repented suggests they knew that what they were doing was wrong, but had not made a decision to turn from their ungodly lifestyle of carnality and sinning to a lifestyle of godly and righteous living. Paul was concerned that his next visit to Corinth would be an unpleasant visit; one where God would call upon him to publicly expose the ungodly lifestyle of some and charge them to repent.

From Paul's words to the Corinthians, from Jesus' words to believers in the book of Revelation, and from other passages of Scripture, it is clear that there are times when believers must engage in the action of repenting from sin. This repenting from sin begins with a wake up call notifying them that their life is not in accord with God's will. This wake up call, whether it comes from the inside or from outside, causes a person to realize they are living a sinful life. This realization leads to a godly sorrow of heart which, in turn, leads to a change of mind about how one is going to live their life. Finally, the person turns away from a lifestyle of sinning in the dark to a lifestyle of godly living in the light.

New Testament repentance begins with an awareness of sin in one's life, is followed by a genuine heart sorrow for that sin, leads to the making of a strong decision of mind to change from sinful living to godly living, and concludes with a complete turn around from a lifestyle of sin to a lifestyle of righteousness. New Testament repentance is not, then, a mental adjustment on a variety of subjects or a renewing of one's mind in important truth. New Testament repentance is, rather, a purposeful decision of mind and deliberate act of will to turn away from sinning and toward righteousness after one becomes aware of the sinfulness of their life.

Repent if You Are Sinning

It is significant that both in the book of Revelation where Jesus corrected believers in various churches who were living in sin and in First and Second Corinthians where Paul dealt with the young man living in sin and with the whole church in Corinth, no instruction was issued or even a mention made that believers should confess their sins so that they could be forgiven. Jesus didn't tell the believers in Pergamos and Thyatira, "I am not going to forgive your sins unless you confess them to God." Paul didn't tell the Corinthian church or the young man living in incest, "You need to confess your sins to God or He won't forgive you." No instructions about confessing sins were given by Jesus or by Paul to believers who were sinning. Strong admonitions were offered, however, to repent. In other words, charges were issued to, "Wake up to the reality that you are sinning, be sorrowful in a godly way for your sins, make an adjustment of heart and a change in your thinking, set your mind to amend your ways, and then make a strong, purposeful, and permanent change from sinning to righteous living."

If you are a believer who has been living a sinful lifestyle, the action you must take is to repent of your sins. That means you must become aware that your sinful lifestyle is wrong and you are grieving your heavenly Father and your Lord Jesus. After you become aware of the fact you have been contrary to God and have been sinning, you should be sorry from your heart about how you have been living and should apologize sincerely to your Father for grieving Him and for damaging your fellowship with Him. After that, you should make a strong decision of mind to turn from sinning and to live righteously in the future. Finally, you should take the action that your heart and mind are urging and make a complete turn away from your lifestyle of sinning and toward a lifestyle of godliness in the light. This repentance and godly lifestyle choice will be, as Paul wrote, a decision, "not to be repented of."

If, like the prodigal son, you have wandered away from the Father and have been living in darkness, engaging in sin, and rolling around in the mud and the muck, you should repent of your sins. Agreeing with God that you have sinned (*homologeō*) is not the complete action you need to take. Even feeling sorry for your sins and apologizing to God is not the complete action you need to take. You must be sorrowful enough for your sins that you make a strong decision of mind to turn away from sin and turn back to the Father and to righteous living. Finally, you must follow through on your decision by making that change from a lifestyle of sinning in the dark to a lifestyle of godliness in the light. That is what it means to repent of your sins and that is what you should do!

Sins You Commit Must Be Forgiven

There are some in the body of Christ who teach that all the past, present, and future sins of all believers are already forgiven. Scripture is clear, however, that although all the past sins of believers were forgiven the moment they believed in Jesus Christ, their future sins were not pre-forgiven. It is true, of course, that because of the finished work of Jesus in His suffering and death and because of the blood that He shed on the cross, there is a sufficient supply to meet any "forgiveness demands" that may arise in the future. In other words, everything necessary for the forgiveness and cleansing of every sin of every sinner and every sin of every believer in every generation and in every place has already been provided through the incredible and super-abundant one time and once for all sacrifice of Jesus Christ. This exceedingly profound and praise-worthy reality does not mean, however, that the future sins of believers are "pre-forgiven."

We can state with certainty, however, that believers will be forgiven and cleansed of any sins they commit in the future because the necessary provision for the forgiveness of those sins has already been put in place. The blood of Jesus Christ is available and is effectual to cleanse any sin that any believer may commit (I John 1:7). God the Father is faithful and just to forgive believers' sins and to cleanse them (I John 1:9). Jesus is believers' advocate with the Father, ready to represent them concerning any sins they may commit (I John 2:1). And Jesus is the propitiation not only for the sins of sinners, but also for the sins of believers (I John 2:2). Because all these things are true and because all this provision is in place, we can say with full confidence that believers will be forgiven and cleansed of any sins they commit in the future.

We could compare the abundant provision that the heavenly Father prepared for the forgiveness of all men's sins to the abundant provision of a wise young man who, because of his generous heart and keen foresight, made a financial deposit into a special account that was so substantial, it would be sufficient to cover every possible need that might arise in the life of any child that would ever be born to him. All school tuitions, food and clothing, health insurances, life insurances, medical bills, lawyer's fees, legal aid, and any other need that might ever arise in the lives of any children born to him in the future could be met by this substantial financial provision. Whenever a bill for services would come due, or if there ever was a debt that needed to be paid, a withdrawal could be made from that special account and every debt or bill could be immediately paid in full. Although the substantial provision to cover every bill, to pay every debt, and to meet every need was put in place before it was needed and before any children were even born, no bills would actually be paid and no debts would actually be covered until those bills or debts came due.

What the young man in this example did for his future children is exactly what our heavenly Father did for us. Before the foundation of the world, He designed a plan to meet the needs of all lost sinners and to meet the needs of every child who would be part of His family. In His plan, He ensured that everything that would ever have to be dealt with, be covered, or be paid for, including every sin of every sinner and every sin that His own children might commit, could be dealt with, forgiven, and paid for. The New Covenant account the Father God opened and funded with the shed blood of Jesus is an account so richly funded that there will never be a debt incurred by any sinner or by any saint that cannot be immediately paid in full. That means, as the apostle John revealed in I John 1:7, in I John 1:9, and in I John 2:1-2, that true believers will continually experience, in real time, the forgiveness and cleansing of any sins they commit. Although the sufficient provision for the forgiveness and cleansing of those sins was put in place before the Father God had any children, the sins that His children commit are not forgiven and cleansed before they are committed. Rather, the sins that His children commit are forgiven and cleansed after they are committed.

In I John 1:9, John wrote that God, "is (present tense) faithful and just to forgive us our sins, and to cleanse us from all unrighteousness." The reason John did not write that God, "was (past tense) faithful and just to forgive us our sins and to cleanse us from all unrighteousness," is because he was neither referring to the forgiveness of sins that takes place when a sinner is first saved or suggesting that God had already forgiven the future sins of believers. It is clear, even from John's words in I John 1:9, that the forgiveness and cleansing of believers' sins occurs after those sins are committed. That means, of course, that future sins are not yet forgiven.

Near the end of his first epistle, John wrote these interesting words,

"If any man see his brother sin a sin which is not unto death, he shall ask, and he shall give him life for them that sin not unto death. There is a sin unto death: I do not say that he shall pray for it."
I John 5:16

John informed his spiritual children that if they saw one of their brothers commit a sin that was not unto death, they could make a request to God and God would, "give him (that brother) life." If it were true, as some say, that the future sins of believers are already forgiven, then the only action a believer should take if they saw their brother sin would be to tell that brother, "Don't worry about it, brother; it's all pre-forgiven!" John's words in I John 5:16 confirm, however, that the future sins of believers are not pre-forgiven.

The apostle James, often considered to be the most down to earth,

every day life spiritual leader in the early church, wrote these interesting words,

> *"Is any sick among you? Let him call for the elders of the church; and*
> *let them pray over him…and the prayer of faith shall save the sick,*
> *and the Lord shall raise him up; and if he have committed sins, they*
> *shall be forgiven him."*
>
> *James 5:14-15*

When James referred to, "any sick among you," he was not referring to sick sinners who might appeal to the elders of the church to
pray for their healing, but was referring to believers who were sick; to,
"any sick among you." Concerning sick believers among them, James
wrote that the prayer of faith would save them, that the Lord would
raise them up, and, "if he has committed sins, they shall be forgiven
him." The words, "shall be," are not past tense, but future tense. If
all the future sins of believers were already forgiven, James would
have written, "And if he have committed sins, just inform him that
his sins have been pre-forgiven." The reason James didn't write those
words is because he understood, as did all the great leaders of the New
Testament, that although Jesus' shed blood was completely sufficient
to cleanse all the sins of all sinners and completely sufficient to cleanse
all the sins believers would commit, the sins that sinners commit are
not cleansed until they believe on Jesus Christ as Savior and the sins
that believers commit are not forgiven and cleansed until after they
are committed.

The Father God, in His keen foresight and great wisdom, planned
and put in place the necessary provision to deal with the sins believers
commit after they are saved. According to His great wisdom, He sent
Jesus to suffer once for all sins, to die once for all sins, and to shed His
blood once for all sins. Although Jesus' remedial work in that aspect is,
indeed, a finished work, His blood is yet effectual and working today;
for both sinners and believers. According to God's great wisdom, the
same precious and powerful blood of Jesus Christ that provides for
the forgiveness and cleansing of every sin of every sinner who comes

to Him in faith is also effectual to provide for the forgiveness and cleansing of every sin that every believer might commit. According to His great wisdom, God set Jesus in place as believers' advocate with the Father; to represent them before Him if they sin. According to His great wisdom, God made Jesus the propitiation for the sins of all believers; to deal with and to move out of the way any sins that might get in the way of their fellowship with Him. And according to His great wisdom, the Father Himself is faithful and just to forgive the sins of true believers and to cleanse them from all unrighteousness. The substantial New Covenant forgiveness of sins provision that the Father God put in place is able to fully meet whatever forgiveness-needs might ever arise—including believers' need to be forgiven and cleansed of sins they commit after they are saved!

Do Not Fear That You Are Unforgiven

The familiar and common interpretation of I John 1:9—that believers must admit each and every one of the sins they have committed to God in order to be forgiven of those sins—has caused some believers to be uncertain and even fearful about the status of their relationship with God. Some worry that if they fail to admit even one of their sins to God in a time of confession, they will not be forgiven of that sin and their relationship with God will be compromised. Some worry that every time they sin, they become unrighteous and unclean until they sorrowfully admit their sins to God and are "re-cleansed" and "re-instated" to right standing with Him. Some are anxious because they believe that when they sin, their fellowship with God is broken and remains broken until they confess their sins. Some, contemplating the difficulties in their lives, wonder if the reason they were not healed, or the reason their prayers were not answered as they hoped, or the reason they are struggling and feeling down and out is because they have unconfessed sin in their life. Some are even fearful about what their eternal destiny might be if they die with "unconfessed sin" in their life.

It is very important to understand that John's words in I John 1:9 do not teach that we, as believers, are only forgiven of the sins we commit if and after we admit every one of those sins to God. The truth of the New Covenant, rather, is that we who are true believers are forgiven of the sins we commit because of the effectualness of the shed blood of Jesus, because of Jesus' present work as our advocate and propitiation, and because our Father God is faithful and just to forgive us and cleanse us. We are forgiven of the sins we commit because God is faithful to His promises and just to act in agreement with the legal covenant He made with us through His Son. We are forgiven of the sins we commit because our all-wise Father put in place, as a necessary and significant aspect of the wonderful New Covenant, a divine remedy for any sins we would commit. We are forgiven of the sins we commit because we are true believers in covenant with God!

Because our Father is all wise and all knowing, He knew that we would sin after we were saved and knew that our sins would have to be dealt with; they would have to be forgiven and cleansed. In designing the New Covenant, He made sure that every necessary provision was in place to deal with every sin that every one of His children might ever commit. He ensured that the work of His Son Jesus in His suffering, His shedding of blood, His death, and His resurrection was so complete and that the New Testament contract was so foil proof that all the sins believers would ever commit could be forgiven and cleansed. He prepared for the matter of sins that believers might commit even more fully by setting Jesus in place as advocate with the Father and the propitiation for believers' sins. The abundant provision and the necessary means to deal with every sin that every believer might commit was "pre-put-in-place" by our loving, all knowing, and all wise Father God!

Your heavenly Father does not want you to live in fear that if you have "unconfessed sin" in your life, your relationship with Him is broken, you are unclean and unrighteous, and your eternal destiny is in jeopardy. He does not want you to live in fear that if you sin, but fail to properly confess your sin to Him, your sin will not be forgiven and your fellowship with Him will be broken. He does not want you to live in fear, based on a wrong interpretation of I John 1:9, that if you don't admit each and every sin you commit to Him, you might be eternally lost.

If you have sinned, understand that according to I John 1:7 the blood of Jesus Christ is continually effectual to cleanse you of that sin. Not only are all your past sins forgiven; any sin that you commit today or tomorrow or any time in the future will also be forgiven. This is a blessed reality for you because you are a true believer. Because you are born of God, are a partaker of the better New Covenant based upon better promises, and are walking with God in the light, God will not and, in fact, cannot impute your sins to you. Every sin you have ever committed and every sin you will ever commit will be cleansed because of the one time and once for all sacrifice of Jesus Christ.

If you have sinned, remember that you have an advocate with the Father; "Jesus Christ the righteous" (I John 2:1-2). As your advocate, Jesus represents you before the Father, presenting to Him all the legal realities of the New Testament, skillfully defending your righteous status. He pleads the powerful merits of His redemptive work. He argues the complete efficacy of His own blood that not only cleansed you of all past sins when you first believed, but is sufficient to cleanse you of every sin you commit as a believer. He argues that you have a legal right, on the basis of His shed blood and His finished work, to be forgiven of whatever sins you have committed and to be cleansed from any stain of unrighteousness that has touched you. He argues that because of His finished work as Savior of the world, all penalties have been paid, any required punishment has been meted out, and full justice has been served. Your advocate, Jesus Christ the righteous, testifies to the Father of these things and reminds Him to be faithful and just and to forgive your sins. As your advocate with the Father, Jesus pleads your case when you sin, doing all He can do to win a "Not guilty" verdict for you. And He will win that verdict for you every time!

If you have sinned, remember that Jesus is the propitiation for your sins. The apostle John wrote these beautiful, powerful, and comforting words to his spiritual children to assure them that things remained okay between them and God, even if they had sinned,

> *"And he* (Jesus) *is the propitiation for our sins: and not for ours only, but also for the sins of the whole world."*
>
> I John 2:2

Notice that John said Jesus, "is the propitiation for our sins," not that Jesus, "was the propitiation for our sins." We often acknowledge that Jesus is the propitiation for the sins of the whole world, but fail to realize that Jesus is the propitiation for our sins as well. John informed his spiritual children that Jesus was the propitiation for their sins because he wanted to be sure they understood that if they sinned, the same Jesus Christ who propitiated concerning their sins when they first believed would also propitiate concerning the sins they might commit as believers, keeping those sins out of the way of their relationship with God. The Father wisely ordained that Jesus be the propitiation for our sins because He knew that after we were born of Him, cleansed of all our past sins, and made righteous in our nature, we would still sin and our sins would have to be dealt with. Jesus' role as the propitiation for our sins is part of God's prescient, excellent, and complete New Covenant provision to deal with the sins we might commit, ensuring that no sin will ever stand in the way of our fellowship with God.

If you have sinned, remember that according to I John 1:9, God is faithful and just to forgive your sins and to cleanse you from all unrighteousness. The apostle John used strong legal and covenant language to describe the Father God who forgives your sins. He didn't say that God would forgive your sins because He is merciful and kind. He didn't say that God would forgive your sins because of your heartfelt verbal admission to Him of each and every one of your sins. He didn't say that God would forgive your sins if you did some kind of spiritual penance or if you were appropriately sorrowful. He said that God would forgive your sins because God is faithful and just!

God is faithful to keep the terms of the New Covenant that He established, based upon the finished work of Jesus Christ. He is faithful to the words He prophesied when He said, "Your sins and your iniquities I will remember no more." God does what is just. He has sworn with an oath. He has made a promise and given His word. He crafted a new and better covenant and that covenant was put in force through the shedding of Jesus' blood. God will act faithfully and justly, according to the terms of the New Covenant. He will not violate spiritual law and He will not violate the New Covenant. John's statement that God is faithful and just to forgive your sins is an absolute bedrock of truth for your strong confidence that God will always forgive you if you sin!

It is very important for you to know and to understand that if you sin and do unrighteously, you do not forfeit your righteous status with God or lose your righteous new nature. Just as the prodigal son did not lose his rightful status as a son when he left his father's house, so you will not become legally unrighteous or lose your sonship if you participate in sin, walk a distance away from the Father, or even live for a season in the dark. But just as the prodigal son got dirty and sustained personal losses in his life when he sinned, you will "get dirty," will be temporarily stained, and may sustain losses if you engage in a lifestyle of sin.

If you are a believer who is presently living a lifestyle of sinning, you should do what the prodigal son did. You should come to your senses, acknowledge your wrong doing, return to the Father's house and to His embrace, and be cleansed of your unrighteousness, allowing the Father to robe you in a clean and righteous robe. Having to be "cleansed from all unrighteousness" does not indicate that you lost your right standing with God when you sinned, or that you became permanently stained by your sin. Having to be "cleansed from all unrighteousness" simply reveals that the sins you committed and the unrighteous ways you were living stained your life and you needed to be cleansed from the effect of your unrighteous actions.

Something powerful you should take note of from the parable of the prodigal son is that when the prodigal son returned to his father's house, there was no barrier erected to prohibit him from entering. There was no wall built to keep him out. There was no gate with servants posted at it to prohibit him from accessing his father's estate. The prodigal son had not been rejected, disowned, or deemed *persona non grata* by his father. In fact, just the opposite was true. His father, who had been hopefully watching for his son's return, ran eagerly to embrace him when he saw him coming. He put a new robe on his back, a ring on his finger, and declared a time for celebration. There was no resistance by the father to the return of the dirt-stained son. In fact, the father welcomed him with open arms and with great joy. No matter the dirtying effects of one's sinning, there is no stain of sin or dirt of unrighteousness that is beyond the cleansing effect of the powerful blood of Jesus!

If you have sinned, understand that because of the finished work of Jesus in His suffering and death and the shedding of His blood, and because of His present role as your advocate with the Father and the propitiation for your sins, God has not shut the door on you. He has not turned His back on you. He has not put up a "No Trespassing" sign indicating that you are no longer welcome in His house. He has not told you, "You can't come home because you went too far." Have faith in the cleansing blood of Jesus. Have faith in the New Covenant in which you are a partner through faith in Jesus Christ. Have faith in the fact that God is faithful and just. Just repent, turn from your sin, return to the Father, and get back to the life God called you to. And be assured, as John wrote, that God is faithful and just to forgive you of any sins you have committed and to cleanse you from any stain of unrighteousness.

Because of the apostle John's words in his first epistle, believers who lived more than two thousand years ago could be completely confident that the blood of Jesus would cleanse them of any sins they committed as they walked with God in the light. Because of the apostle John's words in his first epistle, believers who lived more than two thousand years ago could be completely confident that their Father God was faithful and just to forgive their sins. Because of the apostle John's words in his first epistle, believers who lived more than two thousand years ago could be completely confident that their advocate with the Father and the propitiation for their sins, Jesus Christ, was faithfully doing His work of dealing with their sins. But not only could believers who lived two thousand years ago be comforted and made confident by the apostle John's words. We too, as twenty-first century believers, can be comforted and completely confident. We don't have to be worried, be filled with trepidation, or be paralyzed by anxiety and fear if we have stumbled and sinned. Why? Because we know, we understand, and we are fully confident that our Father God, in His keen foresight and great wisdom, made full provision in the glorious New Covenant to deal with any sins we might commit!

If you sin, remember these important words from the apostle John,

> *"I write unto you, little children, because your sins are forgiven you for his name's sake."*
>
> I John 2:12

Notice that John did not write, "Your sins are forgiven for your sake." He wrote, rather, "Your sins are forgiven you for his name's sake." When God forgives you, it is not just for your benefit. It is also for His benefit. It is so that He can remain in intimate and beautiful fellowship with you. And it is also so that no disrepute will ever come to His great name because He has not fully followed through on what He promised.

Conclusion

As a New Covenant believer, it is very important for you to understand that God's action of forgiving the sins you commit and cleansing you is not set in motion by a required act of admitting your sins to Him in a time of confession, but is constantly in motion. It is very important for you to understand that the forgiveness of sins you commit and your cleansing from all unrighteousness is not triggered when you admit your sins to God in a time of confession, but is ongoing and continual because of the finished work of Jesus Christ and because of

His present day ministry as advocate with the Father and the propitiation for your sins. Because you are a true believer, God is faithful and just to keep His covenant, to keep His oath, to keep His Word, and to forgive you. It is important for you to understand that God is not waiting for you to do the work of confessing your sins to Him before He will forgive you. Rather, as you live your life in Christ, the blood of Jesus is continually cleansing you of any sins you commit and the Father is continually forgiving and cleansing you because He is faithful and just. Knowing that you are forgiven and cleansed and knowing that you are continually being forgiven and cleansed is one of the most important "knowings" you can possess!

As a New Covenant believer, it is important for you to understand that you qualify to be forgiven of each and every sin you commit and to be cleansed from any unrighteous actions, not because you engage in a required action of admitting each and every one of the sins you commit to God, but because you believed God's message of salvation in your heart, confessed with your mouth that God raised Jesus from the dead, and embraced His free gift of righteousness through Jesus Christ. Being righteous and clean is your true internal nature and right standing with God is your permanent legal status. The judgment from God of "Not guilty" is His firm and final ruling on your life!

The remedy for sins you commit as a believer is not "the confession of sins to God." The remedy for sins you commit as a believer is the ever effectual blood of Jesus Christ. The remedy for sins you commit as a believer is the work of Jesus Christ in His representative role as your advocate with the Father and the propitiation for your sins. The remedy for sins you commit as a believer is the forgiving and cleansing action of your faithful and just Father God.

The writer of Hebrews offered these beautiful words about the bold confidence we can walk in as New Covenant believers because of the blood that Jesus shed for us and because of the covenant God put in place for us,

"Having therefore, brethren, boldness to enter into the holiest by the blood of Jesus, By a new and living way, which he hath consecrated

for us, through the veil, that is to say, his flesh; And having an high priest over the house of God; Let us draw near with a true heart in full assurance of faith, having our hearts sprinkled from an evil conscience, and our bodies washed with pure water. Let us hold fast the profession of our faith without wavering...for he is faithful that promised..."

Hebrews 10:19-23

Meditate on these powerful words about Jesus' blood, about the New Covenant, and about the confidence all true believers can have to, "enter into the holiest by the blood of Jesus." You can have this boldness because of the new and living way Jesus procured for you and because He is your high priest before God. Because of these powerful New Covenant truths, we can all, "draw near with a true heart in full assurance of faith." Our strong faith is not predicated on us fulfilling a required action of admitting our sins to God, but rests firmly on what God planned, on what Jesus did, and on what Jesus is currently doing! Because of these things, we can be confident. We can, "hold fast the profession of our faith without wavering."

If you believe in Jesus Christ as Savior, then you are a true believer. You don't need to panic or be fearful about your right standing with God, even if you stumble and sin. The completed work of Jesus Christ in His suffering and death and in the shedding of His blood was not only effectual to cleanse you of every sin you committed when you were a sinner; His blood is also effectual to cleanse you of every sin you commit as a believer. When you are established in this absolutely fundamental New Covenant truth, you will never fear being rejected by God, being disowned by Him, or even being shunned by Him if you stumble and sin. You will rejoice, rather, and greatly praise Him because you understand that your wise and loving and faithful and just Father God made provision for you long before you were saved!

Do not be afraid that if you have not verbally admitted each and every one of your sins to God in a confession session, you are in trouble with Him, have lost your right standing with Him, are banned from fellowship with Him, or are unforgiven and unclean. Your relationship with God has not been broken; it is not that tenuous. You have not become unclean like you were before you were saved. You have not become unrighteous in your nature. God is not standing ready to condemn you and He will not declare you guilty. He is just and the justifier of all who believe. Jesus is not waiting to condemn you or looking for ways to punish you for your sins. He already took the punishment for all your sins and for the sins of the whole world. And He ever lives to advocate for you, to propitiate for you, and to intercede for you. Your Father is not against you; He is for you! Jesus is not against you; He is for you! Who can lay any charge to God's elect? No one. There is no reason to fear. So fear not!

Conclusion

Throughout this study, I set forth an argument firmly based in Scripture and supported by good historical evidence that neither of the two familiar interpretations of I John 1:9 are correct interpretations. As well, I offered an interpretation of I John 1:9 that is Scripturally based, historically accurate, well supported by sound logic, and harmonious with the wonderful truths of the New Covenant in Jesus Christ; an interpretation that I believe to be the best interpretation of John's words in I John 1:9. I understand that not everyone will agree with my interpretation, but hopefully each person who read this study has gained valuable information they can consider when conducting their own study of I John 1:9 and has gleaned truth and godly wisdom they can incorporate into their own lives.

In this study, we examined considerable evidence which revealed that the apostle John's familiar words in I John 1:9 were neither an invitation to early gnostic sinners to admit their sins to God so that they could be forgiven, cleansed, and saved or a teaching informing believers that they must admit to God each and every sin they had committed in order to be forgiven and cleansed of those sins. We discovered evidence which revealed, rather, that John's familiar statement in I John 1:9 was one of several important statements he penned in his warning about and teaching against early gnostic error concerning sin and sinning and was one of the important conditional statements he offered in his exquisite polemic against sin and sinning. John's words in I John 1:9 revealed that in stark contrast to the errant early gnostics, true believers did not disagree with God on the subject of sin and sinning or concerning their own sins, saying, "we have no sin," and, "we have not sinned," but aligned themselves with God, agreed with His Word, and spoke with one voice with Him on the subject of sin and sinning and concerning their own sins. The action of true believers that John characterized in I John 1:9 by his use of the Greek verb *homologeō* and the words, "If we confess (*homologeō*) our sins," was not

344   Must We Confess Our Sins?

the action of repeatedly admitting one's sins to God in order to qualify to be forgiven of those sins, but was the action of submitting to, aligning with, agreeing with, and speaking in agreement with God about sin and about one's own sins. That is, in my studied opinion, the best meaning and truest essence of the apostle John's words, "If we confess our sins."

As we discovered throughout our study, God does not forgive believers' sins only if and only after they admit each and every one of their sins to Him in a "confession of sins session." God forgives believers' sins, rather, because He is faithful to the promises He made and just to follow the terms of the New Covenant. In His keen foresight and great wisdom, He put in place for New Covenant believers, for His children, a divine remedy for the forgiveness and cleansing of sins they might commit. That remedy is not the repeated admission of sins to Him, but is the powerful cleansing blood of Jesus. Added to the sufficiency of His precious blood, Jesus Christ is also believers' advocate with the Father, representing them before God in the matter of sins they commit, and is the propitiation for their sins they commit. Along with God's own faithful and just action in forgiving believers' sins, these are the major aspects of the divine remedy for the forgiveness and cleansing of believers' sins that our wise and all knowing Father God put in place for us in the glorious New Covenant.

As we conclude our study, I will ask a simple question and give a simple answer based on everything we have learned about I John 1:9. The question is, "Must New Testament believers confess/admit to God each and every sin they commit before He will forgive their sins and cleanse them from all unrighteousness?" The simple answer to that questions is, "No." No, there is no "confession of sins" action that is required by God in order for believers' sins to be forgiven in the New Covenant. No, the admission by believers to God of each and every sin they have committed is not a Christian requirement or a necessary New Testament practice and is certainly not a mandated precursor to God's forgiveness. No, God is not patiently waiting for believers to admit all their sins to Him in a "time of confession" so that He has liberty to forgive their sins and cleanse them. No, a believer's private request to God to forgive their sins does not initiate His forgiveness and cleansing. No, in I John 1:9, John was not instructing his spiritual children about a required spiritual activity called "The confession of sins to God" that they must engage in to qualify themselves to be forgiven and cleansed of sins they had committed.

What John was communicating to his spiritual children in I John 1:9 was that if they remained aligned with God and continued in agreement with His Word, openly acknowledging that what He had said about sin and sinning was the truth and not denying that they had sinned when they had, in fact, sinned, but agreed with Him that they had sinned and acknowledged it—in other words, if they *"homologeō* our sins"—then, by so doing, they revealed that they were true believers. Because they were true believers, they would be forgiven of all their sins and cleansed from any stain of unrighteousness by their faithful and just God. God would forgive their sins and cleanse them because the forgiveness and cleansing of sins they committed was part and parcel of the New Covenant they were part of through faith in Jesus Christ. That is what John was communicating to his spiritual children in I John 1:9. And that is what I John 1:9 really means.

Thank you for taking the time to read, to study, and to consider what I have written. I hope that this study has added knowledge and insight to your understanding of God, to your understanding of your salvation, and, most of all, to your understanding of the forgiveness of your sins as a New Covenant saint. I hope that what you learned about I John 1:9 has enriched your life of faith and will aid you as you continue to walk with God in the light.

Research Sources

In writing *Must We Confess Our Sins?* I not only did much of my own prayerful and diligent study and careful consideration of I John 1:9; I also consulted a number of sources to provide important historical information concerning the errant early gnostics and to provide other information essential to a correct view of John's first epistle and a correct interpretation of I John 1:9. I thought it would be interesting for you to know some of the sources I consulted.

To help me get an overview of John's first epistle and to garner various scholar's interpretations and opinions of I John 1:9, I researched a number of good Bible commentaries. These commentaries provided an overview of John's first epistle, contributed insight into John's words in I John 1:9, and furnished important historical information about the early gnostics. They also gave me a general sense of John's personality and insight into his writing style. Some of the commentaries I consulted were "Matthew Henry's Complete Commentary on the Bible," "John Gill's Exposition of the Bible Commentary," and "William Barclay's Study Bible Series."

To learn more about the errant early gnostics, I perused several books on early gnosticism and also used an online website called "The Gnostic Society Library" (www.gnosis.org/library.html). To get a better sense of how the first century church viewed early gnosticism and to understand what was transpiring spiritually in those early days of the church in regards to gnostic influence, I read portions of the early church father's writings. Those writings included works like Irenaeus of Lyon's "Against All Heresies" and Tertuliian's "Against the Valentinians."

To help me understand the best meanings of important Greek words, especially those used in I John 1:9, I consulted Strong's Concordance and Vine's Expository Dictionary of New Testament Words as well as other Greek dictionaries. To help bring out the important meaning and the current understanding of the English word "confess" used in I John 1:9, I looked to Webster's English Dictionary and several other dictionaries.

In my endeavor to understand the best meanings of Greek words important to this study, I also researched various academic websites. The information I found in these places helped me understand what Greek words critical to this study meant (most importantly the word *homologeō*) and revealed how they were conjugated. This gave me a good sense of what these important words meant in their various contexts. Along these lines, I found the online work of pastor William E. Wenstrom Jr. from Marion, Iowa (www.wenstrom.org) to be helpful; especially concerning the Greek word *homologeō*.

The information contained in these research sources contributed valuable context and important support to my study and aided me in reaching my conclusions concerning I John 1:9. That being said, most of the important insights I gained and presented in my book—the reality of John's polemic in I John 1:5-2:11, the many uses and contextual meanings of the Greek word *homologeō*, the important relationship between the three analogous statements, the logical implications of the common interpretation of I John 1:9, and the unique interpretation of I John 1:9 I set forth—were not insights I gleaned from other sources, but were conclusions I arrived at following several years of my own careful and prayerful consideration of I John 1:9.

www.ingramcontent.com/pod-product-compliance
Lightning Source LLC
Chambersburg PA
CBHW060745100426
42813CB00032B/3409/J